One More Elephant

Evolution Versus the Text of Scripture

Robert J. Koester

Books

ONE MORE ELEPHANT
EVOLUTION VERSUS THE TEXT OF SCRIPTURE

© 2020 Robert J. Koester

Cover Design: Pamela Clemons
Copy Edit: Lisa Miller
Cover Art: Images by InspiredImages from Pixabay

Unless otherwise indicated, all Scripture quotations are from The ESV® Bible (The Holy Bible, English Standard Version®), copyright © 2001 by Crossway, a publishing ministry of Good News Publishers. Used by permission. All rights reserved.

All rights reserved. No part of this book may be reproduced or transmitted in any form without the prior written permission of the publisher. Contact the publisher for permission to reprint or to use excerpts beyond fair use.

GWA Books
gwabooks@midco.net
09-21-01

ISBN: 978-1-7344319-2-6
Library of Congress Control Number: 2019921128

Table of Contents

List of Clichés v
Introduction 1

Part One: Scripture

Chapter 1—What the Bible Says About Itself 5

The Old Testament was considered to be a single book 5
The New Testament writers on the Old Testament 6
The New Testament writers' interpretation of Genesis 17
The Old and New Testaments share a single purpose 22

Part Two: Historical Criticism

Chapter 2—Growing Pressure on the Bible 33

Early forces: the Renaissance 36
Should critical scholarship be applied to the text of the Bible? ... 41
Forces at work leading up to the Enlightenment 44
The Enlightenment 56

Chapter 3—The Development of Historical Criticism 67

The triumph of the Enlightenment in the Lutheran Church 70
More types of historical criticism 95
Many glasses to choose from 97

Chapter 4—Historical Criticism and Theistic Evolution Today 103

How is historical criticism used today? 103
How theistic evolutionists use Scripture 110
What is at stake? 123

Part Three: The Ancient Near Eastern Argument

Chapter 5—The Ancient Near Eastern (ANE) Argument 127

iii

What is ANE literature? 127

Evaluating the ANE argument 130

Chapter 6—How Does Scripture Actually Describe the Universe? Part One 141

First, Scripture describes in narrative form how God created the universe 144

The meaning of "the heavens" as described in the creation account 145

The creation of dry land 150

The creation of what is under the earth 151

Second, Scripture uses the language of observation 152

Chapter 7—How Does Scripture Actually Describe the Universe? Part Two 157

The ANE argument and Scripture's symbolism 157

The basic way we interpret symbols 159

Symbols for "the heavens" 163

Symbols that supposedly reflect ancient scientific beliefs about the structures in the heavens 173

Symbols that picture the earth 180

Symbols that picture what is under the earth 190

Evaluating the symbols as a whole 192

The purpose of symbols in Scripture 195

Postscript—The Literature of Other Ancient Near Eastern Nations 203

Questions to ask about ANE literature 203

The heart of the matter 206

What is lost by using ANE resources to interpret Scripture 208

Works Referenced 211

Scripture Index 214

Index of Clichés

God has revealed himself in two books—Scripture and Nature. We must let each book help us understand the other. 26

The doctrine of the inspiration of Scripture is a recent development. 38

Remember the Galileo affair! 47

Creationists are against science. 55

The Bible writers accommodated themselves to their readers. 74

We can understand the Bible only if we understand the culture in which the Bible was written. 81

The evangelism card. 85

It is very difficult to become a truly competent Bible reader. 101

We must interpret Scripture as its original readers interpreted it. 118

Scholars say. 122

Artists' illustrations of the ancient three-tiered cosmos don't lie. 198

(Clichés are statements often found in theistic evolutionary writings. Additional clichés and responses to them are included in the first book of this set: *Elephants in the Room: Evolution Versus the Message of Scripture*.)

Introduction

Theistic evolutionists hail from denominations across the religious world. Some are more liberal. Others are more conservative. In *Elephants in the Room: Evolution Versus the Message of Scripture*, the first volume of this two-volume set, we explored the impact of evolution on the basic truths of the Christian faith. We saw that no part of Scripture's message was left unchallenged and unaffected. In this book we look at the affect of evolution on the *text* of Scripture.

What might be surprising is that authors from historically conservative backgrounds are using Scripture in much the same way as liberal authors use it. Books by conservative authors may not have the heavy philosophical feel that books by liberal authors have. But neither do their authors have much sympathy for a straightforward reading of Scripture, which we might expect them to have. These authors claim to be interpreting Scripture literally, but there is something not quite right about their definition of *literal*.

As recently as the 1950s, all instructors at major Evangelical seminaries like Wheaton College, Westminster Seminary, and Fuller Theological Seminary would have championed historic Reformation principles of Bible interpretation. Today, however, many if not most teachers at these institutions accept what is called "historical criticism," a way of approaching Scripture that until recently had been used primarily in liberal seminaries. I think it is fair to say that acceptance of evolution has entered Evangelical Christianity through the door of historical criticism.

Those deciding on whether or not to merge evolution and Scripture will first have to decide whether or not they want to accept historical-critical methods of interpreting Scripture. Unless we understand this way of reading the text of Scripture, we will be forced to evaluate theistic evolutionary arguments with one arm tied behind our back.

In the first book of this set, we identified some "elephants in the room." These elephants undermine the message of Scripture, how God's Son substituted himself in life and in death to overcome sin and restore us to God's family. This volume identifies one more elephant that lumbers into the room when evolution tries to find a place in Scripture. This is the elephant of historical criticism, a method of interpreting Scripture that replaces reading Scripture in a literal or straightforward way.[1]

We will start with a careful look at Scripture and ask: "How does Scripture want to be interpreted?" We will especially want to discover: "How did Jesus and the New Testament writers interpret and use the Scriptures, namely, the books of the Old Testament?"

Then we will offer a primer on historical criticism—what it is and how it entered the Christian church. We will do this in enough detail so you are able to spot historical criticism when theistic evolutionists use it in their books. You will understand historical criticism well enough to be able to evaluate theistic evolutionary claims for its validity.

The last three chapters treat what is perhaps the most powerful historical-critical argument. Theistic evolutionists claim that Scripture is another piece of ancient Near Eastern literature. Ancient Near Eastern literature contains various national myths about how the world came into being. Scripture merely reveals the Hebrew version of the same themes and should be read accordingly. The argument leads to this conclusion: Just as modern science has helped us dismiss Egyptian and Babylonian creation myths, so it has helped us see that the creation account in Genesis 1 and 2 is merely the Hebrew version of those myths and can also be dismissed.

May the Lord bless this study of how *He* teaches us to read his Word.

Part One

Scripture

Chapter 1

What the Bible Says About Itself

Introduction

We can't evaluate theistic evolution without first evaluating what Scripture says about itself—what it is and how it wants to be interpreted. It is good for every Christian to understand this even apart from the challenge of historical criticism. After all, we confess that our eternal salvation is based on what *Scripture* reveals to us.

What spiritual posture should we have when we open our Bible and read it? How do we become competent to understand the words of Scripture? To answer those questions, we must pay attention to another question: "What did Jesus and the Bible writers understand the Bible to be and how did they use it?" Especially important for the subject of this book is the question: "How did they interpret and use the early chapters of Genesis?"

In this chapter we will look at Scripture like a young lady might look at her engagement diamond, turning it over in her hand and looking at each of its facets to get an overall impression of its beauty.

The Old Testament was considered to be a single book

"The Scriptures"

In English translations of the Bible, the Hebrew collection of sacred scrolls found in the Old Testament are referred to as "the Scriptures." The Greek word used for this Old Testament collection literally means "the writings." The English word *Scripture* comes from the Latin translation of that Greek word, and means the same thing, "the writings."

At times Jesus and the New Testament writers referred to this body of writings in the singular, "the Scripture." Today it is easy for us to think of the Bible as a unit because all the content is included between the covers of a single book. But the Hebrew Scriptures were written on a number of separate scrolls, which could be stored in any order. Even so, they were viewed as a unit. For example, John tells us that when Jesus was raised from the dead, "his disciples remembered that he had said this, and they believed the Scripture and the word that Jesus had spoken" (John 2:22).

At other times the New Testament writers referred to the collection in the plural: "the Scriptures," referring to the individual writings that made up the whole. Luke tells us that Paul went into the synagogue in Thessalonica "and on three Sabbath days he reasoned with them from the Scriptures" (Acts 17:2).

Sometimes the writers use the word Scripture in reference to individual verses in the Old Testament. John recorded the soldiers' act of dividing up Jesus' clothing: "'Let us not tear it, but cast lots for it to see whose it shall be.' This was to fulfill the Scripture which says, 'They divided my garments among them, and for my clothing they cast lots'" (John 19:24).

The Scriptures were divided into major sections

Jesus and the New Testament writers identified two or three major groups into which the 39 Old Testament writings were organized. For example, in the account of Lazarus and the rich man, Jesus said to the rich man in hell, "If they do not hear Moses and the Prophets, neither will they be convinced if someone should rise from the dead" (Luke 16:31). When discussing the importance of keeping all of God's Law, Jesus said, "Do not think that I have come to abolish the Law or the Prophets; I have not come to abolish them but to fulfill them" (Matthew 5:17). When he ascended into heaven, Jesus told his followers: "These are my words that I spoke to you while I was still with you, that everything written about me in the Law of Moses and the Prophets and the Psalms must be fulfilled" (Luke 24:44).

Regardless of which division a scroll fell into, all the books in the Hebrew Scriptures were written by "prophets." Paul referred to the entire Old Testament as the word of the prophets: "Paul, a servant of Christ Jesus, called to be an apostle, set apart for the gospel of God, which he promised beforehand through his prophets in the holy Scriptures" (Romans 1:1,2).

The New Testament writers on the Old Testament

The Old Testament was "contemporary" to the New Testament writers

The Old Testament was written over some 15 centuries before Jesus was born, but Jesus and the New Testament writers never give us the impression that the Old Testament was comprised of documents from the past. They give no hint that it was written for different people, living in a different culture, with a different way of reading literature, and with different questions that needed to be answered. Quite the opposite. Jesus and the New Testament writers reference the Old Testament as if it had been written yesterday for people they were serving.

The New Testament writers often proved they were telling the truth, or they established their point, by citing the Old Testament. In Christ the new era foretold by the prophets had arrived.

For example, after describing the "heroes of faith" found in the Old Testament, the writer of Hebrews equates their faith with his own: "These were all commended for their faith, yet none of them received what had been promised. God had planned something better for us so that only together with us would they be made perfect" (Hebrews 11:39,40 NIV84). The earthly needs of those Old Testament believers might have been different from those of the readers of the Book of Hebrews. But both Old Testament and New Testament believers shared the hope of eternal life through God's promises given in the past and fulfilled in Christ. God had promised the Old Testament believers "something better" than the temporary blessings he gave people like Abraham in the years before Christ. The New Testament believers were enjoying these blessings, but the Old Testament believers were commended for their faith in what the future would bring.

The apostle Paul also considered the Old Testament to be a contemporary book, absolutely relevant for New Testament believers. In Romans 15 he wrote, "For whatever was written in former days was written for our instruction, that *through endurance and through the encouragement of the Scriptures* we might have hope" (verse 4). Interestingly, in the very next sentence (verse 5), Paul linked God and his Word, calling God "the God of endurance and encouragement." Endurance and encouragement come from God through his Word.

After pointing out the Israelites' sins and how God had punished them, Paul warned the Corinthians, "Now these things happened to them as an example, but they were written down for our instruction, on whom the end of the ages has come" (1 Corinthians 10:11). The writer of Hebrews warned his readers not to despise God's blessings and become like Esau "who sold his birthright for a single meal" (Hebrews 12:16). James urged his readers to learn from the example of "Job's perseverance" and take to heart "what the Lord finally brought about" for him (James 5:11 NIV84). Jesus encouraged those who doubted him by holding up the example of Abraham: "Your father Abraham rejoiced that he would see my day. He saw it and was glad" (John 8:56).

Jesus and the New Testament writers and the canon of Scripture

The canon of Scripture (the set group of writings that made up the Scriptures) was gradually assembled over the centuries as scrolls were written, and they were made into a permanent and closed collection. Jesus and the New Testament writers considered the collection of books that in their day formed the Jewish "canon," to be "the Scriptures."

There was some dispute among Jewish scholars in the early New Testament years about which books should be included in the canon of the Old Testament. It is fair to say that the apostles and early church leaders were aware of these disputes. Paul had received the best training a Jewish scholar could receive, and he certainly would have understood that some ancient books had been selected for inclusion in the canon while others had not. Also, he would have known that variant readings—caused largely by copyist errors—had crept into the manuscripts. Variant readings refer to differences in the text of the manuscripts scholars had at their disposal. Paul would have been familiar with those variants through his scholarly work on the manuscripts he had at his disposal. And he would also have known that the Greek translation of the Old Testament he used, called the Septuagint, differed in places from the Hebrew text.

This is important for the current debate about evolution. The "problems" associated with the ancient texts are often given as reasons why the Scripture is unreliable. But Jesus, Paul, and the other New Testament writers did not see it that way. They did not express concern about the human element in the assembly of the canon, about the fact that God used human beings to write down and copy his Word, or about the presence of variant readings.

"It is written"

Often Jesus and the New Testament writers gave no indication that they were quoting from the Old Testament writings. They simply said, "It is written." For example, Jesus rebuked his opponents like this: "But he looked directly at them and said, 'What then is this that is written: "The stone that the builders rejected has become the cornerstone"?'" (Luke 20:17). And Paul wrote, "It is written, 'Those who have never been told of him will see, and those who have never heard will understand'" (Romans 15:21).

"It is written" is shorthand for, "We all know there is an authoritative body of writings that we simply assume are true because they come from God. If we quote from them to make a point, no matter from which of the scrolls our quotation is taken, we have established our point." It would be like a person learning car mechanics hearing his teacher say, "Tighten the lug nut with this amount of torque, for it is written 'you must not use more than 75 foot-pounds.'" After the student hears that phrase a number of times, he asks the teacher what book he is referring to. The teacher points to a book on the shelf called the *Bible of Car Mechanics*.

Of course, there is no such book for any area of human learning. We base our instructions on a wide variety of sources built on human knowledge and experience. But Jesus and the New Testament writers assumed that for learning absolute truth there *is* such a book. There is one source people can turn to for instruction from God, and they can be sure that what they read there is true. What's more, they assume their readers know which book they are referring to and that they also believe it is true. For example, Luke relates what Jesus did for two of his followers who didn't understand that he had to die and rise again: "Then he opened their minds to understand the Scriptures" (Luke 24:45). There was no need for Luke to explain to them what he meant by "the Scriptures."

The Scripture is "holy"

Jesus and the New Testament writers had absolute respect for Scripture. They considered it unique. Paul called the Scriptures "holy." To be holy means to be set apart. The content and purpose of Scripture is set apart from the content and purpose of other books. Paul describes the purpose of Scripture in 2 Timothy 3:16: "All Scripture [literally 'every writing'] is breathed out by God and profitable for teaching, for reproof, for correction, and for training in righteousness."

The New Testament writers quoted *only* from the Jewish Scriptures to prove the truth of something they said. Occasionally a Bible writer might quote from a source outside the Scriptures. He might quote a secular Greek poet or an ancient writing not included in the Scriptures. For example in 1 Corinthians 15:32 and 33, Paul makes a point by quoting statements drawn from secular sources: "If the dead are not raised, 'Let us eat and drink, for tomorrow we die.' Do not be deceived: 'Bad company ruins good morals.'" And he refers to a belief shared by some Greek poets, "For we are indeed his offspring" (Acts 17:1). Jude quotes from ancient sources outside the Old Testament Scriptures when he speaks about Moses' body (verse 9) and when he teaches about the Lord's second coming (verses 14,15).

In all these cases, however, the sources remain in the background, unnamed. One shows that the writer's point has been made even by a non-Christian author or that it is supported by common sense. Another provides information about an event not found in Scripture. These references—and only a few of them are found in the New Testament—are never used as authoritative statements that prove the truth of what the New Testament writer is saying. That role is reserved for the Old Testament writings. The writers of the New Testament used the word *Scripture* only in reference to the Old Testament (except for one time when it was used in reference to Paul's letters, 2 Peter 3:16).

Scripture is a voice

The Bible writers knew that human beings wrote the contents of Scripture. But they often personified the Scriptures. In other words, they said "the Scriptures" were saying this or that, not the men who wrote them down. We might say something like, "The plays of Shakespeare still speak to us today."

But the Bible writers go further. Scripture is sometimes described as having its own voice independent of the men who wrote it.

For example, Paul wrote about an event from the life of Pharaoh at the time Moses led the Israelites out of Egypt. "For the Scripture says to Pharaoh, 'For this very purpose I have raised you up, that I might show my power in you, and that my name might be proclaimed in all the earth'" (Romans 9:17). Here's how Exodus reads:

> Then the LORD said to Moses, "Rise up early in the morning and present yourself before Pharaoh and say to him, 'Thus says the LORD, the God of the Hebrews, "Let my people go, that they may serve me. For this time I will send all my plagues on you yourself, and on your servants and your people, so that you may know that there is none like me in all the earth. For by now I could have put out my hand and struck you and your people with pestilence, and you would have been cut off from the earth. But *for this purpose I have raised you up, to show you my power, so that my name may be proclaimed in all the earth.*"'" (Exodus 9:13-16)

Paul could have said that God spoke to Moses and commanded him to be his mouthpiece to Pharaoh. But Paul says that Scripture—in other words, the record of the events—did the speaking.

Paul uses the same way of speaking in Galatians 3:22: "But the Scripture declares that the whole world is a prisoner of sin, so that what was promised, being given through faith in Jesus Christ, might be given to those who believe" (NIV84). Someone might understand this way of speaking as a figure of speech. Regardless, the effect is to give Scripture an independent authority—something written by men, to be sure, but once written down as having the power to speak on its own.

Jesus did the same: "For all the Prophets and the Law prophesied until John" (Matthew 11:13). In this verse the word "Prophets" might be interpreted as the men who did the writing, but it likely refers to the prophetical books themselves. It parallels "the Law," which clearly refers to the content itself. Jesus could have said that Moses prophesied, but he gave Scripture its own voice: "the Prophets and the Law prophesied."

Jesus said, "It is the Spirit who gives life; the flesh is no help at all. The words that I have spoken to you are spirit and life" (John 6:63). The words Jesus spoke were not simply *used* by the Holy Spirit to give life. They themselves *are* spirit and life. Paul spoke in a similar way: "And we also thank God constantly for this, that when you received the word of God, which you heard from us, you accepted it not as the word of men but as what it really is, the word of God, which is at work in you believers" (1 Thessalonians 2:13). The Word of God does not just convey information. It is actually a power at work in believers.

The words of the Old Testament writers are God's words

When the prophets spoke (or wrote), they knew they were simply the mouthpieces of God. Siegbert Becker says that Exodus 4:22 is the first time in Scripture we hear the phrase, "Thus says the Lord," which "almost became a standard prophetic formula, used about 400 times in the Old Testament."[2]

Sometimes God dictated his words to a prophet and told the prophet to relate those specific words to the people. At one point the Lord told Jeremiah to write down everything he had spoken to him up to that point: "Then Jeremiah called Baruch the son of Neriah, and Baruch wrote on a scroll at the dictation of Jeremiah all the words of the LORD that he had spoken to him" (Jeremiah 36:4).

Jesus and the New Testament writers, however, never implied that the content of all the Old Testament books were given by dictation. They spoke of the Scriptures as a seamless combination of human authorship and divine content. There were reasons why the Old Testament writers wrote—situations in life that elicited strong emotions, pressing questions for God, or special reasons to give him glory. Yet God did not merely give the writers ideas, which they were to express in their own words. When they were finished writing, the author's words were the actual words God wanted them to write.

Consider the variety of ways the Bible writers described the relation between God, the human writers, and the Scriptures. Jesus said, "For *Moses* said, 'Honor your father and your mother'; and, 'Whoever reviles father or mother must surely die'" (Mark 7:10). But a few verses later he rebuked the Pharisees for how they avoided keeping that commandment. He said they were "making void the *word of God* by your tradition that you have handed down" (Mark 7:13). Paul described the blessings God had given the Jewish people through Moses and the other Old Testament writers: "The Jews were entrusted with *the oracles of God*" (Romans 3:2).

---

[2]Siegbert W. Becker, *The Scriptures—Inspired of God* (Milwaukee: Northwestern Publishing House, 1971), p. 44.

We saw that Jesus and the New Testament writers often quoted the Scriptures with the simple formula, "It is written." But they often named the prophet who wrote the words. At the beginning of his gospel, Matthew quoted freely from the Old Testament: "Then was fulfilled what was spoken by the prophet Jeremiah" (Matthew 2:17). John the Baptist fulfilled the words of Isaiah: "For this is he who was spoken of by the prophet Isaiah when he said . . . . " (Isaiah 3:3). When Paul wrote about the clarity of the Old Testament message he named the human authors: "First *Moses* says. . . . Then *Isaiah* is so bold as to say" (Romans 10:19,20).

But at the same time, God himself was speaking. David wrote psalms, but he served as the Holy Spirit's mouthpiece. Jesus said, "David himself, in the Holy Spirit, declared, 'The Lord said to my Lord, "Sit at my right hand, until I put your enemies under your feet"'" (Mark 12:36). Peter described the Old Testament prophecy about Judas' betrayal of Jesus and referred to all three elements: the Word, the Holy Spirit, and the human author: "Brothers, *the Scripture* had to be fulfilled, which *the Holy Spirit spoke* beforehand *by the mouth of David* concerning Judas, who became a guide to those who arrested Jesus" (Acts 1:16).

After Peter had miraculously been released from prison, the believers in Jerusalem praised the Lord and displayed their understanding of how the Scriptures were authored: "And when they heard it, they lifted their voices together to God and said, 'Sovereign Lord, who made the heaven and the earth and the sea and everything in them, who *through the mouth of our father David*, your servant, *said by the Holy Spirit*, "Why did the Gentiles rage, and the peoples plot in vain?"'" (Acts 4:24,25).

Luke describes God's authorship of Scripture in a rather unusual way. He writes (as translated in the NIV84), "God in his wisdom said, 'I will send them prophets and apostles, some of whom they will kill and others they will persecute'" (Luke 11:49). The ESV translates the first words of the verse more literally: "Therefore also the Wisdom of God said." God's wisdom is here personified. The Wisdom of God, written down in the Scriptures, was speaking in the Old Testament through the prophets.

The writer of Hebrews is especially fond of attributing the words of the Old Testament directly to God. In the first two verses of his book, he links the voice of God with the voice of the prophets and the voice of his Son, Jesus. He writes, "Long ago, at many times and in many ways, God spoke to our fathers by the prophets, but in these last days he has spoken to us by his Son, whom he appointed the heir of all things, through whom also he created the world" (Hebrews 1:1,2). If God revealed himself to the people in the past through the prophets and in the New Testament continued revealing himself through his Son, Jesus, then the words of the human prophets in the Old Testament carry just as much authority as the words of God's Son.

What the Bible Says About Itself

In the first chapter of Hebrews, the writer gives a list of Old Testament quotations that distinguish between Jesus and the angels. He doesn't name the Old Testament sources; he only notes that God spoke them. He starts with a quotation from Psalm 2: "For to which of the angels did God ever say, 'You are my Son, today I have begotten you'?" (Hebrews 1:5). He continues with a quotation from a prophecy God gave to David through Nathan the prophet. He adds others. He quoted from the song recorded in Deuteronomy that God told Moses to relay to the Israelites; from the anonymous Psalm 104; from Psalm 45, written by the sons of Korah; twice from Psalm 102, written by an afflicted man who was pouring out his complaint to the Lord; and from Psalm 110, written by David. These quotations came from a wide range of human authors, but the writer of Hebrews attributes them all to God. He does the same in chapter 5: "So also Christ did not exalt himself to be made a high priest, but was appointed by him who said to him, 'You are my Son, today I have begotten you'; as he says also in another place, 'You are a priest forever, after the order of Melchizedek.'" (Hebrews 5:5,6, again quoting Psalm 2 and 110).

The writer said that it was Jesus speaking in Psalm 22 and Isaiah 8:18:

> For he who sanctifies and those who are sanctified all have one source. That is why he [Jesus] is not ashamed to call them brothers, saying [through David], "I will tell of your name to my brothers; in the midst of the congregation I will sing your praise." And again, "I will put my trust in him." And again [through Isaiah], "Behold, I and the children God has given me." (Hebrews 2:11-13)

Jesus was also speaking in Psalm 40: "Consequently, when Christ came into the world, he said, 'Sacrifices and offerings you have not desired, but a body have you prepared for me; in burnt offerings and sin offerings you have taken no pleasure. Then I said, "Behold, I have come to do your will, O God, as it is written of me in the scroll of the book"'" (Hebrews 10:5-7).

In chapter 9 of Hebrews, the writer describes some details of the Great Day of Atonement and credits the Holy Spirit with purposefully designing the regulations for that day: "By this the Holy Spirit indicates that the way into the holy places is not yet opened as long as the first section is still standing" (Hebrews 9:6-8).

Although Jeremiah wrote the words quoted in Hebrews that described the meaning of Jesus' sacrifice for sin, it was the Holy Spirit who was behind the explanation:

> The Holy Spirit also testifies to us about this. First he says: "This is the covenant I will make with them after that time, says the Lord. I will put

my laws in their hearts, and I will write them on their minds." Then he adds: "Their sins and lawless acts I will remember no more." (Hebrews 10:15-17 NIV84)

The words of Scripture were breathed by God (inspired)

As noted above, in the hundreds of places in the New Testament where the writers quote from the Old Testament, there is no indication that God inspired only the ideas and not the specific words of the Old Testament.

The New Testament writers turned to the words of the Old Testament for details they needed to make a point. Abraham was about 100 years old when God affirmed the promise of a son and gave him the covenant of circumcision (Romans 4:10). Abraham believed the Lord even though he had no human hope for a son (Romans 5:18,19). The Queen of Sheba visited Solomon and believed him. She will testify against the present generation who refused to believe in Jesus (Matthew 12:42). Details from the lives of Adam; his sons, Cain and Abel; Adam's descendant Enoch and many more people whose lives are recorded in Genesis (not to mention the people who lived after them) are used by the New Testament authors. The New Testament writers considered all of these people to have lived and done what the Old Testament says they did. The New Testament writers read Old Testament history in a straightforward way like you might read a newspaper story of something that took place in your community, namely, as a factual account of things that actually happened. And, we might add, when they recorded what these people did and applied lessons learned from them, they did so without going into long explanations about customs and motives they felt were necessary for their readers to understand the account.

Jesus and the New Testament writers sometimes made specific points based on nothing more than a single word of Scripture. For example, the writer of Hebrews quotes from Psalm 95 and makes a major point on the basis of the word "today": "Again he appoints a certain day, 'Today, saying through David so long afterward, in the words already quoted, 'Today, if you hear his voice, do not harden your hearts'" (Hebrews 4:7).

Jesus based an argument on the word "Lord." He quoted from Psalm 110: "David himself, in the Holy Spirit, declared, 'The Lord said to my Lord, "Sit at my right hand, until I put your enemies under your feet."' David himself calls him Lord. So how is he his son?" (Mark 12:36). In another place, Jesus argued, "If he called them gods to whom the word of God came—and Scripture cannot be broken—do you say of him whom the Father consecrated and sent into the world, 'You are blaspheming,' because I said, 'I am the Son of God'?" (John 10:35,36, quoting Psalm 82:6). This reference also shows Jesus' attitude toward

What the Bible Says About Itself

Scripture as a whole. It "cannot be broken." That is, you cannot successfully pit one part of Scripture against another.

Another example—a more difficult passage, to be sure—is Galatians 3:16. Paul bases his point on the fact God used a singular noun "seed" instead of the plural, "seeds."

The New Testament writers taught that the words of Scripture are God's words and therefore true. Saint Paul wrote, "All Scripture ['every writing'] is breathed out by God and profitable for teaching, for reproof, for correction, and for training in righteousness, that the man of God may be complete, equipped for every good work" (2 Timothy 3:16,17).

The men who wrote the Scriptures were under God's control. God "breathed" into them what he wanted them to write. Christians can use the entire collection of scriptural books to teach, rebuke, correct, and train each other in what God wants them to believe and do. If Scripture was not completely true, it would be impossible, even presumptuous, for believers to confidently use them to correct people's wrong ideas, rebuke their sins and errors, and equip them for every good work.

The apostle Peter wrote this about the Scripture:

> We ourselves heard this very voice borne from heaven, for we were with him on the holy mountain. And we have the prophetic word more fully confirmed, to which you will do well to pay attention as to a lamp shining in a dark place, until the day dawns and the morning star rises in your hearts, knowing this first of all, that no prophecy of Scripture comes from someone's own interpretation. For no prophecy was ever produced by the will of man, but men spoke from God as they were carried along by the Holy Spirit. (2 Peter 1:18-21)

Here Peter recalled the time he was with Jesus on the Mount of Transfiguration, when God the Father spoke from heaven and put his stamp of approval on Jesus' work. Peter contrasts the words he heard God speak on that occasion with another source of God's Word, the prophetic writings. Peter said that these writings were even "more fully confirmed." Other translations for "more fully confirmed" are "firm," "binding," "sure," and "more certain." The prophetic writings were not the result of the prophets' personal "interpretation." That is, the prophets did not present their own understanding of various spiritual topics or state in their own words some message from God. They wrote as they were "carried along by the Holy Spirit." The content of Scripture was not a joint effort between the prophet and the Holy Spirit. Peter calls the words of Scripture "a lamp shining in a dark place" because they were God's words, uncorrupted by the human weakness of their authors.

In another place Peter put some distance between the writers of Scripture and what they wrote down. The Holy Spirit (here linked with Jesus—"the Spirit of Christ"), spoke through them and foretold Jesus' sufferings, death, and resurrection. Peter wrote, "Concerning this salvation, the prophets who prophesied about the grace that was to be yours searched and inquired carefully, inquiring what person or time the Spirit of Christ in them was indicating when he predicted the sufferings of Christ and the subsequent glories" (1 Peter 1:10,11).

The prophets knew they were God's penmen. What they wrote was coming to them from a source outside their own minds. They had to study what the Spirit wrote through them—just as we must study it.

New Testament writers interpreted the Old Testament accurately

Scripture puts the authority of the New Testament writers on the same level as that of the Old Testament writers. Jesus set aside some of his disciples to be "apostles." Their main work was to give a witness to the fact that they had seen Jesus personally after he rose from the dead. The New Testament church was to be built on their eye-witness account that Christ was alive.

Jesus once told them, "The words that I have spoken to you are spirit and life" (John 6:63). Near the end of his life, Jesus promised to remind them of those words: "These things I have spoken to you while I am still with you. But the Helper, the Holy Spirit, whom the Father will send in my name, he will teach you all things and bring to your remembrance all that I have said to you" (John 14:25,26). The Spirit gave the apostles an unfailing memory of what Jesus had told them. And those New Testament writers who were not apostles themselves worked and taught alongside the apostles and wrote under their auspices.

Can we be sure that the New Testament writers were accurately interpreting the Old Testament? This is a key question in the current debate and many theistic evolutionists would answer, no.

The apostle Paul said that when he spoke or wrote, he did so under the direction of the Spirit: "We have not received the spirit of the world but the Spirit who is from God, that we may understand what God has freely given us. This is what we speak, not in words taught us by human wisdom but in words taught by the Spirit, expressing spiritual truths in spiritual words" (1 Corinthians 2:12,13 NIV84).

The apostles themselves, along with the church, understood their writings to be on the same level as the writings of the Old Testament prophets. Peter wrote:

> And count the patience of our Lord as salvation, just as our beloved brother Paul also wrote to you according to the wisdom given him, as he does in all his letters when he speaks in them of these matters. There

What the Bible Says About Itself

are some things in them that are hard to understand, which the ignorant and unstable twist to their own destruction, as they do the other Scriptures. (2 Peter 3:15,16)

The important phrase for our purpose is "the other Scriptures." Peter is putting Paul's words on the same level as the words of the Old Testament.

The New Testament writers remembered Jesus' words, and they wrote under the Spirit's guidance and direction (John 14:26). They interpreted the Old Testament as Jesus interpreted it, and they can serve as our guides to it's meaning.

Scripture can be understood by all people throughout all time

The New Testament authors assumed their readers could understand the Old Testament. There was never a hint that their readers needed some specialized background material to help the Old Testament become clear or relevant.

Shortly before he ascended into heaven, Jesus told the disciples that they would spread the Word "to the end of the earth" (Acts 1:8). They would spread the Word to people of many cultures, and they could be confident that everyone would be able to understand the Old Testament Scriptures they quoted. The basic teachings of both the Old and New Testaments—temptation, sin, God's punishment of sin, God's forgiveness, the promised Savior, the call to remain faithful to him, and the reward in store for those who remained faithful—were culture neutral and would be understandable and relevant to all.

For example, a man from the African country of Ethiopia was a convert to Judaism. He eagerly listened to the evangelist Philip explain the gospel to him. Philip explained to him the meaning of Isaiah 53, written seven hundred years earlier to people living in a culture far different from that of the Ethiopian.

Certainly Scripture needs explanation. The Ethiopian needed Philip's help to understand Isaiah 53. But he did not need special insights into Hebrew culture to grasp the meaning of the message once Philip explained it to him.

The New Testament writers' interpretation of Genesis

The people referred to in the early chapters of Genesis

Theistic evolutionists want their readers to consider Genesis, especially the early chapters, as sacred myths written to teach theological truths. They believe that this is the "literal" way to interpret Genesis. And it would be, if Genesis was mythology. But according to Jesus and the New Testament writers, Genesis is not mythology. It is a narrative account of events that took place in the past. This section will explore how they viewed Genesis.

Scripture makes no distinction between the people found in Genesis 1-11 and those found afterward. First Chronicles 1 lists ten men from Adam to Noah, the same men found in Genesis 5. First Chronicles then continues with the genealogies of Noah's sons, tracing the descendants of Noah's son Shem down through Abraham. The genealogy refers to Adam and Abraham in the same way. If Abraham was a literal person, so was Adam.

Luke traces Jesus' genealogy back to Adam. Note that the translations usually add "son of" to the list of names, ending in "Adam, the son of God." But the original simply has "of." Accordingly, the end of Luke's genealogy reads, "of Enosh, of Seth, of Adam, of God." Adam was a person like those in the rest of the list. The only difference was that he had his origin in an act of God (Luke 3:38).

With Adam's genealogy in mind, Jude refers to Enoch as "the seventh from Adam" (verse 14). The writer of Hebrews also treats Enoch as a specific individual: "By faith Enoch was taken up so that he should not see death, and he was not found, because God had taken him. Now before he was taken he was commended as having pleased God" (Hebrews 11:5,6).

Paul treats Adam as a specific individual. In Romans 5:14 he writes, "Yet death reigned from Adam to Moses, even over those whose sinning was not like the transgression of Adam, who was a type of the one who was to come." As Romans 5 progresses, we learn how Adam was a type of Christ. Adam, a single human being, introduced sin into the world. Christ, the Son of God who became a human being, performed one act of righteousness that brings salvation for all people. In Romans 5:15-17 Paul's entire line of thought depends on the existence of a real, not mythological Adam, whose personal sin affected the entire world:

> But the free gift is not like the trespass. For if *many died through one man's trespass*, much more have the grace of God and the free gift by the grace of that one man Jesus Christ abounded for many. And the free gift is not like the result of that one man's sin. *For the judgment following one trespass brought condemnation,* but the free gift following many trespasses brought justification. For if, *because of one man's trespass, death reigned through that one man,* much more will those who receive the abundance of grace and the free gift of righteousness reign in life through the one man Jesus Christ. (Romans 5:15-17)

In verses 18 and 19, Paul parallels the result of Adam's sin and Christ's work, which overcame those results: "Therefore, *as one trespass led to condemnation for all men,* so one act of righteousness leads to justification and life for all men. For as *by the one man's disobedience the many were made sinners,* so by the one man's obedience the many will be made righteous" (Romans 5:18,19). According to Paul, human beings are condemned, not because they imitate Adam's sinfulness but because they are connected to Adam by birth. Human beings are saved, not because they imitate Christ's righteousness but because "in Christ Jesus you are all sons of God, through faith" (Galatians 3:26).

In 1 Corinthians 15:22, Paul compares and contrasts Adam and Christ, treating both as literal people: "For as in Adam all die, so also in Christ shall all be made alive." The comparison/contrast continues later in the chapter. We all received human life—became "living beings"—in Adam. Those who have become God's children through faith in Christ share in the new, spiritual life given us by Christ:

> Thus it is written, "The first man Adam became a living being"; the last Adam became a life-giving spirit. But it is not the spiritual that is first but the natural, and then the spiritual. The first man was from the earth, a man of dust; the second man is from heaven. As was the man of dust, so also are those who are of the dust, and as is the man of heaven, so also are those who are of heaven. Just as we have borne the image of the man of dust, we shall also bear the image of the man of heaven. (1 Corinthians 15:45-49)

Here Paul is taking us back to Adam's creation in Genesis 2. Our being "in Adam" determined our earthly makeup, just as our being "in Christ" determines our heavenly makeup.

In speaking to the philosophers in Athens, Paul traced the origin of the human race back to a single man, Adam: "And he made from one man every nation of mankind to live on all the face of the earth, having determined allotted periods and the boundaries of their dwelling place" (Acts 17:26).

Paul referred to Adam's wife, Eve, as a literal person in two places. In 2 Corinthians 11:3, he referred to Eve's temptation: "But I am afraid that as the serpent deceived Eve by his cunning, your thoughts will be led astray from a sincere and pure devotion to Christ." In 1 Timothy 2:13,14, Paul made a point about the roles of men and women by pointing out that "Adam was formed first, then Eve; and Adam was not deceived, but the woman was deceived and became a transgressor."

The writer of Hebrews refers to Abel as a real person and his sacrifice as a real act of faith: "By faith Abel offered to God a more acceptable sacrifice than Cain, through which he was commended as righteous, God commending him by accepting his gifts. And through his faith, though he died, he still speaks" (Hebrews 11:4). Abel's blood cried out for vengeance. Jesus shed his blood, and because his blood was shed for the world's sins, he is able to speak forgiveness, "a better word than the blood of Abel" (Hebrews 12:24).

The apostle John referred to Cain as a real person and his sin as a real act of unbelief: "We should not be like Cain, who was of the evil one and murdered his brother. And why did he murder him? Because his own deeds were evil and his brother's righteous" (1 John 3:12).

The events of creation

Old Testament writers take for granted that the Garden of Eden existed. Moses said that before its destruction, the land around Sodom and Gomorrah was like "the garden of the LORD" (Genesis 13:10). Isaiah also referred to "Eden" as "the garden of the Lord" (Isaiah 51:3). Joel and Ezekiel referred to the Garden of the Lord and Eden (Joel 2:3; Ezekiel 28:13).

In Psalm 90 Moses referred to death in terms of the creation of Adam from the dust of the earth: "You return man to dust and say, 'Return, O children of man!'" (verse 3).

Jesus and the New Testament writers referred to the Old Testament account of creation and the people involved in it no differently than the events and people referred to throughout Scripture. Jesus referred to Satan's temptation of Eve in Genesis 3. He called the devil a "murderer from the beginning" and "a liar and the father of lies" (John 8:44).

In his description of Old Testament people of faith, the writer to the Hebrews presented a list of people who give us examples of taking God at his word. Each of these people acted "by faith," that is, they all served God by believing and acting on something he told them. However, the first time the writer used the term "by faith," he did not refer to an act of faith performed by a person in the Old Testament. The writer gives all God's people credit for believing—for "understanding"—something they have not seen, namely, that the world was created out of nothing by God's command.

In 2 Peter 2:3-8, Peter listed a number of times God carried out his judgment on sin. He listed accounts from early chapters of Genesis as well as events that happened much later in Abraham's day. All the accounts referred to there are treated as historical.

In Matthew 19:3-6 some Pharisees came to Jesus to test him. They asked, "Is it lawful to divorce one's wife for any cause?" Jesus answered, "Have you not read that he who created them from the beginning made them male and female and said, 'Therefore a man shall leave his father and his mother and hold fast to his wife, and the two shall become one flesh'? So they are no longer two but one flesh. What therefore God has joined together, let not man separate." Incidentally, in these verses Jesus uses Genesis 2 not as a separate account of creation but as an expanded account of the creation of Adam and Eve in Genesis 1.

As noted above, Paul traced the origin of all people back to Adam: "And he made from one man every nation of mankind to live on all the face of the earth, having determined allotted periods and the boundaries of their dwelling place" (Acts 17:26). Recall that Adam named his wife Eve, "because she was the mother of all living" (Genesis 3:20). Eve sounds like the Hebrew for "life-giver" and resembles the word for "living."

In Romans 1 Paul wrote, "For what can be known about God is plain to them, because God has shown it to them. For his invisible attributes, namely, his eternal power and divine nature, have been clearly perceived, ever since the creation of the world, in the things that have been made. So they are without excuse" (verses 19,20). Ever since the world began—and this is the significant point—God has been putting his eternal power and divine nature on display. This could be true only if two things had happened simultaneously—first, that the Lord created mankind completely finished with the ability to observe and come to rational conclusions, and second, that the Lord had placed mankind in a world that was completely finished so they could draw the conclusions Paul speaks about.

In Revelation God promises to restore the creation to how it was in the beginning. In heaven we will again experience the blessing of the "tree of life, which is in the paradise of God" (Revelation 2:7; cf. Revelation 22:14,19). In the new heavens and earth, the tree of life will produce fruit for the healing of the nations (Revelation 22:2). Everything will be restored to its original condition: "No longer will there be any curse" (Revelation 22:3 NIV).

The flood

Because the account of the flood is included in the early chapters of Genesis, it would be helpful to see how the Bible writers referred to Noah. Quoting God, Isaiah writes,

> "This is like the days of Noah to me: as I swore that the waters of Noah should no more go over the earth, so I have sworn that I will not be angry with you, and will not rebuke you. For the mountains may depart and the hills be removed, but my steadfast love shall not depart from you, and my covenant of peace shall not be removed," says the LORD, who has compassion on you. (Isaiah 54:9,10)

In this verse the Lord was comparing the future days of his mercy in Christ with the mercy he showed the world by promising never to send another flood.

Ezekiel included Noah in a list of two other historical individuals: "Even if these three men, Noah, Daniel, and Job, were in it [a country that sins against him], they would deliver but their own lives by their righteousness, declares the Lord God" (Ezekiel 14:14).

Jesus described the end of the present world as being similar to the end of the ancient world in the days leading up to the flood:

> For as were the days of Noah, so will be the coming of the Son of Man. For as in those days before the flood they were eating and drinking, marrying and giving in marriage, until the day when Noah entered the ark, and they were unaware until the flood came and swept them all away, so will be the coming of the Son of Man. (Matthew 24:37-39)

Peter spoke of the flood in the same way. He tells us that Jesus, after he rose from the dead, preached to the people in Hell who had refused to listen to his message through Noah:

> He went and proclaimed to the spirits in prison, because they formerly did not obey, when God's patience waited in the days of Noah, while the ark was being prepared, in which a few, that is, eight persons, were brought safely through water. Baptism, which corresponds to this, now saves you, not as a removal of dirt from the body but as an appeal to God for a good conscience, through the resurrection of Jesus Christ. (1 Peter 3:19-21)

In his second letter, Peter referred to the flood as an act of God in which he did not spare the "the ancient world," and he named "Noah" a "herald of righteousness" and indicated how many—"seven others"—were saved with him in the ark (2 Peter 2:5).

The writer of Hebrews refers to specific acts of Noah and the motives that prompted him to do these things. Noah acted "by faith" when he was warned about the coming flood. He acted in "reverent fear" by building an ark to save "his household." By faith he "condemned the world" and "became an heir of the righteousness that comes by faith" (Hebrews 11:7).

The Old and New Testaments share a single purpose

All of Scripture leads us to Christ

The Bible writers of the Old and New Testaments were dead serious about the words of Scripture because they were dead serious about God's plan of salvation. They preached repentance and faith in the forgiveness of sins won by Jesus for all people, and they taught that Christ was the only way to eternal life. That's why Scripture demands our utmost respect and attention.

God told Satan that someday a person would overcome what he had done: "He shall bruise your head, and you shall bruise his heel" (Genesis 3:15). God

What the Bible Says About Itself

had promised Abraham, "In you all the families of the earth shall be blessed" (Genesis 12:3). The promise was repeated by the prophet Nathan to King David: "When your days are fulfilled and you lie down with your fathers, I will raise up your offspring after you, who shall come from your body, and I will establish his kingdom. He shall build a house for my name, and I will establish the throne of his kingdom forever" (2 Samuel 7:12,13). David knew that God was speaking about the coming Savior. He prayed: "And now, O LORD God, confirm forever the word that you have spoken concerning your servant and concerning his house, and do as you have spoken" (2 Samuel 7:25).

Even a cursory reading of the gospels shows that Jesus was intent on keeping God's will as revealed in Scripture—on fulfilling God's promises to Adam and Eve, to Abraham, to David, and to all the people in Old Testament times. Fulfilling these prophecies—indeed, fulfilling the whole Old Testament—was the purpose for which he was born.

Jesus took part in the weekly synagogue services, in which the Old Testament Scriptures were read and interpreted to the people. On one occasion he read from Isaiah 66 and explained to the worshipers that he was fulfilling the promises found there: "Today this Scripture has been fulfilled in your hearing" (Luke 4:21). To the religious leaders of his day, Jesus said, "You search the Scriptures because you think that in them you have eternal life; and it is they that bear witness about me" (John 5:39).

On the Mount of Transfiguration, two of the Old Testament's greatest leaders, Moses and Elijah, met with Jesus and spoke of his departure, which he was about to accomplish at Jerusalem" (Luke 9:31). These two men were vitally interested in what Jesus would do in Jerusalem, namely, die for the sins of the world. Although they lived long before Jesus, their right to live in God's presence was based on what Jesus would do in Jerusalem, that is, "depart" this world after he had given his life for them.

It was no accident that Jesus died on the Jewish Passover. He was God's Passover Lamb. Paul wrote, "For Christ, our Passover lamb, has been sacrificed" (1 Corinthians 5:7). A quick look at the book of Hebrews shows how many other Old Testament laws pictured Jesus and his sacrifice for sin.

Jesus' followers were slow to understand the events of his life. On one occasion he had to rebuke two of them: "'O foolish ones, and slow of heart to believe all that the prophets have spoken! Was it not necessary that the Christ should suffer these things and enter into his glory?' And beginning with Moses and all the Prophets, he interpreted to them in all the Scriptures the things concerning himself" (Luke 24:25-27).

Jesus' own disciples were slow to grasp the obvious: "Then he said to them, 'These are my words that I spoke to you while I was still with you, that everything written about me in the Law of Moses and the Prophets and the Psalms must be fulfilled.' Then he opened their minds to understand the Scriptures" (Luke 24:44,45).

The New Testament writers understood their relation to the Old Testament and to Jesus. Paul referred to himself as a "servant of Christ Jesus, called to be an apostle, set apart for the gospel of God, which he promised beforehand through his prophets in the holy Scriptures, concerning his Son" (Romans 1:1-3).

The Scripture calls people to repentance and faith

The second chapter of Ezekiel shows how serious God is about his creation, in particular, the people he has created in his image. Ezekiel was commissioned to speak God's Word to the Jewish people. It would be a battle of words: words of the false prophets against the words God was speaking through Ezekiel. Only the absolute truth—the divine words that the Lord put into the mouth of Ezekiel—could turn the people from their wicked ways. And only God's promises of mercy could restore them as his children. Only if Ezekiel was convinced that his Words were God's words could he preach fearlessly. God gave Ezekiel that assurance:

> And he said to me, "Son of man, I send you to the people of Israel, to nations of rebels, who have rebelled against me. . . . I send you to them, and you shall say to them, 'Thus says the Lord GOD.' And whether they hear or refuse to hear (for they are a rebellious house) they will know that a prophet has been among them. And you, son of man . . . be not afraid of their words, nor be dismayed at their looks, for they are a rebellious house. . . . Be not rebellious like that rebellious house; open your mouth and eat what I give you." And when I looked, behold, a hand was stretched out to me, and behold, a scroll of a book was in it. And he spread it before me. And it had writing on the front and on the back, and there were written on it words of lamentation and mourning and woe. (From Ezekiel 2)

Jesus preached God's Word in that same spirit. Jesus rebuked the callous hearts to whom he was preaching: "Have you not read . . ." how David on one occasion ate the consecrated bread? "Have you not read . . ." in Moses' law about how God gave the priests permission to work on the Sabbath? (Matthew 12:3-5). Don't you remember Jonah's three days and nights in the belly of the fish, which is a sign of my three days and nights in the grave (Matthew 12:40)? Have you forgotten the testimony of the Ninevites, who repented at Jonah's preaching

(Matthew 12:41)? Have you forgotten the Queen of Sheba who came to faith when she heard the wisdom of Solomon (Matthew 12:42)?

And to those who rejected him, Jesus gave warnings from Scripture in no uncertain terms: "You hypocrites! Well did Isaiah prophesy of you . . ." that you honor God with your lips but not your heart (Matthew 15:7). Why do you dishonor what "God commanded" when he told you to honor your father and mother (Matthew 15:4)? You Sadducees are in error "because you know neither the Scriptures nor the power of God" (Matthew 22:29).

Christians believe the Scriptures because only the Scriptures lead us to Christ

Every Christian can make this confession: "I believe that I am a sinner, condemned to hell. But I believe that God himself came into this world to suffer for my sins, to enable me to become his child and serve him with my life, and to give me an eternal home with him. What is more, he has used the words of Scripture to lead me to realize my need for forgiveness, repent, and receive the benefit of his Son's work of salvation. And the Holy Spirit works on me daily through God's Word to strengthen my faith and to keep me on the road to eternal life. What the Scriptures have done for me and for countless others corresponds to what the Bible says about its truth and its power."

Question: "Why do you believe the Bible?" Reply: "Because the Bible says it is true."

Question: "How can you be sure that your interpretation of the Bible is correct in its report of the world's origin?" Reply: "Because I'm interpreting the early chapters of Genesis as Jesus and the writers of Scripture interpret it."

Question: "How can you be sure their words were accurately recorded?" Reply: "Because their words are found in Scripture, and Scripture is true."

Question: "But how can I be sure that the Bible's statements about its own truthfulness are true?" Reply: "Because that's what the Bible teaches."

Question: "But that's circular reasoning, isn't it?" Reply: "You're right; it is."

A missionary to Japan once explained his approach to the charge of circular reasoning. A man asked him, "But how can I believe this Bible of yours is true?" The missionary would only say, "Just read it and decide for yourself." Put a little differently, Siegbert Becker confesses:

> Scripture's message comes to me with the same words that were used by the Old Testament Prophets to introduce what they had to say, namely, "Thus said the Lord!" Far from being an argument in a circle, it is really a take-it-or-leave-it proposition.[3]

---

[3] Siegbert W. Becker, *The Scriptures—Inspired of God* (Milwaukee: Northwestern Publishing House, 1971), pp. 80,81.

Conclusion

Christian leaders have often pointed out that you cannot say Jesus is merely a great man or a profound teacher. Either he is who he says he is—the Son of God, Savior of the world, and Judge of all people. Or he is a lunatic and liar for making such claims.

We can apply the same logic to Scripture. One cannot say the Bible is a great collection of writings that form the epitome of mankind's religious thought and moral development. It is either a book given to us by God in his own words, through which he personally tells us about his actions in the past and his gracious will for us today. Or it is a book written by liars whose claims for its absolute truth and divine origin should warn anyone with common sense to avoid taking it seriously.

Should we accept Scripture as the truth revealed to us by the perfect Creator of our world, or should we consider it, at least in part, to be the product of his creatures' imperfect attempts to serve as his mouthpiece? This is the choice theistic evolution forces Christians to wrestle with. As you continue reading about what theistic evolutionists say about Scripture, keep in mind what Scripture says about itself.

A cliché

Throughout this book we will occasionally pause to consider arguments used by theistic evolutionists that seem to back up their claims. These arguments are repeated over and over again in the literature. They have become clichés. They can be quite convincing. They need some analysis.

Before we continue with our primer on historical criticism, we'll look at a popular method used to give scientific conclusions about the world equal status with Scripture. The argument supposedly comes from Scripture itself. This cliché will help us see the importance of what we have done in this chapter—carefully looking at what Scripture says about itself and its unique authority.

> **Cliché: God has revealed himself in two books—Scripture and Nature. We must let each book help us understand the other.**
>
> The argument goes like this. Scripture teaches that there are two "books," the book of Scripture itself and the book of Nature. We should read each one for what it teaches us.
>
> To evaluate this cliché, we should begin with what the Bible actually says about the "two books."

What the Bible Says About Itself

Scripture tells us that what God has made displays certain things about God—he is divine, he is powerful, he is eternal, and he shapes and guides all things. Saint Paul wrote in Romans 1:20, "For his invisible attributes, namely, his eternal power and divine nature, have been clearly perceived, ever since the creation of the world, in the things that have been made. So they are without excuse." The psalmist David wrote, "The heavens declare the glory of God, and the sky above proclaims his handiwork" (Psalm 19:1). David also praised God when he thought about his body: "I praise you, for I am fearfully and wonderfully made. Wonderful are your works; my soul knows it very well" (Psalm 139:14). Paul appealed to the knowledge of God's providence that all people have: "And he made from one man every nation of mankind to live on all the face of the earth, having determined allotted periods and the boundaries of their dwelling place, that they should seek God, and perhaps feel their way toward him and find him" (Acts 17:26,27).

The relation between what we read in Scripture and what we see in creation is quite simple: Scripture says that God is glorious. What we see in creation affirms that fact. Case closed.

Or it should be.

In the minds of theistic evolutionists, this simple idea has morphed into something more complex. As the "two books" concept becomes more complex, it slowly creates an illegitimate conflict between Scripture and science. Here is how the discussion goes:

(1) Scripture teaches that there are two books that tell us about God. One book contains everything God has revealed. The other book contains everything scientists have discovered about the world.

(2) Since the content of these two books comes from God, they both convey information that is completely true.

(3) The title of the first book could be expanded: *The Truth Taught in Scripture*. The full title of the second book could be: *The Truth Learned From Observing the World*.

(4) Since both books are "The Truth"—God's truth—neither book can take precedence over the other.

(5) Over the years, the content of both books has been expanded. We have witnessed *The Truth Taught In Scripture* interpreted and reinterpreted. It is now a book that no longer contains just the

words of God, but it includes a large number of interpretations Bible scholars have added to it over the centuries.

The content of *The Truth Learned From Observing the World* has also been expanded. It no longer contains observations of creation that illustrate God's power and wisdom. It also includes the various ways scientists have organized and interpreted their observations of the data. The theory of evolution is one of those ways, which today has replaced older ideas about the origin of the world.

(6) Once the content of both books has been modified and expanded, the door is open to theistic evolutionist logic: The truth found in each book does not contradict the truth found in the other book. It is only the *interpretation* of the truth found in the two books that seems to contradict the other. Scientists have drawn some wrong conclusions about the truth found in the book of Nature. But theologians have also come to wrong conclusions about the interpretation of Scripture. So we must maintain an open-minded humility and admit that contradictions between the two books are due to our faulty thinking.

(7) The logic results in this approach to Scripture: In order to discover the truth, we must draw on both Scripture and nature. Sometimes we must let Scripture guide our understanding of nature. But sometimes we must let what we observe in nature correct a wrong interpretation of Scripture. Think about Galileo. His discoveries forced the church to redo its interpretation of many passages on the relation of the sun and the earth. In the case of the current debate over creation and evolution, the truth of evolution must force us to reevaluate how we understand creation as described in Genesis.

If you have felt swept along by this way of thinking, you might be scratching your head and thinking, "I know that all truth is God's truth. Since the description of creation in *The Truth Taught in Scripture* is in conflict with the truth about creation taught in *The Truth Learned From Observing the World*, perhaps I should reevaluate my thinking about a six-day creation as taught in Scripture. After all, evolution is based on hard, observable data, while my ideas about creation are based on words, which we all know have been interpreted differently over the centuries."

If this is how you are tempted to think, consider slowly backing out of the argument. Theistic evolutionists take the idea that there are two books and redefine those books in a way that creates the potential for them to contradict each other and force their readers to make a choice between them. Remind yourself (1) that Scripture is God's Word and is not a mixture of the text of Scripture itself plus a muddle of conflicting human interpretations of what it says. Then remind yourself that (2) observations of nature are just that—observations of things people can actually see. They are not a muddle of what people see plus their speculation of how what they see came into being.

Scripture never calls what we see around us a "book." This is a theological idea, which, in a non-evolutionary age might be harmless. But today it is not. The book of Scripture identifies what we are to learn from nature. The glory of God's creation and how he shapes the lives of his creatures is nothing more than a testimony to the glory of God as described in Scripture itself.[4]

---

[4] For more on this point, see Andrew S. Kulikovsky, *Creation, Fall, Restoration: A Biblical Theology of Creation* (Ross-shire, Scotland: Mentor, 2009), pp 15-26.

Part Two

Historical Criticism

Chapter 2

Historical Criticism:
Theistic Evolution's Tool of Interpretation

Growing Pressure on the Bible

Introduction

Trying to keep the marriage going

For centuries Scripture and science had enjoyed a relatively successful marriage. Genesis had been read in a straightforward way. It was accepted as an accurate description of how God created the universe. Natural philosophers attempted to draw conclusions from their observations accordingly. (Natural philosopher is a old term for scientist.)

But the world began to change. The Renaissance followed by the Enlightenment began to create a new worldview in which science and Scripture as traditionally understood would have to go their separate ways. Natural philosophy began insisting on the right to analyze its findings without concern for Scripture. The general attitude of the natural philosophers was, "You can't argue with what you see." Scripture agreed, but only as long as "what you see" was interpreted in a way that did not contradict the literal reading of Scripture.

The marriage came into real danger when natural philosophers began speculating about the origin of things: at first about minerals and rock formations and later about the origin of plants and animals. Their speculation always included time frames and methods that conflicted with a straightforward reading of Scripture.

At first, the natural philosophers knew they were merely speculating. But over time, they became more and more insistent that, even if their speculations might be chronologically off target in scriptural terms, "something like this simply *had to* have happened." Scripture, however, would put its foot down and say that "something like that *did not* happen." A divorce seemed inevitable.

Or was it? Many theologians thought the marriage could be saved. But if it were to be changed, Scripture would have to become more agreeable. In the end, it did, and the marriage continued. The second part of this book is the story of that change—how Scripture was made agreeable to evolutionary science.

Introduction to the effort to change the meaning of Scripture

As mentioned above, long before Darwin natural philosophers became interested in the rocks and rock formations they observed around them. They began to speculate about how these formations came to be, which naturally led to speculation about how the world and the universe came into existence. Their speculation about the formation of the universe required much more time than a literal reading of Scripture allowed. Then, near the end of the 18th century, the origin of plants and animals came under consideration. They, too, needed long periods of time to develop. Thousands of years turned into tens of thousands, then hundreds of thousands, and then millions—an astounding length of time in those days.

The length of time required by evolutionary science made it impossible to accept Scripture and evolution. The chronology of Scripture simply could not be expanded enough to accommodate the tens of thousands of years necessary for even the earliest scientific theories. It would have been easy simply to discard Scripture in the face of these speculations. But many refused to do that. They treasured Scripture. Many wanted to remain faithful to the early chapters of Genesis, but they also wanted to pursue their ideas about how the universe developed.

From the very beginning, scientists and theologians realized that there were only two ways to maintain the truth of Genesis without abandoning their speculation about the earth's age. Either (1) they had to accept the traditional narrative *approach to the early chapters of Genesis and find alternate meanings to the words and sentences* used there. Or (2) they had to rethink *what kind of literature* the early chapters of Genesis contained.

Some began to work with word and passage meanings, and some still try to do that today. For example, what does the word "day" in Genesis 1 refer to? In Scripture, the word "day" can mean a 24-hour day or a long period of time. Natural philosophers began arguing that "day" in Genesis 1 and 2 must mean a long period of time. Methods for reinterpreting the "kinds" of Genesis 1 also had to be developed. The phrase "in the beginning" in Genesis 1:1 had to be reinterpreted so it no longer referred to a point in time.

But many found, and still find today, that debates about word meanings are too often strained and result in odd interpretations that conflict with a common sense approach to language. To early promoters of evolutionary ideas, it became clear that they had to interpret too many words and sentences of Scripture in ways Scripture simply could not support. There were too many statements in Scripture that still begged to be read in a traditional, literal way.

It would be much easier simply to change one's approach to Scripture as a whole. And that is what happened. As early natural philosophers were struggling to combine evolutionary ideas with Scripture, the nature of Scripture itself was being redefined by theologians in academic circles. We should not think, however, that the pressure to redefine Scripture came only from natural philosophers who wanted to make it compatible with early evolutionary ideas. Scripture was being redefined for more general reasons. Forces were at work in the Western world that went beyond those generated by science. They came from two broad movements, the Renaissance, and in particular the Enlightenment, which would sweep the Christian West in the 18th century. Intellectual forces at work in the Western world moved scholars to work out a way of redefining and reinterpreting Scripture that was conveniently at hand when natural philosophers needed it, particularly in the wake of Darwin.

The formal re-creation of Scripture began in the early18th century and by the middle of the 19th century it affected almost all of European Christianity. In fact, some of the early emigrants to the United States left Europe in order to avoid parish life shaped by a re-created Bible. But the new way of reading Scripture followed them. Beginning in the late 1800s, it was imported into American religion. Throughout the 20th century it has continued to spread from one American denomination to another.

In recent years, most books by theistic evolutionists begin with the author's statement that they are using a newer, more scholarly way of interpreting Scripture. They give the impression that this new way of interpreting Scripture began in fairly recent times. It is billed as a new discovery based on the studies and findings of the best modern Bible scholars. Just as the old is giving way to the new in all areas of learning, the old way of interpreting Scripture is giving way to a new and more productive approach with the help of such things as archaeological research and computer-assisted text analysis.

The fact is, however, that what modern "critical" scholars are teaching about the Bible is nothing new. It is merely a thinly veiled modern version of methods for redefining Scripture that were under development some three hundred years ago.

In order to read theistic evolutionary literature, it is almost mandatory to have a basic grasp of the history of the redefinition of Scripture. What follows in the next three chapters is a primer on that history. It is a combination of the history of the movement, anecdotes to show how the movement has affected Bible study today, and a discussion of the clichés based on the new way of interpreting Scripture that one finds throughout theistic evolutionary literature.

When you are finished reading this section, you will be able to spot historical criticism when you come across it.

Early forces: the Renaissance

The new way of viewing Scripture is called historical criticism. Here the word *criticism* does not mean just being critical of the Scripture. It refers to tools developed to analyze the text and discover its meaning. The word *historical* refers to the attempt to discover the history of Scripture, which, it is claimed, is the key to unlocking its meaning.

The development of historical criticism began in earnest in the 18th century and reached its most intense period in the 19th. It's roots, however, are found in an earlier movement called the Renaissance. The Renaissance began in Italy in the 1300s, spread throughout Europe, and continued until about 1600. The European Renaissance was a time of rapid growth in learning and the arts. Renaissance leaders worked to rediscover knowledge and skills that had been lost since the collapse of the Greek and Roman empires. Perhaps the most well-known Renaissance figure is Leonardo da Vinci (1452–1519), whose life and work epitomizes the Renaissance spirit.

The Renaissance was not primarily a religious movement. Nor did it have a direct influence on how church leaders of the day interpreted the Bible. Kings and princes merely wanted to beautify their cities and make them centers of learning. Many Renaissance leaders were in high positions in the Catholic Church and wanted to use the learning of the past in service to the church—to beautify church buildings and enhance the training of the clergy. Ancient manuscripts from Greece and Rome revealed a culture much more glorious than the culture of medieval Europe. Renaissance scholars worked to rediscover the art, sculpture, architecture, and philosophy of ancient Greece and Rome. A catchphrase of the Renaissance was *ad fontes*, "back to the sources," that is, back to the documents produced in ancient Greece and Rome. Many documents were already well known. Renaissance scholars scoured ancient monastic libraries looking for more.

Tools to study these documents were needed. Scholars developed a variety of ways to examine newly found manuscripts to see if they were what they claimed to be. This is what it meant to study them "critically." Manuscripts were subject to a barrage of questions: Did the work fit into the time period in which it claimed to have been written? For example, is the vocabulary of the manuscript appropriate to that time, or does it give evidence that the book was written at a later date? Was the manuscript really written by the person whose name was attached to it; did the manuscript's vocabulary and style correspond to that of other manuscripts written by the same author? If several manuscripts of the same work existed and there were small changes in wording among the manuscripts, which of the "variant readings" had been in the original manuscript? These are all legitimate questions. Similar questions are asked in modern courts of law to distinguish genuine documents from fakes.

The Reformers themselves benefited from Renaissance learning. The Renaissance scholar Desiderius Erasmus studied the various Greek manuscripts at his disposal and produced the Greek text Luther used to make his German translation of the Bible. Philip Melanchthon, Martin Luther's most valued coworker, was a Renaissance scholar, and he used his understanding of Greek and the ancient skills of logic and rhetoric to advance the Lutheran Reformation.

Nevertheless, there was a dark side to the otherwise legitimate analysis of ancient documents. Scripture, after all, is an ancient document, and some scholars believed they should subject Scripture to the same critical examination as other ancient documents.

Before we turn to that topic, we should note a more general dark side of the Renaissance. The Renaissance began to shift how people thought about God. Prior to the Renaissance, the Christian world focused on the Word of God, which pointed people to the glories of the world to come. By contrast, the Renaissance focused on the glory of the human body and mind and fostered what we would call a more "secular" world-view.

Renaissance culture began to think that man, not God, was the measure of all things. In other words, truth became a relative concept, determined by how human beings, not God, defined it. In Renaissance studies, "one felt *no weight of the supernatural* pressing on the human mind, demanding homage and allegiance. Humanity—with all its distinct capabilities, talents, worries, problems, possibilities—was the center of interest."[5] Accordingly, the Renaissance has been called a humanistic movement.

Moreover, the Renaissance desire to learn from the past brought Greek attitudes and philosophies to the church's doorstep. Paul had to warn the Corinthians: "Jews demand miraculous signs and Greeks look for wisdom, but we preach Christ crucified: a stumbling block to Jews and foolishness to Gentiles" (1 Corinthians 1:21-23). That warning once more became necessary in the Renaissance, when the wisdom of the Greeks was once more a major topic of study.

---

[5]"Humanism," The Cambridge Dictionary of Philosophy, 2nd Edition (Cambridge University Press, 1999), p. 397 (emphasis added).

Cliché: The doctrine of the inspiration of Scripture is a recent development.

Francis Collins, the head of the human genome project and a theistic evolutionist, uses the tools of historical criticism in his interpretation of Genesis. He believes that this way of approaching Scripture has been the standard practice in the Christian church since its beginning and that the teaching that every word of Scripture is inspired by God is a recent development. He wrote:

> It is clear that the ultra-literal YEC [young earth creationist] views are in fact not required by a careful, sincere, and worshipful reading of the original text. In fact, this narrow interpretation is largely a creation of the last hundred years, arising in large consequence as a reaction to Darwinian evolution.[6]

Some theistic evolutionists support this idea. Some mention that the early church father Origin did not read the words of Scripture literally but merely used the words as a jumping-off point to teach deeper, spiritual truths. Some point out that Augustine, a highly respected church father, sometimes used non-literal methods of interpretation. For these reasons they claim that a non-literal method of interpreting Scripture became the official position of the Catholic Church.

To be fair, most theistic evolutionists know that this is not the case. They know that in spite of some exceptions, a literal reading of Genesis 1 and 2 based on the verbal inspiration of Scripture was the norm in the Christian church up to the Enlightenment.

Martin Luther reacted against Augustine's non-literal interpretation of Genesis, and he argued that Moses' words are to be interpreted in a straightforward way:

> Nor does it serve any useful purpose to make Moses at the outset so mystical and allegorical. His purpose is to teach us, not about allegorical creatures and an allegorical world but about real creatures and a visible world apprehended by the senses. There, as the proverb has it, he calls "a spade a spade," i.e., he employs the terms "day" and "evening" without allegory, just as we customarily do.[7]

---

[6] Francis Collins, *The Language of God* (New York: Free Press, 2006), p. 175.

[7] Martin Luther, *Luther's Works, Vol. 1, Lectures on Genesis Chapters 1-5*, edited by Jaroslav Pe-

Growing Pressure on the Bible

Some accuse the Lutheran dogmaticians of concocting a doctrine of verbal inspiration that went far beyond Martin Luther. But Luther scholar Robert Preus says, "Except for a few rather free-thinking Catholic theologians like Erasmus and Albert Pighius, most Catholics before the seventeenth century spoke of the origin of Scripture [that is, as being verbally inspired by God] in terms very like those employed by the seventeenth century Lutheran dogmaticians."[8]

In the higher critical *Dictionary of Biblical Interpretation,* John Barton, who is one of the foremost modern advocates of historical-critical methods, wrote in his article on verbal inspiration, "It can reasonably be said that verbal inspiration in some form has been the majority opinion about the nature of scripture throughout most of Christian history."[9]

Luther and the other reformers rejected the Catholic practice of finding allegories throughout Scripture. And they rejected the Catholic teaching that Scripture had to be supplemented by the decrees of the pope and church councils. But they did not disagree with the Catholic Church on the teaching that the entire Hebrew and Greek Scriptures were inspired by God and therefore completely true. Significantly, when the Lutherans wrote their confessions, they found no need to add a section on Scripture to distinguish Lutheran teaching from Roman Catholic teaching.

In his article on verbal inspiration in the *Dictionary of Biblical Interpretation* referred to above, John Barton gives an honest appraisal of what the teaching of inspiration means:

> It is hard to see how we can avoid calling the inspiration of Scripture verbal, since the Bible, being a book or collection of books, is composed of words. There is a considerable paradox in saying that a book is divinely inspired while denying that the inspiration extends to the words which comprise it.
>
> Even the theory that it is not the words, but the content of the Bible that is inspired, is difficult in the light of the recognition, in modern linguistic study, that the content of a text cannot be separated from the words through which

---

likan (Saint Louis: Concordia, 1958), p. 5.

[8] Robert Preus, *The Inspiration of Scripture: A Study of the Theology of the 17th-Century Lutheran Dogmaticians,* 2nd Edition (St. Louis: Concordia, 1957), p. 26.

[9] John Barton, "Verbal Inspiration," *A Dictionary of Biblical Interpretation*, ed. R. Coggins and J. Houldon (London: SCM Press, 1990), p. 721.

that content is expressed. If the words were different, the content or "message" would necessarily be different, too.[10]

Martin Luther could not have said it better.

Those who claim that the Fundamentalists of the early 20th century were the first to teach verbal inspiration on which the 24-hour creation day was built, have not done their homework. When the Fundamentalists came on the scene, nearly all American denominations taught verbal inspiration and those that didn't had fairly recently given up that teaching.

This is certainly true of the early Lutheran churches in the United States. Present teachers in the Evangelical Lutheran Church of America (ELCA) are, in general, strong proponents of historical criticism. But as recent as 1938, in an adult instruction manual commissioned by the Board of Christian Education of the American Lutheran Church (the ALC is one of the Lutheran bodies that merged into the ELCA), we find this statement about the Bible: "The Bible thus is different from all other books in the world, because its source and authorship is different. This book is from God in an altogether different way from that of any other good book we might mention. It is inspired in the special sense that God chose these men for their work and revealed to them what they should say and write. Therefore what they wrote is an infallible revelation of God."[11] The author's statement on creation follows suit, as we noted in the Introduction.[12]

Francis Collins' statement reverses the truth. It is not the "ultraliteral" young earth creationists who came up with the teaching of a 24-hour creation day. Rather, it is the much more recent methods of higher criticism that have altered this ancient way of interpreting Genesis 1.

---

[10] John Barton, "Verbal Inspiration," *A Dictionary of Biblical Interpretation*, p. 721.

[11] Martin Anderson, *The Adult Class Manual* (Minneapolis: Augsburg Publishing House, 1938), p. 1.

[12] Martin Anderson, *The Adult Class Manual*, p. 12.

Should critical scholarship be applied to the text of the Bible?

During the Reformation

There was nothing wrong with how Renaissance scholars developed and used critical tools to judge the manuscripts they had unearthed. The natural question was whether those tools should be used to evaluate—and judge—the Scriptures.

Scripture and secular ancient manuscripts do have some things in common. God did not provide the church with a Bible written on stones and then stand over them throughout the centuries testifying that these words were written by him. God used human beings to write down his Word.

Nor did God inspire a book and then come down from heaven and announce to everyone, "This book belongs in the Bible." Rather, he worked through Christian leaders to assemble his writings into the "canon" (that is, the set of books that do, in fact, belong in his Scripture).

God did not establish a divine publishing house with a sole license to copy his Word. He transmitted the text throughout the centuries by whatever copying technique was in use at the time. Before the printing press was invented, God used human copyists, who made one copy of the Bible at a time.

God's method of revealing his Word, assembling the canon, and transmitting it down through the centuries has forced the church throughout its history to answer a number of questions. For example, How can each human author reflect his own style, vocabulary, and emotions yet still be writing under God's inspiration? Why are there verses in a particular book of the Bible that seem to have been inserted by a later writer or editor? Why were some books included in the Old Testament while others referred to there were not? Why was the inclusion of certain books into the canon of the New Testament questioned here and there in the early Christian church—a fact that forced the early church to make some decisions about these "disputed books" and whether they belonged in Scripture? It is a fact that there are small differences between various ancient copies of the Bible. These differences are called variants. For the most part, they are copyist errors. But every Bible scholar, ancient and modern, has the task of deciding which of the variants were in the original manuscript written by the Bible writer. The question is: Why did God force the church to make such decisions? And what is the relation between the variant readings and the Scripture's teaching of verbal inspiration?[13]

---

[13] The process of making decisions about variants has also been called literary criticism or text criticism. This is practiced by all denominations in the Christian church. The word *criticism* does not mean to be critical about the Bible but to make judgments about the variants. This work is also called lower criticism in distinction from higher criticism, another term for historical criticism. (Note that literary criticism is also used for a specific kind of historical criticism, which

All these issues can be addressed in a humble spirit that trusts in the verbal inspiration of Scripture. In some cases, the simple answer "we don't know" is legitimate. On the other hand, these issues can be handled in ways that imply that Scripture is not completely true: Who *actually* wrote the books of the Bible (asked with the assumption that the book may not have been written by the author named in the book itself or provided elsewhere in Scripture)? When were the books of the Bible *really* written (asked with doubt about the chronology found in Scripture itself)? How do we deal with *inconsistencies* in the Bible (under the presupposition that inconsistencies exist)? How can we be sure that the church was correct when *it chose* which books should be in the Bible (implying that the church, and not God, was behind the decisions)?

The Reformers were not oblivious to these questions or to the fact that some were hard to answer. They thought about these questions carefully. But they always answered them in the light of what Scripture says about itself: that it is revealed by God and that its every word is inspired. Reasonable answers were not difficult to find for most of the problems. Some questions eluded completely satisfactory answers and were answered with as much information as Scripture itself provides—and left at that.

As we noted in the last chapter, the New Testament writers themselves faced these very issues when they studied the Old Testament Scriptures. They faced questions about the canon of Scripture, about variant readings among the manuscripts, and about matters of vocabulary and style. The New Testament writers didn't let these matters bother them. They quoted from the Old Testament canon that had been passed down to them. Even though there were some variants among the manuscripts, they quoted the human authors of Scripture as God's spokesmen, whose words were true. The Reformers approached Scripture in the same way.

But in the context of the Renaissance, when scholars were examining critically ancient Greek and Roman manuscripts, Bible scholars came under increasing pressure to examine Scripture with the same critical tools.

Already in Luther's day the waters were being muddied. Andreas Karlstadt (1486–1541), one of Luther's colleagues at the University of Wittenberg, was the first within Protestantism to engage in critical analysis of Scripture. He expressed certain concerns about the formation of the canon and how to evaluate the different writing styles found within books by the same author. He raised questions about the Mosaic authorship of sections of the Pentateuch, like the death of Moses.

---

will be mentioned later in this book.)

Karlstadt did not think he was departing from Reformation principles. But he began to ask the same questions that would be asked again and again in later historical-critical research, and he was not averse to dealing with Scripture in ways similar to how historical-critical scholars of the future would deal with it. As one example, Karlstadt doubted that Ezra wrote the book of Ezra since he didn't think Ezra would have praised himself as he does in 7:6,25. Ezra wrote: "He was a scribe skilled in the Law of Moses. . . . And you, Ezra, according to the wisdom of your God that is in your hand, appoint magistrates and judges." Karlstadt's doubt about the authorship of Ezra was a matter of opinion, based on Karlstadt's own view of what is proper or improper for a person to say about himself.[14]

After the Reformation

In the years after the Reformation, most people accepted what Jesus and the New Testament writers said about the inspiration and truth of Scripture. But more and more scholars in the church questioned this. They struggled to answer the questions raised about Scripture during the Renaissance that we noted above, and they began to doubt the reliability of the Bible. During the first 150 years after the Reformation, many of them came to two conclusions about Scripture. First, they became convinced that Scripture can be evaluated like any piece of ancient literature. Second, they denied the verbal inspiration (and, therefore, the truth) of Scripture.

A quick look at a number of men who lived in the post-Reformation years will give us a feel for what was beginning to happen.[15]

The words compilation and redaction were first used in a book published in 1574 by *Andreas Masius* (a Roman Catholic lawyer, 1514–1573). The concept of "compilation" is the idea that the Scripture was a collection of many ancient documents, which at some point were assembled by a "redactor" (or editor) to create our Bible. This way of approaching Scripture was later developed by historical critics under the name "source criticism."[16] This concept plays havoc with what Scripture itself says about who wrote it and when it was written.

The *Socinians*, an anti-Trinitarian group that began in the late 1500s, claimed that the Old Testament is not literal history and that it was treated as history for the first time by the writers of the New Testament. This, of course, destroys

---

[14] Hans-Joachim Kraus, *Geschichte der Historisch-Kritischen Erforschung des Alten Testaments* (Neukirchen Verlag, 1956), pp. 25ff.

[15] Hans-Joachim Kraus, *Geschichte,* for Kraus' complete list, see pp. 34-64.

[16] Hans-Joachim Kraus, *Geschichte*, p. 35.

both the historicity of the Old Testament and the credibility of Jesus and the New Testament writers.[17]

Hugo Grotius (1583–1645), a lawyer and Reformed theologian, tried to establish a truly objective way of interpreting the Old Testament. To do this he denied that the New Testament writers had the right to interpret the Old Testament.[18] This idea, of course, makes the Old Testament a document written only for people of one time and culture. It also denies the purpose of the Old Testament to foretell and reveal the Savior's work.

Seventeenth century *English Deists* (who taught that God exists but has little to do with his creation) put the Old Testament laws on the level of those developed by other nations in the ancient Near Eastern world. This effectively turned the Bible into one human document among many.[19] This approach to Scripture gained popularity as historical criticism developed, and it plays a major role in how modern theistic evolutionists rely on ancient Near Eastern literature to evaluate Scripture (which we will address in the last three chapters of this book).

The Jewish philosopher *Baruch Spinoza* (1632–1677) was the first to develop a full-blown historical-critical method of interpreting the Old Testament.[20] Spinoza listed difficult questions about Scripture and suggested methods of approaching those questions in line with the tools being used to critique other ancient manuscripts.

Although the Catholic Church did not adopt historical criticism until the end of World War II in our century, in the 17th century some *Jesuit theologians* used various methods we would label as historical critical. Their goal was to devalue Scripture in order to elevate papal authority.[21]

Forces at work leading up to the Enlightenment

These writers did not gather large followings and were often suppressed by religious and secular authorities. By 1700, however, new ways of thinking about the world—about law, economics, social institutions, religion, and mankind—were developing throughout Europe. The mild force of the Renaissance was being replaced by the more powerful thinking of the radical Enlightenment.[22]

---

[17] Hans-Joachim Kraus, *Geschichte*, pp. 37-39.

[18] Hans-Joachim Kraus, *Geschichte*, p. 47.

[19] Hans-Joachim Kraus, *Geschichte*, p. 52.

[20] Hans-Joachim Kraus, *Geschichte*, p. 57.

[21] Robert Preus, *The Inspiration of Scripture*, p. 26.

[22] The term radical is not a personal comment about Enlightenment thought. It is a somewhat technical term for the early Enlightenment's challenge to the status quo. It refers to the philosophers of the first hundred years of the movement who challenged European culture and religion. Modern scholar Jonathan Israel titled his book on the whole history of the Enlightenment,

Growing Pressure on the Bible

The Enlightenment had a profound affect on Christianity as practiced in Europe, and it opened the door to the use of historical-critical methods within mainstream Christianity.

Enlightenment thought itself and its methods of interpreting the text of Scripture did not arise in a vacuum. We will look at the Enlightenment later in this chapter. But first, we should note a cluster of forces at work in the days following the Reformation. All these forces contributed to the general desire to think about life in more "enlightened" ways, and this included new ways of understanding Scripture.

European Christianity was no longer a united force

Following the Reformation, the Lutheran and Reformed churches continued to debate their doctrinal positions. Both struggled to maintain their identity against the Catholics. The Catholic Church began a Counter Reformation, built on a fresh doctrinal statement drafted at the Council of Trent (1545–1563). Led by the Jesuits, Catholics worked to regain the territories they had lost to the Protestants.

In the European world, the Catholic Church for centuries had been a "state church." Under that arrangement, the church and the state saw themselves in a mutually beneficial relationship. The church was to uphold the moral fabric of society and pray for the state, and the state was to protect the church and punish heretics. A threat to one side of this relationship was a threat to the other. After the Reformation, the Lutherans and the Reformed churches, largely for their own survival, also adopted the state-church system.

But this created a problem. The secular authorities in each state were now responsible for protecting their territories against the other two religions. There was only one way to solve the problem. The stability of the state-church system demanded that the doctrinal differences between the Protestants and Catholics be resolved. One way was through force of arms. Everyone fully expected the Reformation to end in a major armed conflict, which it did. That conflict broke out in 1618 and came to be called the Thirty Years' War (1618–1648). Various European nations joined in the conflict, which was fought entirely on German soil. The war began for clear religious reasons, but by its end it had become as much political as religious. The Thirty Years' War solved little, and it even made the church-state system more complicated. In the Peace of Westphalia (1648), it was agreed that the prince of each territory would decide which religion was

---

beginning already in the 17th century, *The Radical Enlightenment: Philosophy and the Making of Modernity 1650–1750*. Israel was not singling out a few Enlightenment philosophers who were particularly radical. In those first hundred years of the Enlightenment, they were all radical, hence the term.

to be the state church in his territory—the Evangelical (Lutheran) church, the Catholic church, or the Reformed (Calvinist) church, which had become a new member on the list of approved churches. Members of religions other than the official state church of a particular territory could live there, but they were restricted in how they could worship and discuss their faith.

What does this have to do with the challenge to God's Word? By the late 1600s the religious world was fractured. What's more, people were getting tired of Christians fighting over the meaning of Scripture. People wanted peace. Christians were urged to be more tolerant of each other's teachings.

In that environment it was difficult to claim that Scripture was an objective source of truth. Serious Christians certainly understood that differences of belief lay with faulty interpretations of Scripture, not with Scripture itself. Most, however, only saw three church bodies, each claiming that their interpretation of Scripture was correct. They began to ask if Scripture could really yield a single meaning. They concluded that Scripture was not clear, or perhaps was not even the kind of literature that was able to, or even meant to, yield a single meaning. They began looking for methods that could assure a more "objective" interpretation, outside the arena of quibbling theologians.

The European political landscape was changing

In line with the humanistic impulse that began during the Renaissance, a new breed of philosophers urged people to view themselves as autonomous, to chart their own course in life, and to decide for themselves the best way to live. God was usually somewhere in the picture, but his role in human life took a back seat to humanistic self-determination. This was readily accepted by many European princes, who used it for political ends. After all, a prince has more freedom to do what he wants if he isn't required to answer to God. While many princes in the days after the Reformation concerned themselves with the religious life of their people, the new form of leadership became more and more concerned with secular matters. More and more, political leaders stocked their courts, churches, and universities in their realm with pastors and teachers who shared the humanistic mind-set.

The Scientific Revolution

The 17th century was the century of men like Galileo and Newton, who were at the heart of what's called the Scientific Revolution.

The Scientific Revolution was termed a "revolution" not just because of the large number of new discoveries made during that period or because those discoveries were considered by some to be a "revolt" against Scripture. It was called a revolution because it resulted in a new way of understanding the universe.

For the previous two thousand years, the Christian West had viewed the world through the eyes of the ancient philosopher Aristotle. The Catholic Church, largely through the work of Thomas Aquinas (1225–1274), had incorporated much of Aristotle's philosophy into its theology and also into *how it read Scripture's statements about the natural world*. For example, in line with Aristotle's earth-centered universe, the Catholic Church interpreted passages that spoke about the sun rising and setting to prove that the earth was at the center of the universe and that the sun revolved around the earth.

For this reason, when Aristotle's view of the universe began to be challenged, Catholic theology itself was being challenged. Some in the church dug in their heels against Galileo's idea that the earth revolved around the sun on the basis of what they considered a literal reading of Scripture. As Galileo's ideas became more and more firmly established, it became clear that if the Catholic Church's interpretation of Scripture was correct, then either Scripture could not be read literally, or it had to be read as a book that contained outdated ideas about the universe.

> **Cliché: Remember the Galileo affair!**
>
> Almost all theistic evolutionists include the "Galileo affair" somewhere in their books. The use of the Galileo affair is a true cliché—usually used without much research or thought. I don't mean to be harsh, but it is almost impossible to put a good spin on the way most theistic evolutionists use this account.
>
> Here's how the Galileo affair is presented: Galileo discovered that the earth revolves around the sun. In spite of Galileo's clear evidence for this scientific truth, the Catholic Church blindly and stubbornly condemned Galileo. The Church argued that the Bible clearly says that the earth cannot be moved and that the sun revolves around the earth. Consider the fact, Church leaders argued, that Joshua commanded the sun, not the earth, to stand still until he defeated Israel's enemies (Joshua 10:12,13). As a result, the Church foolishly arrested and tried Galileo for merely reporting what he saw.
>
> Theistic evolutionists apply the Galileo affair to the creation/evolution debate: In the face of the clear evidence for evolution, those who accept Genesis 1 and 2 as literally true make the same blind and stubborn mistake the Catholic Church made in its reaction against Galileo's indisputable conclusion that the earth revolves

around the sun. The Church of that time was shown to be wrong and forced to change its traditional interpretation of passages like Joshua 10:12,13. Christians today in the light of modern scientific observations that prove evolution should follow suit and change their outdated view of a literal reading of Genesis 1 and 2.[23]

But what exactly was the Galileo affair? Books have been written on Galileo's life. The story of his problems with the Catholic Church is readily available on the internet. But a few comments will alert you to the complex nature of the story and the unscholarly way theistic evolutionists often use it.

It wasn't that one day Galileo built a telescope and said, "Look, I see the earth revolving around the sun," only to have the whole Catholic Church rise up in arms against him because the Bible clearly says the sun revolves around the earth.

The telescope did provide some close-up details of the heavenly bodies that supported a sun-centered universe. However, Galileo himself was mostly working with the same observational data that his predecessors had relied on.

The basic scientific argument against the earth moving around the sun was the fact that you can't feel it move. Galileo's most important book *Dialogue Concerning the Two Chief World Systems* (1632) had originally been titled *On the Flux and Reflux of the Sea*. At that time Galileo's primary argument for the earth being in motion around the sun was not what he saw through his telescope, but the phenomenon of tides, which were a sort of "sloshing around" of the oceans due to the earth's movement. You may not be able to feel the earth move, he claimed, but you can observe the results of its movement in the tides. It would take Isaac Newton (1643–1727), not earlier scientists like Galileo, to work out the physics that made the heliocentric view of the universe entirely convincing.

Much more was at stake, however, than several Bible passages that might be interpreted to say that the earth was at the center of the universe. Galileo was challenging the entire understanding of reality as taught by the Roman Catholic Church. That's why the scientific ideas of men like Galileo were considered revolutionary.

The Western Christian view of reality was not based only on Scripture. It was also based on the writings of the ancient philosopher

---

[23] Denis O. Lamoureax, *Evolutionary Creation* (Eugene, Oregon: Wipf & Stock, 2008), p. 25.

Growing Pressure on the Bible

Aristotle (384–322 B.C.). The early Catholic teacher Thomas Aquinas (1225–1274) had synthesized the Catholic Church's theology and Aristotle's philosophy. Included in the synthesis by Aquinas was Aristotle's understanding that the earth was at the center of the universe. Aristotle reasoned that everything was made up of four elements, with earth being the heaviest. Heavier elements went down and lighter elements rose above the heavier ones: invariably water rested above earth, air above water, and fire rose upward above the air. The heavenly bodies were the lightest of all and circled around the earth far above it. According to Aristotle's logic, the earth had to be immovable and at rest in the center of the universe. The heavenly bodies, which were the lightest of all, could do nothing other than circle the earth.

Aristotle's philosophy was a comprehensive and tightly woven system. If one part was proven wrong, the entire philosophy would fall. Aquinas integrated Scripture and Aristotelian philosophy so tightly that if Aristotle were ever proven wrong, much of Catholic theology was in danger—not just its idea that the earth was at the center of the universe.

But the matter is still more complicated. Long before Galileo, Nicolaus Copernicus (1473–1543) taught the same as Galileo, that the earth revolved around the sun. His book *On the Revolutions of the Heavenly Orbs* (1543) is one of the greatest works in the history of science. The preface to this work puts to rest the idea that the Church as a whole was digging in its heels against scientific discovery, even if those discoveries did challenge Aristotelian philosophy or the literal reading of Joshua 10:12 and 13.

In fact, in deference to the teachings of his church, Copernicus was hesitant to publish his findings until he was encouraged to do so by some Catholic leaders. Copernicus wrote:

> These [my own] misgivings and actual protests have been overcome by my friends. First among these was Nicolaus Schoenberg, cardinal of Capua, a man renowned in every department of learning. Next was one who loved me well, Tiedemann Giese, bishop of Kulm, a devoted student of sacred and all other good literature, who often urged and even importuned me to publish this work which I had kept in store not for nine years only, but to a fourth period of nine years. The same request was made to me by many other em-

inent and learned men. They urged that I should not, on account of my fears, refuse any longer to contribute the fruits of my labors to the common advantage of those interested in mathematics. They insisted that, though my theory of the earth's movement might at first seem strange, yet it would appear admirable and acceptable when the publication of my elucidatory comments should dispel the mists of paradox. Yielding then to their persuasion I at last permitted my friends to publish that work which they have so long demanded.[24]

The book was dedicated to Pope Paul III.

Yet the book did fly in the face of Aristotelian physics, which was deeply embedded in church doctrine. Historian Lawrence Principe of Johns Hopkins University in a set of lectures on the history of science up to 1700 said, "In the end, there were probably no more than a dozen thinkers committed to Copernicus' heliocentric system during the 50 years after its publication."[25]

Today Copernicus is justly famous because of his pioneering discoveries. But Tycho Brahe, one of the three greatest astronomers of the late 1500s and early 1600s (along with Kepler and Galileo), did not accept Copernicus' view that the earth rotated around the sun. Principe says, "Tycho rejected Copernicus' idea of a moving earth as physically absurd and theologically untenable. In 1588, he [Brahe] presented his own planetary system with the earth at the center, the moon and sun revolving about the earth, and the other planets revolving about the sun."[26] So even contemporary scientists, in addition to being "theologically untenable" saw heliocentric views of the universe as "absurd." The Galileo affair was hardly a knee-jerk reaction of the Church to a scientific study that should have been a no-brainer.

It would not be right to defend the Catholic Church for everything it did to Galileo. But Galileo committed errors himself. He lived at a time when ideas were very much in flux. Not just the Catholic

---

[24] Quoted in Margaret C. Jacob, *The Scientific Revolution: A Brief History With Documents* (Boston: Bedford/St. Martin's, 2010), p. 46.

[25] Lawrence Principe, *History of Science: Antiquity to 1700, Course Guidebook*, p. 118. Lecture and Guidebook produced by "The Great Courses," Chantilly, Virginia, 2002.

[26] Lawrence Principe, *History of Science: Antiquity to 1700, Course Guidebook*, p. 125.

Growing Pressure on the Bible

Church but the entire scientific community was wrestling with the implications of the Scientific Revolution. Much was at stake.

The book that got Galileo into trouble, *Dialogue Concerning the Two Chief World Systems* published in 1632, was actually sanctioned by Galileo's close friend Cardinal Maffeo Barberini, who became Pope Urban VIII in 1623. Barberini had opposed the Church's condemnation of Galileo in 1616. As Pope Urban, he allowed Galileo to publish his findings, but he attached a couple of conditions. It was not Galileo's heliocentric ideas that got him in trouble with the pope but the way Galileo fulfilled the pope's second condition. You can explore this basic history yourself. The information is no farther away than the Wikipedia article on Galileo.

Again, we cannot justify everything the Catholic Church did to Galileo. But the chief error of church leaders stemmed from combining their interpretation of Scripture with Aristotle's philosophy. If the Galileo affair teaches us anything, it should warn churches against wedding their interpretation of Scripture to the current philosophy of the day, which, in fact, is what theistic evolutionists urge the church to do. This should also warn us against wedding ideas of creation science to statements of Scripture that don't clearly teach those ideas.

Theistic evolutionists should be more sensitive to three more issues.

First, they should be sympathetic to the fact that at stake in the Galileo affair were passages whose interpretation doesn't have anything to do with salvation. But at stake in the evolution controversy is the interpretation of a wide range of passages that have a direct impact on our salvation in Christ.

Second, some theistic evolutionists imply that throughout history, the church has had to change its interpretation of other passages as a result of new scientific findings. But, personally, I have yet to find a theistic evolutionist citing another instance similar to the Galileo affair.

Third, theistic evolutionists will often quote a comment Luther made about Copernicus. Luther's comment is not found in his doctrinal or exegetical works but in a collection of his "table talks," things he is reported to have said in after-dinner conversations.

> When someone at the table mentioned Copernicus' theory, Luther is said to have remarked,
>
>> Whoever wants to be clever [referring to Copernicus] must agree with nothing that others esteem. He must do something of his own. This is what the fellow does who wishes to turn the whole of astronomy upside down. Even in these things that are thrown into disorder I believe the Holy Scripture, for Joshua commanded the sun to stand still and not the earth.[27]
>
> This was from 1539, four years *before* Copernicus' book *On the Revolutions* was published. As we noted above, Tycho Brahe, one of the greatest astronomers of the period, lived *after* Copernicus' book had been published. If Brahe could hold as his formal educated scientific opinion the same idea that Luther tossed out one night at the dinner table a number of years *before* Copernicus' book had been published, I think we can give Luther a break.
>
> The Galileo affair is complicated. Theistic evolutionists who throw it into the creation/evolution debate are simply trying to score an easy point.

The scientific revolution and the Galileo affair give us insights into historical criticism. The Catholics had used the ideas of the ancient Greek philosopher Aristotle to help define and shape its theology. That is, it had erected a platform over Scripture on which to stand in order to build Catholic theology. The new insights gained by the natural philosophers were competing with Aristotle's insights. As such, natural philosophy became yet another platform built over Scripture on which to stand in order to analyze and interpret it. This is the spirit of historical criticism and what makes it so dangerous to Scripture. Scripture is not allowed to be its own interpreter.

The growing importance of Bible background material

During the 1600s, an emphasis on the importance of background material for understanding Scripture entered the church somewhat unnoticed. The reformers, in the face of the strained allegorical interpretations of Scripture common in their day, insisted that faith be based on the literal meaning of the words of Scripture. They relied on the study of Scripture itself to provide that literal meaning.

---

[27] Martin Luther, *Luther's Works, Vol. 54, Table Talk* (Fortress Press: Philadelphia, 1967), p. 358.

But with the three churches—Catholic, Lutheran, and Reformed—all claiming that their interpretation of Scripture was the literal one, Bible scholars from each church felt pressured to get the edge on the competition. This pressure grew as the 17th century progressed. Jonathan Sheehan wrote, "The Bible that shaped Protestantism . . . was insufficient on its own to confirm the authenticity of the Protestant religions."[28]

Bible scholars felt they needed outside help to prove that their interpretation was the right one. Scholars worked hard to discover more accurate meanings for the words used in the Bible. They struggled to uncover information on Israelite culture and a better understanding of the cultures of the nations around Israel. Such study and research was not wrong, of course. The danger lay in the misplaced role given to such study. The conviction that Scripture could interpret Scripture was being lost. It was no longer considered a document that contained everything the Christian interpreter needs to understand the Christian religion. Scripture had to be helped along by insights not found in Scripture itself.

Again, that is the heart of historical criticism: the search for a platform outside of Scripture on which one can stand in order to interpret Scripture objectively.

The "religion of the heart"

In the latter part of the 17th century, a broad-based spiritualist movement began surfacing in the Christian world. In England it was called Puritanism. In Germany it was called Pietism. Other church bodies, including the Catholic Church, experienced similar movements. Ted Campbell calls this collection "the religion of the heart."[29]

The experiential dimension of these movements affected how Christians used the Scriptures. At the end of the 17th century, the Pietistic movement in Germany arose as a rival to Orthodox Lutheranism. On the surface, the Pietists appeared orthodox. Like the orthodox, they were concerned about propositional truth taught in Scripture. But the experiential nature of the movement shifted their purpose for studying Scripture. More and more they studied Scripture to affirm their experience and to find direction for their Christian journey through life.

Campbell described a group of English spiritualists called the Cambridge Platonists. For them, truth was based on experience. They claimed that "just as knowledge of material things comes by way of the 'bodily' senses, so knowledge

---

[28] Jonathan Sheehan, *The Enlightenment Bible* (Princeton: Princeton University Press, 2005), p. 27.

[29] See Ted A. Campbell, *The Religion of the Heart: A Study of European Religious Life in the Seventeenth and Eighteenth Centuries* (Columbia, SC: University of South Carolina, 1991).

of spiritual things comes by way of a 'spiritual sense' (or 'sensation')."[30] This comment could be applied, as least in part, to the other "heart" religions.

One's relationship with God came to be grounded in personal experiences rather than on the promises and assurances found in God's Word. This is another example of a platform built above Scripture on which people could stand to interpret it.

The rise of radical philosophy

Radical philosophy refers to a wide range of philosophies that flew in the face of established views of society, politics, and religion. Baruch Spinoza, whom we have already met, was one of the early radical philosophers. In previous centuries, the Catholic Church and the Catholic secular powers had forcefully suppressed such thinkers. But the breakdown of religious unity in Europe allowed radical philosophers to find safe havens in which to promote their teachings. Holland was tolerant of radical thinkers and became a home for many of them. Some were arrested and their books confiscated. But their ideas spread as their writings found their way, often through underground channels, into more and more personal libraries. Inevitably their ideas coalesced, came out into the open, and provided the foundation for the Enlightenment.

The radical philosophers were more interested in natural religion than in the religion of the Bible. To many, Scripture was just one source of truth among many, no better, no worse. Natural philosophers—again, an older term for those who study nature, "scientists" as we call them—were part of this movement. More and more they studied the universe without reference to God's creating activity as recorded in Genesis. At the end of the 17th century, the conflict between Scripture and philosophy surfaced in the denial of the inspiration of Scripture. The search went on for new platforms for interpreting Scripture that would allow the new philosophies, including the new philosophies about nature, to exist alongside it.

Summary of the forces leading up to the Enlightenment

The religious wars and heated doctrinal debates of the 17th century caused many to tire of Scripture. The radical philosophers, who divorced their thoughts from Scripture, were gradually entering the mainstream religious and political world. The idea that reason was sufficient to guide the state appealed to statesmen who wanted to be free from church control, and they less and less fulfilled their age-old function of protecting orthodox religion. In the 18th century, princes began appointing to their universities and churches professors and pastors who

---

[30]Ted Campbell, *The Religion of the Heart*, p. 64.

were open to the new ways of thinking being popularized by radical philosophers. A new set of religious movements emphasized personal experience and, along with that, a more individualistic process of Bible interpretation. The Catholic Church's adoption of Aristotle's philosophy was being successfully challenged by the Scientific Revolution. In the process the Catholic Church's views of the universe, seemingly gotten from Scripture, were being relegated to the past.

This was the dawn of the Enlightenment. Scripture was now on the defense. Michael Legaspi describes what many were thinking:

> In the decades surrounding the turn of the eighteenth century, the prestige of the Bible in the Western world was at an all-time low. Skeptics, rationalist critics, and proponents of the new science published widely and influentially on the state of its textual corruption, the unreliability of its historical narratives, the crudeness of its style, and, in some cases, the fanciful, even childish quality of its stories. It was, to many elites, a book no longer worth believing.[31]

Hans-Joachim Kraus observes: "The abandonment of the historical teaching of inspiration happened slowly, in part concealed by the way matters were taught. But the change could not be stopped."[32] Confidence in Scripture as a source of truth was at a low ebb. The power of human reason was jumping in to fill the vacuum. New ways had to be found to understand the Bible.

Cliché: Creationists are against science.

This is a cliché I am almost embarrassed to bring up.

It is hard to believe that some theistic evolutionists still claim that a statement against the theory of evolution is a statement against science. But many still say that. It is often an undercurrent that runs through their books.

But it's a straw man. Those who believe in a six twenty-four-hour day creation are just as interested in scientific discovery as those who don't, and they applaud the many ways scientific discoveries have benefited our world. They are only against two things: The evolutionary interpretation of some of what can be observed in nature and the conclusions of some scientists about how the world began.

---

[31] Michael C. Legaspi, *The Death of Scripture and the Rise of Biblical Studies* (New York: Oxford University Press, 2010), p. 5.

[32] Hans-Joachim Kraus, *Geschichte*, p. 80.

The Enlightenment

What was the Enlightenment?

The Renaissance had created a wave that swept through Europe—a wave of optimism about the human mind and spirit. The Enlightenment was the crest of that wave. The Enlightenment took place in the Western world roughly between 1700 and 1800. The radical philosophers, some of whom were already at work before 1700, set the pace for the Enlightenment with their reliance on the power of human reason.

The Enlightenment was not an event. It was a movement, closely tied to the forces we noted above. Movements often lie concealed for decades in the minds of visionaries. But gradually it becomes clear that something permanent has come into being and that new ideas were here to stay. In the Lutheran church, by 1725 both orthodox German scholars and their Pietist rivals realized that something new was going on around them. Both sides were forced to spend less time debating each other and more time understanding the new movement and warning their people against it.

The Enlightenment is the story of philosophers, writers, playwrights, and politicians. It encouraged exploration and discovery, political and economic rethinking, and even social revolution. On an individual level, it encouraged people to discover afresh who they are.

The goal of the Enlightenment was to rethink everything the world had inherited from the past. In order to do that, Enlightenment thinkers believed they had the right "to question everything."[33] Enlightenment thinker Immanuel Kant gives us a feel for the spirit of the Enlightenment. In a short essay, "What Is Enlightenment?" Kant wrote,

> Enlightenment is one's exit from a self-incurred immaturity. Immaturity is the inability to think on one's own without another's control. This immaturity is self-incurred [by a lack] of resolution and the courage to think on one's own without another's control. Dare to think on your own! is thus the watchword of the Enlightenment.[34]

The Enlightenment was much more than specific ideas that came from the pens of its leading thinkers. It was not the *result* of their thinking that was important but *the way* their thinking was done. Enlightenment historian Ernst Cassirer writes, "The true nature of Enlightenment thinking cannot be seen

---

[33] Roy Harrisville, *Pandora's Box Opened: An Examination and Defense of the Historical-Critical Method and Its Master Practitioners* (Grand Rapids: Erdman's, 2014), p. 47.

[34] Immanuel Kant, "Beantwortung der Frage: Was Ist Afklaerung?" quoted in Roy Harrisville, *Pandora's Box Opened*, p. 47.

in its purest and clearest form where it is formulated into particular doctrines, axioms, and theorems; but rather where it is in process, where it is doubting and seeking, tearing down and building up."[35]

The process was all important. Enlightenment thinkers disagreed among themselves on just about everything. But they all agreed on one thing: It was every person's right and responsibility to tear down the traditions of the past and to build a new future. And, of course, there was always more to tear down and more building to do. The overarching principle was that "every apparent goal attained by reason is but a fresh starting-point."[36]

The Enlightenment's impact on the gospel

The goal of the Enlightenment could only be achieved by a tool that was accessible to all people and the same for all. This tool was human reason. Reason was considered to be much more than one's ability to use his or her mind to solve problems or store up facts. Rather, human reason was thought to have access to the eternal truths or principles behind all areas of human life.

Reason alone, it was believed, could answer such questions as how the universe is constructed and how it works. Human reason alone could accurately observe the world and then reduce observations to general principles—the natural laws—under which the universe operates. Reason alone could determine how people should direct their personal lives and what social, political, and economic systems were best for society.

There is nothing wrong with trying to understand how the world works, from its physical to its social systems. In the beginning Adam and Eve were to "have dominion over the fish of the sea and over the birds of the heavens and over the livestock and over all the earth and over every creeping thing that creeps on the earth" (Genesis 1:26). That responsibility entailed the constant use of their reason to explore God's creation and to make decisions about the best way to care for it.

But Enlightenment thinkers went far beyond this. Human reason alone, they contested, had the ability to understand right and wrong. Needless to say, such things as sin, the need for reconciliation with God, and the death of Jesus as restitution for sin found little place in Enlightenment thinking.

---

[35] Ernst Cassirer, *The Philosophy of the Enlightenment*, trans. Fritz Koelln and James Pettegrove (Princeton: Princeton University Press, 1951), p. ix.

[36] Ernst Cassirer, *The Philosophy of the Enlightenment*, p. 22.

One More Elephant

The Enlightenment's new version of the "past"

Yet it would be a mistake to envision everyone in Europe tossing their Bibles into the trash and going out to buy the latest philosophical publications. People respected the Bible and wanted it to influence their lives. But many insisted on a Bible that was compatible with Enlightenment thought. They wanted a Bible that would allow for the free use of human reason. For that to happen, Scripture could no longer stand alone as the source of absolute truth. Rather, it had to be considered one of many documents produced by human beings in the past—a witness to how the people of that day used their reason to answer the questions of life.

How could this be accomplished? Kraus summarized this in a few words. He wrote, "An important hermeneutic fostered in the Enlightenment was 'the past.'"[37] That is, the Enlightenment generated a new understanding of human history. Let's examine this important insight. It is lurking in the background of every book promoting theistic evolution.

Up until this time, the past had been viewed as Scripture views it. Men and women were created with all the intellectual gifts and reasoning abilities we possess today. Cultures of the past may have been different from ours, but culture was considered to be only the outward trappings of the same basic human society that had existed from the beginning.

The Enlightenment could not exist alongside that definition of the past. The driving spirit of the Enlightenment was to enlighten the world. To do this, it had to define the past as a time of darkness. The Enlightenment wanted to create a new world. But it couldn't do that without first creating an old world.

It had to answer a basic set of questions: What made the 1700s different from previous centuries? What enabled people living in the present time to do what previous generations had been unable to do? Have our powers of reason somehow suddenly become more sophisticated? And if so, how did that happen?

There was only one way to answer these questions. Human history had to be viewed as *a time of development*. It had to be understood as a slow, gradual movement out of ignorance. The Enlightenment envisioned the past as a time when mankind was more naïve and when their reasoning ability was less developed. It was a time of hunter-gatherers who could not be expected to have a sophisticated worldview. Writing, art, technology, and most notably religion were all at a primitive stage of development. The past was not merely the time when exploration and technology were getting their start at the hands of intelligent societies, which was coming to completion in the modern 18th-century world;

---

[37] Hans-Joachim Kraus, *Geschichte*, p. 98.

rather, it was a time when people's minds were undeveloped and incapable of moving ahead as quickly as people could in modern times.

Kraus' point is that Enlightenment scholars had to create a "past" for Scripture to coincide with the past they had created for mankind in general. So they promoted the idea that to understand the Bible, you *could not* think of it as a contemporary document. It was an old document, written in the past by people who were not as developed as 17th- and 18th- century Europeans. As such, it is not as relevant to people today as it was to the people for whom it was originally written. In fact, one could not even be sure of what its words meant to people who lived long ago and whose minds were still developing. The writers of Scripture gave answers that people in the past could understand and relate to. But those answers may or may not be relevant to modern people.

To understand Scripture, it was claimed, we must first re-create Scripture's "past" and then transport ourselves back into that time. We can do this with the help of Bible background material. When we understand the day-to-day concerns faced by the people to whom Scripture was originally written, we can glean from Scripture lessons that will benefit us today. But if our reason says we cannot apply those lessons to ourselves, then we must follow our reason and leave that part of Scripture in the past.

To illustrate the remaking of the past in Enlightenment terms, consider how German Enlightenment philosopher Gotthold Lessing (1729–1781) described the advance of religion from Old Testament to modern times. Jonathan Sheehan explains Lessing's thoughts using Lessing's own words (in his explanation Sheehan puts quotation marks around Lessing's words). Lessing considered the Old Testament to be a primer that "embodied the aboriginal relationship of man and God."[38] Sheehan describes the sequence:

> The revelations of the Old Testament—"education, which affected and still affects the human race"—nurtured mankind in its childhood, gradually leading to knowledge of the true God. But just as children outgrow their first toys and books, after a time a maturing mankind sensed the inadequacy of the Old Testament. At this point, "a better teacher had to come and rip the exhausted primer from the hands of the child—Christ came." His primer, the New Testament, would become the textbook for an adolescent humanity groping its way toward full autonomy. Over the centuries of its maturation, this humanity took the New Testament as the "*non plus ultra* [the last word] of its knowledge" and used it as a scaffold for its own development. In time, though, even this primer wore thin for a humanity finally approaching adulthood. The eighteenth cen-

---

[38] Jonathan Sheehan, *The Enlightenment Bible*, p. 131 (emphasis original).

tury was on the cusp of this final metamorphosis, ready to give up the New Testament and begin moving toward "the time of a *new eternal Gospel*," the last age of man, the "time of perfection."[39]

The time of perfection, of course, was the time of the Enlightenment.

The Enlightenment had to find ways to extract timeless truths from Scripture. Human reason was central to the process. Faced with the fact that the Bible "so poorly coincides with the timeless truths of reason," one must use "the concepts of *development* and *accommodation*."[40] Roy Harrisville explains,

> The idea of *development* assumed that the perfect clarity of the *religion of reason* could be attained only at the end of a long progression from the darkness of superstition and mysticism.... The idea of *accommodation* could help connect reverence for Jesus with the criticism of his teaching. God could only make himself understood by accommodating himself to the thought-forms and conditions of the various ages involved.

Therefore, Christians in their present level of development are not bound to accept everything Jesus said. Jesus was naturally accommodating himself to the thought-forms and conditions of his listeners. Therefore, we can respect Jesus even while we deny certain things he taught. (This is precisely how many modern theistic evolutionists approach the teachings of Jesus and the New Testament writers on the Genesis account of creation.)

If this is so, how can we decide which parts of Scripture are relevant for the modern world? To answer that, Scripture must first be examined in its historical context. Harrisville writes, "Historical criticism was thus the means by which these truths of reason could be wrung from the Bible and brought into the clear light of day."

The Enlightenment, science, and Bible interpretation

Much of Enlightenment thought dealt with abstract concepts such as morality, social systems, and the role of reason. The Enlightenment, however, was also deeply interested in the work of the natural philosophers (scientists), who in the late 17th century were beginning to collect and analyze rock samples, geological formations, plants, and animals. Natural philosophers began to uncover what seemed to be evidence that the world had taken a long time to arrive in

---

[39] Jonathan Sheehan, *The Enlightenment Bible*, p. 131 (emphasis author's). The words in quotations are Lessing's, the rest are Sheehan's. From Gotthold Lessing, *Education of the Human Race*, 1780. Sheehan calls this "historical fantasy."

[40] The quotations in this and the next two paragraphs are from Roy Harrisville, *Pandora's Box Opened*, p. 48 (emphasis added).

its present form. The slow development of geological formations seemed to call for more years than Scripture would allow. Therefore, the natural philosophers had to create a past that was very different from the one described in Genesis, namely, that God in relatively recent history, had created the world in six literal days. The Enlightenment idea that human beings developed out of intellectual darkness fit well with the natural philosophers' growing conclusion that the physical world—later the biological world would be included in the discussion—was the product of gradual change over time. The general population might have trouble grasping why Enlightenment intellectuals needed to recreate the past. But they had no trouble understanding why the natural philosophers needed to do it—they need more time for things to evolve.

In the following quotations from *The Philosophy of the Enlightenment*, Ernst Cassirer explains the tension in the 18th century between Scripture's description of creation and the evolutionary ideas of the natural philosophers.

The pressure to combine Scripture and evolutionary science surfaced sooner than we sometimes think. Already in the 1600s, Thomas Burnet (ca. 1635–1715) speculated about the structure of the earth, doing so in theistic evolutionary terms. Cassirer writes,

> In his works, *The Sacred Theory of the Earth* in 1680 and *Philosophical Archaeology* in 1692 Thomas Burnet is still striving to confirm the objective truth of the Biblical account of creation. But to this end *he has to abandon the principle of verbal inspiration and take refuge in an allegorical interpretation* which permits him to disregard all measurements of time in the Bible. In place of the individual days of the Biblical creation Burnet assumes whole epochs or periods to which any length of time required by the empirical findings can be attributed.[41]

As the geologic data began to suggest more strongly that the world had slowly evolved, the pressure to somehow combine this idea with Scripture grew. Cassirer writes,

> The whole eighteenth century is permeated by this conviction, namely, that in the history of humanity the time had now arrived to deprive nature of its carefully guarded secret, to leave it no longer in the dark to be marveled as an incomprehensible mystery but to bring it under the bright light of reason and analyze it with all its fundamental forces.
>
> To do this, however, it was above all necessary to sever the bond between theology and physics once and for all. Much as this bond had been loosened in the eighteenth century, it had by no means been entirely broken.

---

[41] Ernst Cassirer, *The Philosophy of the Enlightenment*, p. 49 (emphasis added).

> The authority of Scripture was still eagerly defended even in matters of pure natural science.... Orthodoxy had by no means given up the principle of verbal inspiration, and in this principle the inference was implied that a genuine science of nature was contained in the Mosaic story of the creation.[42]

Cassirer notes the close relationship between the advance in the sciences of geology and biology and the advance in historical-critical studies:

> Clear methodological differentiation between theology and science makes its way slowly. Geology takes the lead in this matter by breaking down the temporal framework of the Biblical story of creation.... *[Bible] Criticism becomes more serious after definite empirical results, especially paleontological [fossil] discoveries, are there to support it.*[43]

It was only as the 18th century was coming to an end, however, that one Enlightenment naturalist, Comte de Buffon (1707–1788), went so far as to completely separate Scripture and the physical sciences. Cassirer explains:

> In Buffon's great work *The Epochs of Nature* [1778]... a physical account of the world had been outlined which avoided religious dogmatism and claimed as its sole basis the observable facts and general principles of natural science. The stronghold of the traditional system had finally been breached.... Such demolition was the indispensable precondition of the new edifice of physics.

> This was the first important victory of the philosophy of the Enlightenment. It finished in this respect what the Renaissance had begun; it marked off *a definite field for rational knowledge within which there was to be no more restraint and authoritative coercion* but free movement in all directions.[44]

Cassirer takes us back to the Galileo affair in the light of what would happen in the Enlightenment. Galileo was already a servant of the forces that would culminate in Buffon's position:

> The Church was not assailing individual accomplishments of scientific investigation.... In reality it was not the new cosmology [of Galileo] which church authorities opposed.... What was not to be tolerated, what threatened the very foundations of the Church, was the new con-

---

[42] Ernst Cassirer, *The Philosophy of the Enlightenment*, pp. 47, 48.

[43] Ernst Cassirer, *The Philosophy of the Enlightenment*, p. 48 (emphasis added).

[44] Ernst Cassirer, *The Philosophy of the Enlightenment*, p. 49 (emphasis added).

cept of truth proclaimed by Galileo. Alongside the *truth of revelation* comes now an independent and original *truth of nature*.[45]

Convictions about the power of reason, Cassirer says, led to "the almost unlimited power which scientific knowledge gains over all the thought of the Enlightenment."[46]

Scripture in the Enlightenment stew

Enlightenment thinkers were cooking a stew. The Enlightenment reliance on reason was first into the pot. This was the broth. Next in was the meat of the reconstruction of human history in terms of its gradual emergence from a dark past. Next came the beans of growing speculation that the earth and its inhabitants had evolved over millions of years. Along with that came the peas and carrots of reconstructed political, social, and economic systems.

Everyone knew the Scriptures had to be part of the stew. But Scripture, as it had been understood for centuries, was like a rock sitting on the counter. And rocks are not thrown into stews. So Scripture had to be turned into a potato, so to speak, before it could be thrown into the pot.

In more scholarly terms, Jonathan Sheehan says that the Bible had to be reinvented "for a post confessional Europe."[47] Or as Martin Luther wrote in more poetical terms: "The Word they still shall let remain. Nor any thanks have for it."[48]

What had to be done with Scripture? First, *the purpose of the Bible* had to change, and second, *the nature of the Bible* had to change.

First, the *purpose* of the Bible had to change. It could no longer be the place where God revealed the way to salvation—that we are saved through faith in the forgiveness of sins won by Christ. The idea of sacrifice for sin was part of mankind's developing past.

Sheehan writes that in 1700, if a person was asked why he or she should read the Bible, the answer would overwhelmingly be "because it reveals the means to your salvation." But by the middle of that century, "answers given to that question began to proliferate, jostle, and compete with the standard one."[49] The value of any section of Scripture was determined by whether it had "relevance to human morality, aesthetics, *and history*."[50] If it didn't, it could be ignored. As we will

---

[45] Ernst Cassirer, *The Philosophy of the Enlightenment*, p. 42 (emphasis added).

[46] Ernst Cassirer, *The Philosophy of the Enlightenment*, p. 45.

[47] Jonathan Sheehan, *The Enlightenment Bible*, p. 27.

[48] *Christian Worship: A Lutheran Hymnal* (Milwaukee: Northwestern Publishing House, 1993), Hymn 201:4: "A Mighty Fortress Is Our God."

[49] Jonathan Sheehan, *The Enlightenment Bible*, p. xiii.

[50] Jonathan Sheehan, *The Enlightenment Bible*, p. xiv (emphasis added).

see, much of the Old Testament was deemed useless and even harmful for an enlightened person in the 18th century trying to live a moral life in service to God.

Second, the *nature* of the Bible had to be redefined. If human reason was to tear down the past and rebuild the future, it could not be hindered by the Bible. Scripture *had to* be seen in terms that would allow it to be put under the control of reason. Scripture *had to be* seen as a piece of ancient literature that reflected the weaknesses of its human authors. It *had to be* stripped of its divine origin and divested of its claim to absolute truth. Hans-Joachim Kraus describes a truth that would become more and more obvious as Europe moved forward into the Enlightenment: "The doctrine of inspiration, and everything that doctrine implied for how Scripture should be interpreted, was why the critics struck out as they did. Making the Scripture divine brought the humanists onto the plain of battle."[51] Only if Scripture was demoted to a piece of ancient religious literature would it be ripe for analysis. Then scholars could examine it with the same critical tools Renaissance scholars had used in their study of the ancient documents of Greece and Rome. Only then could it be thrown into the Enlightenment stew.

Enlightenment assumptions about the past

Here is a list of contrasts that summarize how the historical critics turned the Bible from a rock into a potato.

- *Scripture:* God created mankind with the highest level of intellectual gifts.

    Historical criticism: Human beings emerged from an uninformed, naïve past.

- *Scripture:* Beginning with Moses, God began revealing himself to people through his Word.

    Historical criticism: Ancient people had a long history of oral traditions to explain various aspects of the physical universe and of life. Israelite oral traditions were collected and written down, perhaps by a man named Moses.

- *Scripture:* Jesus and the Bible writers knew that the events of the Old Testament are literally true.

    Historical criticism: In order to be heard and understood, the writers of Scripture had to accommodate themselves to the worldview of their readers, which included a six-day creation.

---

[51] Hans-Joachim Kraus, *Geschichte*, p. 34.

- *Scripture:* The cultures of the people found in Scripture are different from ours, but no matter what their cultural trappings look like, people are all the same. Scripture's purpose is to reveal God's plan of salvation, which deals with the truths of sin, guilt, forgiveness, and hope. Those needs are universal as are the words Scripture uses to teach about them.

    Historical criticism: Bible readers must first decide what a particular passage taught to the people to whom it was first written. Only then can readers determine what, if anything, that passage teaches us today. For that reason, modern Bible readers must thoroughly understand the history and culture of the people to whom Scripture was first written.

- *Scripture:* Every word of the original manuscripts was inspired by God.

    Historical criticism: Verbal inspiration is an illusion. The human authors of Scripture left their mark on the text. We can say that Scripture contains the word of God, but not that it is the Word of God.

- *Scripture:* Jesus and the New Testament writers accepted the Old Testament canon, even though God had used the church to assemble the canon into its present form. We accept the canon of the New Testament, even though God gave the early Christian church a role in establishing it.

    Historical criticism: We must not assume that every book we find in our Bible should be there. After all, human beings created the canon using human criteria. Christians of all ages have the right to reevaluate those decisions of the past.

- *Scripture:* Scripture is a one-of-a-kind book. We interpret Scripture on the basis of what Scripture itself tells us.

    Historical criticism: We must analyze Scripture with the same critical tools we use to analyze other ancient documents.

- *Scripture:* Scripture teaches us about God's salvation in Christ. All Scripture is written for our instruction and encouragement.

    Historical criticism: Scripture contains many lessons valuable to life. But much of Scripture, especially the Old Testament, must be ignored as irrelevant or even harmful.

Not all these themes surfaced at the same time and place. Not all were accepted by every scholar. Not all were taught as absolute truth, nor were they all taught with the same intensity and conviction. But by the middle of the 19th century, Bible scholars were more and more using some or all of those ideas in their interpretation of Scripture. We will trace the development of historial criticism in the next chapter

Chapter 3

Historical Criticism:
Theistic Evolution's Tool of Interpretation

The Development of Historical Criticism

John and Joan

Before we start tracing the development of historical criticism, we'll set the stage with a story of two fictional characters who are trying to understand the Bible. The first person, John, is reading the Bible *without* "the Enlightenment past" in mind. For him, the Bible is a contemporary document, and he reads it as God's Word for all people of all ages. The second person, Joan, is being taught to use "the Enlightenment past" and the historical-critical methods based on it as her principle of interpretation.

We'll start with John. John grew up in a fairly conservative denomination and has patterned his approach to the Bible accordingly. His parents were his chief spiritual influence, and after their deaths, the church's longtime pastor has helped John maintain their approach to Scripture. Here's an example of John reading his Bible.

> John is reading Moses, who delivered Israel from Egypt and parted the waters of the Red Sea to save them from the Egyptian army. He thinks about God's power on display—walls of water on one side and the other. He imagines himself walking through that corridor along with the Israelites.
>
> After finishing the story, a note in his Bible directs him to a psalm that helps him praise God for his help in the past and for continuing to help his people today. He pictures the Israelites walking through the desert with God's pillar of cloud in the lead. He imagines himself walking with the Israelites on their journey to the Promised Land. Someday he, too, will be in the Promised Land. He also recalls that Jesus referred to Moses as the lawgiver.
>
> Before he closes his Bible, he looks at the table of contents. He finds a quick review of the books of the Bible helpful. He sees the books of history from Genesis to Esther lined up one after the other. They record the history of God's Old Testament people. He relates them to the New Testament history books, Matthew through Acts, which record Jesus' words and deeds

and outline the growth of the early church. He looks over the prophetical books and mentally places as many as he can into Israel's history.

John knows his Bible was written a long time ago. But he feels the Bible was written just for him. God's promise of mercy to Adam and Eve is no different from the mercy God has given him. He understands that the Old Testament laws—as strange as some of them seem to him—were given for a purpose, namely, to lead Israel until the Savior came. And over the years he has come to understand the reason behind many of them. He reads about God's judgment on the Canaanites, and as gruesome as it was, he sees it as an example of God's judgment on sin, idolatry, and unbelief. Sometimes he struggles with these events, but he sees their value in helping him avoid God's judgment in the future. He sees the Old and New Testaments as one grand story about God's plan of salvation, written by many people but having God as their author.

He knows the people of the Bible lived in a different culture than his, but the basics of life with God—repentance over sin and faith in God's promises of grace—have been the same for all people since the world began. The people he reads about are just like him—their trust in God's Savior, their struggles and temptations, their hope of eternal life, and their confidence in God's daily guidance. Their clothing, customs, and countries are different. But their actions, motives, and words are the same as his.

John grows to understand his Bible by attending Bible study at his church. Occasionally, John will read an article in his Bible encyclopedia, and he welcomes the background information he finds there. In fact, his pastor once had a study on the history and practices of the Assyrians and Babylonians, which really helped him picture what it must have been like when they took God's people captive. But most of the time he just sits in his easy chair, reads his Bible, and understands it quite well. To him, the Bible was written a long time ago, but it lives in the present—in his present.

Now let's examine Joan's experience. She too likes to sit in her easy chair and read her Bible. Joan just started a Bible study at church: "Introduction to the Bible." The title piqued her interest. The study is being taught by a retired professor of biblical studies at a well-known denominational college located in the town where she lives.

The first class starts with a "get to know-you" time. The people in the class introduce themselves. Some have been members of that church for a long time. Others have joined recently. Most have come from other churches in the denomination. But a few have come from other church bodies, some of which have been a bit more conservative than this congregation. The teacher is getting a pretty good feel for his class. Their background isn't much different from the new group of students he faced each semester in his college classes.

The teacher (his name is Jack) reciprocates by telling a little about himself. He graduated with an M.A. in history. He did his Ph.D. work under a well-known Bible scholar at a major university, graduating with a degree in ancient Near Eastern studies. He has been teaching Bible introduction courses and other courses on the Bible ever since.

Jack is a sensitive man. His teaching background has given him a solid feel for the religious climate from which the students in this new class have come. He knows he is facing a group with different backgrounds. Some will easily fit into his course. But some may be more like John, whom we described above.

Jack has developed a "first class day" routine that will help the students ease into the course. He introduces his approach to Scripture with tact and consideration. He begins with a rather benign statement. "React to this statement," he says: "'You cannot understand the Bible unless you understand the world in which the Bible was written.'" The reactions are generally approving. Joan, who had a fairly traditional religious upbringing at the country church she attended as a child, had never heard it put quite like that. But she understands the value of the background material her pastor included in many of his sermons, so she nods politely to Jack's statement.

Jack moves to his next point. He says, "You know, in recent years scholars have made tremendous strides in understanding the world of the Bible. Studies of the ancient Egyptian language have yielded much more precise meanings for the words used in Scripture. Archaeology has uncovered information about the Holy Land that is simply amazing. Many of the actual places referred to in Scripture have been unearthed and studied. The dates given them by modern scientific dating techniques allow us to date these places quite accurately, and for the first time we can construct a precise timeline of Bible events." Joan likes history, and the promise of really understanding the timeline of Scripture appeals to her.

Jack continues, "The more we can set the ancient Hebrew people into the context of the ancient world of their day, the more we will understand how they thought. And the more we understand how they thought, the better we will understand what the Scriptures meant to them. The more we understand that, the more we can determine what lessons we moderns can learn from the Holy Scriptures."

Jack finishes his introduction: "Over the years, the hardest part of teaching Bible introduction is to get students on board with this approach to the

Bible. Sometimes I have to work hard to show the importance of modern Bible scholarship for understanding Scripture."

That last statement sounded a bit ominous to Joan. Nevertheless, she knows what she believes about the Bible. And she is excited and looks forward to learning what archaeologists have unearthed. She anticipates sitting down in her easy chair with a fresh appreciation of what the Word God is saying to her.

John and Joan are on divergent paths. For John, the Bible will remain in the present—connected with his spirit of repentance and faith, a spirit he understands as transcending time and culture. For Joan, her Bible will increasingly be tied to its "past," which in the coming weeks her teacher will systematically reveal to her on the basis of current Bible scholarship. Almost imperceptibly, however, the great, overarching themes of sin and grace, which she wants to better understand, will move into the background.

John Barton, a leading historical-critical scholar, describes the shift from John's mind-set to the mind-set Jack will be instilling in Joan. Barton draws from Hans W. Frei's study of 18th- and 19th-century Bible interpretation. There was a time, Barton says, when the historical accounts of the Old Testament "caused no problem for the Christian reader. . . . It was simply assumed that these books presented correct accounts of earlier stages in world-history—that they told of earlier parts of a story that was still our story."[52] The rise of historical criticism changed that "naïve" assumption, and readers were taught they could not simply relate to the story without further analysis:

> It became clear that much in the biblical books was not true as it stood, at the level of straightforward historical accuracy. People also came to realize that the world of the biblical narrators was not our world anyway, but a pre-scientific, pre-critical world which worked with different categories and concepts from ours. The historical books, like the rest of the Bible, became documents from an ancient and rather alien culture, not something to which we could relate unselfconsciously.[53]

The triumph of the Enlightenment in the Lutheran Church

Ironically, the German Lutheran Church, which prided itself for treasuring the text of the Bible most highly, was the church most responsible for re-creating

---

[52] John Barton, *Reading the Old Testament* (Louisville: Westminster John Knox Press, 1996), pp. 160, 161, referring to Hans Frei, *The Eclipse of Biblical Narrative: A Study in Eighteenth and Nineteenth Century Hermeneutics* (New Haven and London, 1974), no page reference given.

[53] John Barton, *Reading the Old Testament*, p. 161.

the Bible for inclusion in the Enlightenment stew. No other church played as central a role in the development of historical criticism of Scripture. No group of scholars so doggedly built on each other's work over the course of some 150 years. No one else would publish the mass of books that spread historical-critical ideas throughout the world.

The legacy of the German redefinition of Scripture is still with us, and it is central to the theistic evolution debate. Modern Bible scholarship, so often appealed to by theistic evolutionists, is based on the work done in the German universities in the 18th and 19th centuries. Any claim to the effect that modern Bible scholars are producing new, groundbreaking research to prove that Scripture can support evolution is historically inaccurate. The methods may be new to a particular denomination or college, or they may be new variations on the theme, but the theme itself was written and finished over a hundred years ago, for the most part in Germany.

The University of Halle, where it all started

In the early 18th century, Enlightenment philosophers throughout Europe mostly worked behind closed doors and usually attracted only small circles of followers brave enough to openly identify with them. These philosophers knew their books would be condemned, as did the book houses that published them. But they forged ahead. Holland's toleration of Enlightenment thinkers made it a haven for radical philosophers and a place where a fairly robust underground sale of Enlightenment books could begin.

But as the 18th century progressed, Enlightenment thought started to become fashionable in many universities and courts. It could no longer be suppressed by the church or controlled by conservative state authorities. A few decades into the 18th century, Enlightenment philosophers and Lutheran theologians in sympathy with them could work openly to re-create Scripture for use in an enlightened age.

Our journey to discover how this happened takes us to a small town in east-central Germany named Halle and the newly formed university there. What happened there deserves to be told in some detail because it has become a kind of "everyman" story. That is, for the next three hundred years, what took place there—the triumph of historical criticism—would take place in dozens of denominational seminaries and colleges throughout the world. This includes many conservative institutions in the United States, some of which were established to escape the historical-critical environment in Europe.

The University of Halle was founded in 1694 by Frederick III, elector of Brandenburg, whose court was located to the north in the city of Berlin. Brandenburg was a Reformed territory. And there was no love-loss between the

Elector of Brandenburg and the strong orthodox Lutheran princes to the south in the territory of Saxony.

Frederick was determined to stock his new university with the best possible teachers. Like most universities, the University of Halle contained two kinds of instructors: those who taught theology and those who taught secular subjects. Frederick stocked both departments with brilliant professors who had no love for Lutheran orthodoxy.

He filled the theology department with Lutheran Pietists. The Pietists were one of those religions of the heart mentioned earlier, who contended that the orthodox Lutheran church had departed from the spirit of Luther and that its leadership was largely unconverted. The Pietists chosen by Frederick were exceptional men, especially their leader, August Hermann Francke, who was a world-class linguist with a tremendous gift for organization and innovation.

Frederick stocked the secular departments, like the departments of mathematics and philosophy, with equally brilliant men. Among them were Christian Thomasius and Christian Wolff, scholars who were in the forefront of the new thought and would later be recognized as important Enlightenment scholars.

The showdown at Halle

Halle soon became a divided university. The Pietists were against Lutheran orthodoxy, but all the early Pietist leaders had been taught at orthodox Lutheran universities. They valued Scripture and were committed to it as God's inspired Word.

This commitment was not shared by Christian Wolff, who had been called to Halle in 1707 to teach mathematics. In a few years, he was teaching all the philosophical disciplines. Unlike the Pietists, Wolff taught that human reason could discover truth "rationally," independent of outside help.

As the second decade of the century progressed, the Pietists began to realize that Wolff was teaching the opposite of what they were teaching. His rationalistic thoughts were opposed to the Bible.[54] In 1721 the Pietists got into an open dispute with Wolff. The Pietist leaders at Halle—August Francke, Paul Anton, and Joachim Lange—persuaded the new Prussian King, Frederick-Wilhelm I, to have Wolff removed. They prevailed, and in 1723 Wolff lost his position and was unceremoniously commanded to leave Halle. This event was perhaps the most significant confrontation between culture and religion in Europe during the 18th century. Enlightenment rationalism had been pitted against traditional religion and lost.

---

[54] In Germany, Enlightenment thought was called Rationalism.

The Development of Historical Criticism

Or had it? What happened next at Halle is the pattern for what has been happening at conservative Christian universities and colleges ever since. We will let some of the key players in the rise of historical criticism trace the story for us.

Accommodationism—Siegmund Baumgarten (1706–1757)

After Wolff left Halle, the conflict seemed to have come to an end. However, in 1730 a Halle graduate, Siegmund Baumgarten, who had sat at Wolff's feet and accepted his philosophy, began teaching at Halle. By this time most of the original Pietist leaders who had been instrumental in forcing Wolff out of Halle had died. What's more, by 1730 the scholarly tastes of the students at Halle had changed. The hard line Pietistic insistence—that one must depend on Scripture as God's inspired Word, must demonstrate a conversion experience, and must lead a highly disciplined life—was losing favor. The path of rationalism, that is, discovering truth through personal thought and reflection, was becoming the preferred method.[55]

Only one member of the old guard remained, Joachim Lange. Lange believed something was not quite right with how Baumgarten was handling Scripture, and he complained to the university board. Baumgarten defended himself, claiming that his views on Scripture were no different than Luther's. Baumgarten was convincing. In the early days, when many Enlightenment scholars had grown up at the feet of mainstream orthodox teachers, their vocabulary and way of expressing themselves often made it difficult to expose their errors. Added to this was Lange's own lack of a clear understanding of the new ways of thinking, which were only beginning to surface. The board dropped Lange's complaint.

But Lange was right. In many ways, Baumgarten was the first university professor in Germany to organize and express a new way of viewing Scripture. Baumgarten also was among the first to openly question the verbal inspiration of Scripture.

David Sorkin describes Baumgarten's approach to Scripture, which we recognize as consistent with Enlightenment goals. To Baumgarten, "the purpose of Scripture was practical."[56] Sorkin quotes Baumgarten: "The goal of the entire holy Scripture . . . consists in the application and observation of the truths it contains, and in producing right conduct."[57]

Sorkin describes Baumgarten's approach to Scripture:

---

[55] Johannes Wallmann, Kirchengeschichte Deutschlands (Tuebingen: J. C. B. Mohr, 1988).

[56] David Sorkin, "Reclaiming Theology for the Enlightenment: The Case of Siegmund Jacob Baumgarten (1706–1757)" in *Central European History 36, no. 4* (2003): 503-30, p. 510.

[57] David Sorkin, "Reclaiming Theology for the Enlightenment," p. 510.

> As the foundation for extracting truth from Scripture the exegete needed to employ an exacting philological and historical method that began with determining the meaning of words and then connecting those meanings with historical circumstances (speaker, audience, time, location, and cause), a step that Baumgarten called "grammatical" exegesis.[58]

Sorkin continues: "Baumgarten's historical awareness enabled him to recognize that the authors of the Bible were human and endowed with discernibly human intentions." Although he "unequivocally affirmed the divine contents of the books themselves," he departed from the 17th-century Orthodox Lutheran "'inspiration' theory that held every aspect of Scripture to be literally inspired."[59]

Baumgarten's departure from the verbal inspiration of Scripture allowed him to make "extensive use of the principle of *accommodation*—that in dealing with humankind God 'accommodated' himself to time, place, and particular mentalities—to account for those aspects of Scripture that were of a purely temporal nature and those accounts that were subject to error."[60]

Baumgarten linked his theory of accommodation to the idea that "Scripture was certain and unerring in regard to the truths that were necessary for salvation, but in respect to secondary or extraneous matters, e.g., history, chronology, or science, it was fallible."[61]

This, of course, supported the growing consensus among the natural philosophers that the earth had taken shape over long periods of time.

> **Cliché: The Bible writers accommodated themselves to their readers.**
>
> The appeal to accommodation is often found in theistic evolutionary books. The argument goes like this: "In order to be understood, the Bible writers often accommodated themselves to the views of their contemporaries, even if those views were inaccurate. If the writers had lived today, they would have modified their message for a modern audience."
>
> For example, accounts of miracles can be considered stories written for people who were unable to discover natural reasons behind these events. Or, Old Testament civil laws (how people should conduct themselves in their day-to-day lives) and ceremonial laws

---

[58] David Sorkin, "Reclaiming Theology for the Enlightenment," p. 511.

[59] David Sorkin, "Reclaiming Theology for the Enlightenment," p. 511.

[60] David Sorkin, "Reclaiming Theology for the Enlightenment," p. 512 (emphasis added).

[61] David Sorkin, "Reclaiming Theology for the Enlightenment," p. 512.

The Development of Historical Criticism

(particularly laws of sacrifice) were laid down according to what ancient people would consider appropriate behavior. Moral statements, particularly New Testament statements about such topics as homosexuality and the roles of men and women, were written to match the moral sensitivities of the day, at least those of Jewish culture.

The apostle Paul, it is claimed, may have known that Genesis 1 and 2 were the Hebrew version of a common ancient Near Eastern creation myth. But when he wrote to a Jewish audience that accepted Genesis as a literal account of how God made the world, he did not want to jeopardize his point by telling them that the account was mythology.

Some will argue, however, that there is no doubt that Paul himself believed the creation literally happened as the Bible describes it. In that case it was God who was accommodating himself to both Paul and Paul's audience. God did not want to jeopardize the truth by forcing Paul and his audience to think in unfamiliar ways.

Accommodationism was one of the earliest and most popular ways of avoiding what the Bible writers say on a variety of topics. In fact, by the end of the 18th century, it had started its own minor controversy in the theological world. Gottfried Hornig notes that between 1763 and 1817, no fewer than 31 books had addressed the subject.[62]

Hornig identifies evolution as the main reason for this: "We can say with certainty that the accommodation theories of Enlightenment theology were proposed, above all, to explain the lack of agreement between the Bible's statements about nature and the conclusions of modern natural science."[63]

Let's think about accommodationism in two ways. First, we will sort out various types of accommodationism. Second, we will examine the claim that accommodationism is designed to successfully merge God's message with ancient primitive world views.

A. First, some forms of accommodationism are legitimate and some are not. What theistic evolutionists do is to lump them all together and then use the legitimate forms found in some places in Scripture

---

[62] Gottfried Hornig, *Die Anfaenge der historisch-kritischen Theologie* (Goettingen: Vandenhoeck & Ruprecht, 1961), p. 211, note 1.

[63] Gottfried Hornig, *Die Anfaenge der historisch-kritischen Theologie*, p. 219.

to justify finding accommodation in places where Jesus or the authors are confessing the truth of Genesis.

Legitimate forms of accommodation include the following:

1. At the most basic level, God accommodated himself to us by communicating in human language. He used the author's style of writing, vocabulary, and even his emotions and struggles to speak his Word to us. This form of accommodationism has always been taught in the church.

2. We might say that God accommodates himself to how we use figurative language. For example, Scripture says "God is a rock." We know God is not a literal rock. God is merely accommodated himself to our way of speaking to describe something about himself.

3. At another level is Paul's accommodating himself to help the spread of the gospel. He became "all things to all men so that by all possible means [he] might save some" (1 Corinthians 9:22). Depending on his audience, he sometimes changed his way of speaking and acting so as not to turn people away from his teaching. But we realize that he never altered or misrepresented God's Word when he did this.

4. At another level is God's use of the language of appearances. For example: "The sun rises and sets." God accommodates himself to our way of looking at the world around us. He speaks in terms of the relationships between the earth and the heavenly bodies as we see them.

But accommodationism becomes illegitimate when it gives us reason to dismiss what Jesus or a Bible writer says.

5. It is claimed that God accommodated himself to ancient ideas about the universe. For example, he allowed his writers to use the ancient belief in a flat earth with a dome above it and pillars to support it. By speaking in these terms, God was purposely speaking inaccurately so as not to confuse an ancient reader. Once we realize this, the argument goes, we can dismiss such statements as untrue.

6. Sometimes we find Jesus and the New Testament writers actually basing points of teaching on the events recorded in the early chapters of Genesis. Those statements are explained away like this: It is not important for making the point whether the report is about events that actually happened or is mythology. For example, we say, "Slow and steady is the best policy. Remember the tortoise and the

The Development of Historical Criticism

hare." We know there was no such race, but the lesson we learn from the fable is valid. Theistic evolutionists claim that Jesus and the New Testament writers were doing just that, basing their teaching on Old Testament stories they knew were not literally true, like Adam and Eve's fall as recorded in Genesis 3. But the eternal lessons the story tells us—in that case that human beings at some point fell into sin—are still true.

7. The most dangerous level of accommodationism is the same as the previous level but with a twist. Sometimes the point a Bible writer draws from an account can be true *only if the account literally happened*. For example, in Romans 5:12 Paul wrote that "sin entered the world through one man" and follows that with this teaching: "For just as through the disobedience of the one man the many were made sinners, so also through the obedience of the one man the many will be made righteous" (Romans 5:19). Paul is basing his point on the fact that there was a literal man, Adam, as recorded in Genesis 1-3, and that all other humans descended from him. If Adam and Eve were not the first pair of humans, Paul himself has been misled, Paul's argument is nonsense, and Scripture is not a book we can trust.

The point is this: Be careful when theistic evolutionists use the legitimate uses of accommodationism found in Scripture to convince you to look for accommodationism in other places in order to avoid the fact that Jesus and the New Testament writers believed in Scripture's account of creation.

B. We now look at accommodationism from a second standpoint. Theistic evolutionists claim that the account of creation is an accommodation to the readers' primitive worldview. In other words, Moses wrote the account of God's creating activity in a way that could easily be understood by the humble farmers and desert nomads under his care.

Does that claim even make sense?

Why would Moses in his account of creation locate the creation of plant life ahead of the creation of the sun? Even a little Hebrew child given some seeds and a pot would observe that his plant grew best when the sun was shining. Some theistic evolutionists argue that the "creation" of the sun, moon, and stars was merely God making them visible for the first time. But that makes even less sense. Imagine a little Hebrew child being given that explanation. He would ask, "Why did God create plants that depend on the light of the sun and then hide the sun? How long did he hide it for?" It would have been much easier for the little child to understand that God created the sun first and then the plants or that God created the plants and then the sun in quick succession, as Scripture teaches.

If Moses knew that God created the world over long periods of time, he was doing the opposite of accommodating his description to what ancient farmers could understand. He was writing an account that any Hebrew farmer would consider nonsense.

Let me indulge in a little speculation. If creation had occurred through the process of evolution and God wanted to describe his creation in terms humble farmers and desert nomads could understand, why did God risk his own credibility by having Moses describe the creation as he did? Why didn't he have Moses write something like this:

> You know that the gods of the people living around you have tried to explain how the world began. The world, they say, was created by the many gods they worship. But those stories are false, as are the gods they claim exist.
>
> Here is the account of how I, the God of Abraham, Isaac, and Jacob created the world.
>
> Long ago in ages past, over the course of more years than you can imagine, I created everything you see. First, I made the raw materials. Then I created the sun, moon, and stars. After many ages had passed, I began to fill it with the beautiful things you see around you. I created the sky in which you see the sun, moon, and stars. I created clouds in the sky to send rain on the earth. Then I created plants. I filled the sea with fish. I created everything that lives on the earth, from the smallest insects to the largest beasts of the forest and the animals that graze on the hills.
>
> After many more years of work, I created you out of one of those animals. But you are far greater than any animal. I gave you my image. I gave you special gifts so that you could work alongside of me and care for my creation. I created you to know and love me just as I know and love you. You are the crown of my creation.

The Development of Historical Criticism

> What other god has done such things for his people? What other god knows the past and can foretell the future like I can? Your God, O Israel—yes, your God Jehovah—created this world for his glory and to show his love to the life he created upon it. My people, worship me alone.

Such an account would have made perfect sense to people who knew nothing about the modern teaching of evolution. Such a description would also have left the door open for scientists to fill in the blanks as more information about evolution became available. And God would have made the "theological" points that many theistic evolutionists teach was God's main purpose for including the creation account in Genesis.

Some say that God described the creation in terms consistent with the observation of an ancient people. But that also makes little sense. Moses' statement that on the first day God created light when there was no sun was not something the Israelites had observed or could even envision based on what they saw in the heavens. No one in Moses' day had observed a source of light other than the light that came from the sun, moon, and stars. They had to accept the creation as recorded in Genesis 1 on faith, apart from what they observed, just as we must do.

We return to Halle. Christian Wolff would not be denied his professorship at Halle. The new king of Prussia, Frederic Wilhelm II (Frederic the Great, who assumed office in 1740), was determined to allow Enlightenment thought to reign at his court. So he quickly reinstated Wolff at his university.

Wolff's reentry into Halle was a glorious event, at least as Wolff described it:

> A great multitude of students rode out of the city to meet me.... All the villagers along the roadside came out of their towns, and anxiously awaited my arrival.... When we reached Halle, all the streets and market-places were filled with an immense concourse of people, and I celebrated my jubilee.... In the street, opposite the house which I had rented as my place of residence, there was gathered a band of music, which received me and my attendants with joyous strains....
>
> My arrival was announced on the same evening to the professors and all the dignitaries of the city. On the following day they called upon me, and gave me warm greetings of welcome and esteem. Among all the rest I was received and welcomed by Dr. Lange [the Pietist leader who had been partly responsible for ousting him], who wished me the greatest

success, and assured me of his friendship; of course I promised to visit him in return.[64]

This event caught the attention of all of Europe. It was highly symbolic. The tables had turned. From this point on, there was nothing to stop German scholars from redefining Scripture for use in Enlightenment rationalism.

The Death of Scripture and the Rise of Biblical Studies[65]— Johann Michaelis (1717–1791)

Christian Wolff became chancellor of the university. Siegmund Baumgarten would teach theology there until his death in 1757. In 1740 Johann David Michaelis, the son of a Halle professor, began teaching at Halle. Five years later he received an offer to teach at the University of Goettingen. He accepted that offer and remained there until his death in 1791.

Michaelis would become Europe's leading scholar on all aspects of the text of the Old Testament. He worked to better understand biblical Hebrew, comparing it to other Near Eastern languages, such as Arabic. He studied the geography of the Holy Land and was among the first to use the findings of archaeology to shed light on the Hebrew text. He was one of the first "to insist that the Old Testament must be read historically, and interpreted in the light of the times and of the situation of those to whom it was addressed."[66]

Christians have always used background material to shed light on the history and customs they read about in the Bible. But Michaelis moved beyond that. Although he tried to maintain an Orthodox understanding of Scripture, his approach was embedded with Enlightenment goals. Kraus says that Michaelis stood between Orthodoxy and the Enlightenment.[67] That is, Michaelis thought he was treating the Bible as Luther had. But his use of material from outside the Bible as an important tool for understanding the Bible led him in directions Luther would not have gone.

For example, on his visit to the Red Sea, Michaelis noted that it had tides of 3.5 feet. Michaelis speculated that Pharaoh caught the Israelites on the shore of the sea when the tide was at its lowest point. Moses raised his arm, and "a strong storm came from the north-northwest, keeping back the tide long enough for the Israelites to cross." The drying up of the sea, Michaelis concluded, "was itself

---

[64] John F. Hurst, *History of Rationalism* (New York: Carlton & Porter, 1867), pp. 108,109.

[65] This is the title of Michael Legaspi's book, *The Death of Scripture and the Rise of Biblical Studies*.

[66] Stephen Neill, *The Interpretation of the New Testament, 1861–1961* (New York: Oxford, 1964), p. 5.

[67] Hans-Joachim Kraus, *Geschichte*, p. 93.

natural, and no miracle, but a work of providence."[68] With the help of background material, Michaelis could give a naturalistic explanation for why the sea dried up, but he could still honor God by giving him credit for his providential timing.

In the days after Michaelis, German Enlightenment scholars would give background material an even greater role. They would dismiss Scripture's own description of its past and begin using historical studies to create a new past for Scripture. Michael Legaspi explains, "They mastered and activated the older scholarship—by then two centuries' worth of philological, text critical, and antiquarian learning—in an effort to embed the Bible in a foreign, historical culture." They "used historical research to write the Bible's death certificate."[69]

Once Scripture was no longer a document whose purpose and meaning were applicable to people of all ages, Enlightenment scholars could "operate on the Bible as an inert and separated body of tradition." They could resurrect the biblical writings "as ancient cultural products capable of reinforcing the values and aims of a new sociopolitical order." In this way Scripture would stop dividing the world and produce a nonconfessional set of ideas, "a common cultural inheritance" that would unify the church.[70] Legaspi summarized his point with this graphic statement: "The Bible, once decomposed, could be used to fertilize modern culture."[71]

The study of Scripture more and more became focused on the "world *of* the Bible rather than the world as seen *through* the Bible."[72] This undermined the average Christian's faith in his or her eternal Savior. To quote Jonathan Sheehan, "Germans were estranged from their familiar texts and made to see the Bible as a bewildering archive of ancient humanity."[73]

> **Cliché: We can understand the Bible only if we understand the culture in which the Bible was written.**
>
> In theistic evolutionary literature, this cliché has reached the level of a mantra. What follows are some thoughts on how Bible background material as it was used before it was repurposed by the Enlightenment.

---

[68] Jonathan Sheehan, *The Enlightenment Bible*, p. 206.
[69] Michael C. Legaspi, *The Death of Scripture*, p. 5.
[70] Michael C. Legaspi, *The Death of Scripture*, p. 5.
[71] Michael C. Legaspi, *The Death of Scripture*, p. 5.
[72] Michael C. Legaspi, *The Death of Scripture*, p. 25 (emphasis author's).
[73] Jonathan Sheehan, *The Enlightenment Bible*, p. 214.

1. As we study the Bible, we should never discount the value of background information. But we must clearly define its role in the study of Scripture.

For example, we may not know everything that we would like to know about the Assyrian Empire. But the insights of historians and discoveries of archaeologists can help us better visualize what the Assyrian attack on Israel and Judah may have looked like. Nevertheless, we find enough information in Scripture itself to get a clear picture of how the Assyrians treated the Northern Kingdom of Israel and what a devastating tool of judgment they were in God's hands.

We may not know everything about how the sects of the Pharisees and Sadducees developed during the Intertestamental Period. And we welcome additional information from that period because it deepens our understanding of them when we meet them in the New Testament. For example, history teaches us that during the Intertestamental Period, a group called the Pharisees took a clear stand for Moses' laws in the face of pressure to adopt Greek culture, and that was good. But our best way to learn what they were like in Jesus' day is from their words and actions as recorded in the New Testament. And the only real way to understand their theology and motives is from how Jesus described them to his disciples.

As another example, we may not know precisely what kind of animal "leviathan" refers to. But from its description in Job 41, we conclude that it was a powerful and fierce creature, and we learn that God can control it even though human beings like Job could not. Someday scientists may discover the remains of such a creature, which would shed light on the account. And that would be nice. But it is not necessary for a basic understanding of God's description of the leviathan in Job 41.

2. To imply that until we have more information about the Old Testament we cannot really understand it, does not ring true with how Jesus and the New Testament writers used the Old Testament. They quoted from it hundreds of times with confidence that their hearers could understand it and take its lessons to heart.

Even as we value insights from history and archaeology, we are confident that Scripture itself gives us everything we need to understand it. Francis Pieper, a conservative Lutheran dogmatician from the early 20th century, said it well: "It must be maintained that the pure understanding of Scripture in no wise depends on the acquaintance with its secular-historical background, since the entire historical background necessary for a correct understanding of the meaning of Scripture is given in Scripture itself."[74] In other words, if a Christian were to be stranded on a desert island with only his Bible, he would have everything he needed to read and interpret it.

The Bible *contains* God's Word—Johann Semler (1725–1791)

Johann Semler matriculated at Halle in 1743. At Baumgarten's urging, Semler began studying theology. In 1752 he was called to teach theology at Halle, and when Baumgarten died in 1757, Semler replaced him as chairman of the theology department. Semler taught at Halle until his death in 1791. He is often called the founder of historical-critical methodology. At the very least, Semler laid the foundation on which historical-critical methods were built.

Semler strengthened the Bible interpreter's reliance on the past. To be a proficient interpreter, one needs help from outside Scripture. Gottfried Hornig wrote,

> Semler completely agreed with the traditional grammatical way of interpreting the text. But he came to the realization that that alone did not guarantee that one understood and explained the text in the original sense intended by the author. This was the epoch-making significance of Semler for the history of hermeneutics and exegesis.[75]

Semler also divided Scripture into more and less valuable sections. Enlightenment thinkers did something similar. They used Scripture, but only as a source of the kind of truth that appealed to reason and served to foster morality. As such, Scripture was a mixed bag. If a section of Scripture supplied that sort of thing, it was considered valuable for people of all times. If not, it was valuable only for the people to whom it was written.

Semler did something like that, but his standard of judgment was how well or poorly in his view a particular section of Scripture taught the gospel. Semler wrote: "I have taught others to differentiate between the books of the Bible on the basis of their content. Do all the books of the Bible contain the gospel?"[76] Regarding the canon of Scripture, Semler said, "For Christians, only the New

---

[74] Francis Pieper, *Christian Dogmatics, Vol. 1* (St. Louis: Concordia Publishing House, 1950), p. 366.

[75] Gottfried Hornig, *Die Anfaenge der historisch-kritischen Theologie*, p. 79.

[76] Gottfried Hornig, *Die Anfaenge der historisch-kritischen Theologie*, p. 199.

Testament's message should be considered normative because Christ is the only ground of faith."[77]

Semler divided the canon into books that were more valuable, less valuable, or had no place in the Bible at all. Hornig wrote, "Semler explained that in some Old Testament books 'God's Word was completely absent.' To this group belonged the historical books of Ruth, Samuel, Kings, Chronicles, Ezra, Nehemiah, Esther, and the Song of Solomon."[78] Semler himself wrote, "The root of evil [in theology] is the interchangeable use of the terms 'Scripture' and 'Word of God.'"[79] In other words, it can be said that Scripture *contains* God's Word but not that it *is* God's Word.

Needless to say, Semler's view of the canon of Scripture had a direct impact on his views of inspiration. As we have seen, long before Semler's time the teaching of the verbal inspiration of Scripture was seriously questioned in most scholarly circles. Semler pretty much killed it. To Semler, Scripture was nothing more than "a human account of God's revelation of himself in the past."[80]

We see the parallel between Semler's position on science and those of modern theistic evolutionists. As a document from the ancient past, the Bible was hardly an authority in areas of knowledge important to Enlightenment historians and natural philosophers: "Moreover, we must realize that from the Holy Scriptures (the Bible) a person cannot derive a general history of the world, nor a precise chronology, nor links to the chronology of other nations. Still less can philosophy, physics, astronomy, mathematics, etc., be assembled and taught on the basis of Scripture."[81]

In 1740 Baumgarten had tried to merge the findings of early natural scientists into his theology.[82] But by the end of the 18th century, it was becoming more difficult for theologians to do that. The world was now in the period of writers like Erasmus Darwin (1731–1802), who were searching for natural explanations for the origin of living things, not just of rocks and minerals. Georges Cuvier's (1769–1832) analysis of fossils was moving the scientific community from philosophical speculation about the evolution of living beings closer to the certainty of most modern scientists that biological evolution is true and based on hard evidence.

---

[77] Gottfried Hornig, *Die Anfaenge der historisch-kritischen Theologie*, p. 65. Also note p. 92. Semler did not completely deny that Christ was to be found in the Old Testament.

[78] Gottfried Hornig, *Die Anfaenge der historisch-kritischen Theologie*, p. 90.

[79] Gerhardt Maier, *The End of the Historical-Critical Method* (St. Louis: Concordia, 1974), p. 15, quoting Semler, *Kanon*, p. 52.

[80] Gottfried Hornig, *Die Anfaenge der historisch-kritischen Theologie*, p. 74.

[81] Gottfried Hornig, *Die Anfaenge der historisch-kritischen Theologie*, pp. 63,64.

[82] Gottfried Hornig, *Die Anfaenge der historisch-kritischen Theologie*. See his note 22, p. 55.

The Development of Historical Criticism

Semler thought it important to keep Christians from looking foolish. Hornig described the problem as Semler and other theologians of the day saw it:

> The real reason for the conflict between theology and the scientific disciplines that were being independently developed lay in the orthodox teaching about Scripture and its idea of truth. . . . Since theology, on the basis of its own principles, felt obligated to defend the traditional view, it came to be seen as the enemy of science. This put the average Christian in a serious dilemma. If he continued to follow orthodox teaching, he was compelled to sacrifice his intellectual integrity. And if he chose to accept the findings of natural science, he had to deny the truth of Scripture.[83]

> **Cliché: The evangelism card.**
>
> The argument goes like this: In these modern times, since evolution is a proven fact, the Christian church will turn away many seekers unless it embraces some variety of theistic evolution.
>
> The argument is based on assumptions. It assumes that the Bible can be interpreted to allow for evolutionary teachings. And it assumes that evolution has no adverse impact on God's plan of salvation.
>
> Moreover, the argument is speculation; namely, it assumes that in the long run more people will be brought into God's family if the Christian church adapts itself to current ideas, even if those ideas are at odds with what Scripture teaches.
>
> The mature Christian position is this: Teach the truth as you find it taught in Scripture. If you believe that Scripture can be reconciled with evolution and has no impact on the nature of Scripture or its message, then go ahead teach that. But if you accept the literal reading of Genesis and see the damage evolution does to the message of Scripture, then teach that and leave the growth of the church in God's hands.
>
> Christians have always known that God will use his truth, and not the popularity of the message, to bring people to faith. That was Paul's position. The message of the cross, he wrote, is foolishness to some and a stumbling block to others, but it is the power of God (1 Corinthians 1:23). Any other attitude, no matter how pious

---

[83] Gottfried Hornig, *Die Anfaenge der historisch-kritischen Theologie*, pp. 54,55.

it sounds, gives no honor to God and his Word, nor does it help people come to faith.

To understand Scripture, we must discover how it came to be—Johann Eichhorn (1752–1827)

In the rest of this chapter, we will touch on how historical criticism of the Bible developed in the early 19th century. We will mention only some of the main scholars. But from these men we will see that, in spite of the claim that modern Bible scholars have developed new and better methods of interpretation, the older German ideas are still very much in the mix and are heavily used by theistic evolutionists in their interpretation of Scripture.

Johann Herder (1744–1803), approached the Old Testament as a poet. He encouraged Bible readers to *experience the text*. Herder treated the account of creation like this: "It is not a scientific cosmology, but a natural primitive view of the universe."[84] Herder explained the experience a Bible reader should take away from the account of creation: It contains "the most basic natural philosophy, the most simple view of the establishment of the world, and the most basic regulations for human life." From Eden we are to take away "an enchanting story of a happy childhood dream, now sadly lost." In the account of the fall into sin we experience the "simplest philosophy about the cursed knot that binds humanity to the dissimilar and twisted ways our lives end."[85]

Nevertheless, most German scholars were taking a more analytical approach. A student of David Michaelis, Johann Eichhorn, took the lead in providing a scholarly way of looking at the Old Testament and he began to organize the historical-critical methods that scholars still use today.

By the end of the 18th century, the Enlightenment concept of "the past" had been firmly entrenched in the study of Scripture. Jonathan Sheehan refers to a comment Eichhorn made about the New Testament. "What a discovery it was, Eichhorn exclaimed, that the New Testament was only 'of local and temporal character, and neither for all times and peoples, nor an indispensable source for Christianity.'"[86]

Eichhorn began where all historical-critical scholars must begin—with the idea of mankind's slow development over the centuries. To him, it took thousands of years for people to realize that creation and life were not regulated by a divine being, but that history is like a long chain of events caused by the

---

[84] Hans-Joachim Kraus, *Geschichte*, p. 117, quoting Herder.

[85] Hans-Joachim Kraus, *Geschichte*, p. 117, quoting Herder.

[86] Jonathan Sheehan, *The Enlightenment Bible*, p. 90, quoting Eichhorn, *Algemeine Bibliothek*, 5.1 (1793): 75.

The Development of Historical Criticism

unchangeable laws of nature.[87] Kraus quotes Eichhorn: "In the development of the world, there has been a natural development of human beings from children to knowing adults. In this context, the Old Testament is located at a time when people were still children."[88] Here we find echoes of Gotthold Lessing, quoted in the last chapter.

Eichhorn played a major role in introducing the concept of mythology into biblical studies. According to Eichhorn, Scripture is composed of ancient myths passed down orally over the centuries by word of mouth. "Myth" is not to be equated with a fairy tale, merely an intriguing story told to entertain. Rather, it is a formal tool used to convey concepts and ideas by encasing them in stories with characters and plots. Scripture, especially the early books, is largely comprised of myths in this sense.[89]

Eichhorn described the process by which he believed the Old Testament was created. He taught that before the exile to Babylon, the Jews had collected a massive library and stored it in the temple at Jerusalem. It is hard to know everything they stored there, but the collection would have contained prophetic writings, historical annals, wisdom literature, liturgical writings, and miscellaneous documents written at the dawn of Israelite history. It must have included far more material than what ended up in the Old Testament.

When the Babylonians took Jerusalem in 586 B.C, they burned everything, including this library. But bits and pieces of the library had been stored in private collections or were rescued from the temple before it was burned. After the Jews returned from Babylon, they attempted to gather together as much of this material as they could to re-create the library. This was due to the goodness of the Persian king Cyrus, who allowed those who returned from Babylon to collect these writings and work on them before the ability to translate them was lost.

The material they found, however, was a "very poor collection" compared with the former, and what was still in existence was a matter of "mere chance."[90] Eichhorn did not deny that the Jews of Jesus' day had an established canon of Scripture. But it came from this work of Jewish scribes after the exile, who collected whatever material was left and pieced it together as they thought best.

Eichhorn's theory was intended to provide an objective platform on which to interpret Scripture. But all it did was make the interpretation of Scripture a

---

[87] Johann Eichhorn, *Introduction to the Study of the Old Testament*, George T. Gollop, trans. (the German original published in 1803, the translation printed by Spottswoode and Co, London, 1988), p. 35.

[88] Hans-Joachim Kraus, *Geschichte*, p. 124.

[89] For a description of Eichhorn's ideas about mythology, see Hans-Joachim Kraus, *Geschichte*, pp. 136-140.

[90] Johann Eichhorn, *Introduction to the Study of the Old Testament*, p. 18.

matter of speculation and opinion. Once Scripture became nothing more than a random collection of ancient material, the study of Scripture depended as much on analyzing why the ancient scribes chose the material they did and how they pieced it together—as it did on the content itself. Gone was the idea of a single writing given to us by a single being, written to reveal a single plan of salvation. What is more, the Old Testament and the New Testament became divided. The Bible commentator could "no longer . . . unify the disparate books of the Bible into a harmonious whole, nor could he read the Bible as the seamless unraveling of God's unified program."[91] A reconstruction of the origin of Scripture that completely discounted Scripture's own statements about its authorship and chronology gave license for a wide variety of interpretations. What is more, commentators writing on one book of the Bible lost the right to let the rest of Scripture influence their interpretations.

Eichhorn insisted that "an explanation of the respective Bible passage is not possible without a precise understanding of the *historical moment*."[92] Kraus gives an example of this in how Eichhorn envisioned the historical moment of Jeremiah's call to be a prophet (Jeremiah 1:4-8). Eichhorn said it happened like this: Jeremiah had been traveling through the land of Judah. He witnessed the people's distress. It was so bad that he concluded God must be trying to tell them something, and he felt the urgency to help them understand the reason for their suffering. In Eichhorn's words, "In order to give this simple message prophetic dignity, Jeremiah constructed a poem about a conversation between himself and God. And what could be more natural? People don't have thoughts unless God puts them there. And if God gives people thoughts, is that any different than if he speaks to them?"[93] In this way Jeremiah believed he was called to be God's spokesman. Of course, this kind of speculation undermined Scripture's teaching that God inspired any of Jeremiah's words.

Eichhorn was a leader in other areas of historical criticism. He advanced the study of "source documents." For example, some sections of Scripture seemed to favor the name Elohim for God, while other places seemed to favor the name Jehovah. Eichhorn and others believed that the difference pointed to different source documents written by different authors, which at some point—likely after the exile—were assembled into Scripture as we know it. The attempt to analyze the origin of Scripture in this way is referred to as "source criticism."

Eichhorn also pioneered the study of the various "forms" in which Scripture was written. This is the study of Scripture's origin and theology from the stand-

---

[91] Jonathan Sheehan, *The Enlightenment Bible*, p. 126.
[92] Hans-Joachim Kraus, *Geschichte,* p. 135 (emphasis added).
[93] Quoted in Hans-Joachim Kraus, *Geschichte,* p. 135.

point of various recurring patterns of thought and expression. This is referred to as "form criticism" and was fully developed years later by another critical scholar, Herman Gunkel.

In all of this we see the mark of historical-critical studies. They are all attempts to find a platform outside and above Scripture on which to stand in order to evaluate and interpret it objectively. When you read the writings of theistic evolutionists, you will hear them appeal to one or more of these techniques of Bible interpretation. The early chapters of Genesis are especially vulnerable to this kind of analysis.

The key to the Bible's past was finally discovered— Julius Wellhausen (1844–1918)

In the following years, archaeological research continued in earnest, as did the study of Near Eastern languages. The discovery of creation and flood documents from Babylon, Egypt, and other cultures would lead to whole new fields of critical study. But at this time the critical study of Scripture was still focused on discovering its sources. If scholars could discover when the books of Scripture were written and assembled, this would enable them to understand better the motives of its writers and editors and the specific problems Scripture was trying to address. This would provide clues for a correct interpretation.

The Pentateuch received much, if not most, of the attention. It makes a big difference for the interpretation of the five books of Moses if Moses actually wrote those books when he led the Israelites out of Egypt, and if Moses actually received God's law at Mount Sinai. It makes a big difference if as an eyewitness Moses recorded what happened when he led God's people to the Promised Land and if the chronology Moses provides in his narrative (which includes the narrative of God's creation of the world) is the true historical framework for the events as they unfolded. If so, the five books of Moses are the history of the early world and of God's making the descendants of Abraham into his chosen nation through which he would bless the world.

But if Scripture is just an ancient piece of literature with an undefined past and its history must be worked out from scratch, it will likely be set in a completely new context and written for a completely different purpose. For example, if the Pentateuch was written after the exile when Jerusalem lay in ruins and the Jews' faith in God needed to be bolstered, the Pentateuch would serve as a body of inspiring stories written to encourage the small, struggling group of Jews in Jerusalem as they worked to take advantage of the second chance God gave them to live as his people. How encouraging it was for the Israelites to hear that their God, not the gods of the Babylonians, created the world! The flood story would inspire them to believe that Israel's God controls the world and has the power to punish wicked people. The Exodus story was written to show that no nation has the power to keep God's people enslaved or keep God's promises to Abraham from being fulfilled.

It makes little difference if God actually created the world in six days, if there was a flood, if Abraham was an actual person, or if the account of the exodus was literal history. The value of these accounts for Israel lay in the encouragement they gave them, and that is what they teach believers of all ages. This is not just a hypothetical example. German scholars, under the leadership of Julius Wellhausen, would ultimately accept this way of looking at the Old Testament.

In the middle of the 19th century when Wellhausen started his work, German scholars still could not see the big picture of when the various books of Scripture were written. Speculation reigned. The Old Testament was like a pile of documents lying on a table. Some scholars thought the pile had come from a large number of independent sources. Some believed fewer sources were involved. Others believed Scripture started out as the work of a single, unknown author and was enlarged over the years by other unknown authors. Prior to Wellhausen, all scholars had was a Bible in pieces—without specific authors, without a timeline, without a unifying theme, and without a starting point for interpretation.

At this point the German scholars were united on only one idea: that the traditional way of reading Scripture was wrong and that their approach, as incomplete as it was, was correct. One of these scholars, Abraham Kuenen, summarized their attitude: "Disunity regarding the truth is always better than being united in error."[94] The German scholars could not put up with speculation. They would not give up until they were confident they knew when and how the Bible came into existence.

That would happen through the work of Abraham Kuenen, Eduard Reusz, Karl Graf, and Julius Wellhausen. Wellhausen was the leading figure. After years of grueling analysis, in 1885 he assembled the conclusions of him and his co-workers in his *Prolegomena to the History of Ancient Israel*.[95] Wellhausen rejected two major ideas that had been popular before him: (1) that the Old Testament was a combination of many ancient fragments and (2) that the Old Testament started out as the work of a single author whose work had been enlarged over the centuries. Wellhausen reduced the sources of the Old Testament to four: "J," the writer who mostly used "Jahveh" as the name for God; "E," the writer who mostly used "Elohim" as the name for God; "D," the writer who wrote the code of laws that found its way into Deuteronomy; and "P," the writer who wrote into

---

[94] Hans-Joachim Kraus, *Geschichte*, p. 235.

[95] Julius Wellhausen, *Prolegomena to the History of Ancient Israel (1885),* Sutherland Black and Allan Menzies, trans. (Evinity Publishing, 2009, Kindle).

The Development of Historical Criticism

Scripture the laws for Israel's priesthood and worship. At some point in time, these four sources were combined by a redactor, or editor, into what we know as the Holy Scriptures. This is called the *Documentary Hypothesis*.

John Barton explains the impact this hypothesis had on Bible interpretation: "Wellhausen's epoch-making insight that 'P' [the source of laws for Israel's priesthood and worship] was the latest, rather than (as had formerly been thought) the earliest of the four Pentateuchal sources," would revolutionize how scholars understood "the relation of post-exilic Judaism to the pre-exilic faith expressed in J, E, and D. Pre-exilic 'Yahwism' now for the first time stood out clearly as something distinct from later Jewish religion."[96]

What does that mean? If a person reads Scripture in a straightforward way, it is clear that God revealed his law to Israel at Mount Sinai and added various additional laws throughout Israel's years in the desert. Already at Sinai, God established the priesthood, the sacrificial system, the tabernacle, the Jewish church year, and all the other ceremonial and civil laws.

Wellhausen denied this and said the Mosaic law was written *after* the Jews returned from exile in Babylon. At that time a powerful and influential priesthood formed. An entirely new set of laws was written to regulate every aspect of Israel's secular and religious life. This was done to preserve the Jews' future, lest they squander the second chance God had given them to live free from idolatry. To give this new system of law authenticity and authority, it was written back into the five books of Moses. By making it appear that the priesthood and the law came through Moses, the new religious practices were given the highest authority possible.

The high point of Israel's history, according to Wellhausen, actually came before the exile, during the time of the prophets, when Israel was taught to worship the Lord "Jehovah" in simplicity, willingness, free from the demands of Moses' law. This is why the "J" source was put first in Wellhausen's list of contributors of the Bible. The low point of Israel's history came after the exile, when the Jews were forced to live under a new and legalistic system of worship and a way of life regulated by the priests. At that time material from the Elohist author, the priestly authors, and the authors of Deuteronomy (the E, P, and D sources) were added to the Scriptures. For German scholars and for scholars throughout Europe, the Documentary Hypothesis (or the Graf-Wellhausen theory as it is also called) successfully established Scripture's past. It established the order in which Scripture was supposed to have been written, edited, and assembled.

Some claim that the German higher critical scholars were only interested in discovering the Bible's history. But they knew that a correct understanding

---

[96]John Barton, *Reading the Old Testament*, p. 30.

of the Bible's origin would also help them read and interpret it correctly. The traditional, straightforward reading of Scripture could in good conscience be abandoned. The restructuring of Scripture's chronology gave the books of Moses, the writings of the prophets, the Psalms, etc., new meanings. Needless to say, any sense that Scripture was inspired was completely lost. An overarching framework had been established for interpreting the Bible. A platform had been built high above Scripture on which a person could stand to interpret it accurately.

As with all Enlightenment thought, Wellhausen's approach builds on the supposed primitive intellectual and spiritual condition of the Israelite people. George Ladd writes, "Wellhausen treated Israel's religion not as the vehicle of divine revelation but as a religious development resulting from the outworking of evolutionary principles manifesting themselves in religious history."[97]

Some say the Documentary Hypothesis has gone out of favor in recent years, along with all other efforts to construct the history of Scripture from its sources. But the basic concepts of the Documentary Hypothesis are still very much present in modern historical criticism. You will often find references to the JEPD theory in theistic evolutionary literature, which is the starting point for discussions about the meaning of the early chapters of Genesis. It effectively turns those chapters into myths intended to bolster the faith of the Israelites during difficult times, rather than Moses' record of what actually happened in the beginning.

To understand Scripture, we must understand its *forms*— Herman Gunkel (1862–1932)

By the turn of the 20th century, German historical-critical scholars had found weaknesses in the Documentary Hypothesis. Under the leadership of Herman Gunkel, they turned from Scripture's *written* sources to its *oral* history, using what is called form criticism. Form criticism was applied to both the Old and New Testaments.

Gunkel saw the Old Testament as an assembly of various *types* of material, which he called "forms." Forms share various characteristics of content and style. Form criticism attempts to construct the history and meaning of Scripture by isolating and analyzing these forms.

The forms had their origin in ancient oral history. The basic assumption is this: Ever since people started to communicate, they began to pass down to the next generation descriptions of special aspects of their lives, such as historic events, basic life truths, the nature of the gods, and how the nations came into being. The way people spoke about these things became standardized. People

---

[97] George Eldon Ladd, *The New Testament and Criticism* (Grand Rapids: Eerdmans, 1967), p. 196.

The Development of Historical Criticism

also created ceremonial rites, which by constant use also took on a standardized form. The authors of Scripture had these pieces of literature at hand when they began to write. Their task was to weave them together into a story.

Form critics try to identify various standardized forms of literature as they come up in Scripture. Form critics believe that if they can determine when and why the various forms were originally written and the truths they were meant to convey, this will help unfold the meaning of Scripture.

One particular kind of form is a little story that teaches a truth or answers questions people have about what they see in the world around them. Gunkel calls these forms "legends," or "myths." In *The Legends of Genesis: The Biblical Saga and History*, Gunkel shows how understanding forms will help in reading Genesis. In the following quotation, we hear Gunkel explain his view of the events of the early chapters of Genesis.

> Many myths attempt to answer questions, being intended to give instruction. This is the case with the primitive legends of Genesis: the story of creation raises the question, where did heaven and earth come from? and at the same time, why is the Sabbath sacred? The story of Paradise treats the questions, where do man's reason and his mortality come from? and along with this, where do man's body and mind come from? Where does his language come from? Where does the love between the sexes originate? Why do women experience so much pain in childbirth, why must man till the stubborn field, why does the serpent crawl on its belly, and so on. The legend of Babel asks the question, why is there such a variety of languages and why do the nations live in various places? The answers to these questions constitute the real content of the respective legends. In the case of the legend of the deluge this is different, but there is an etiological, or explanatory feature at the close: Why is there never such a flood again? And what is the meaning of the rainbow? All these questions interest not Israel alone, but the whole world.... Here is a place in which the ancient race is able to treat universal human problems, the profoundest questions of mankind.[98]

Of course, Gunkel's system is also based on an evolutionary view of mankind and civilization. Gunkel writes: "Legends come from ages and stages of civilization which have not yet acquired the intellectual power to distinguish between

---

[98] Herman Gunkel, *The Legends of Genesis: The Biblical Saga and History*, W.H. Carruth, trans. (Chicago: Open Court Publishing Co. 1901, Kindle Version by Nisyros Publishers, 2014), loc. 247, 256. I edited the translation slightly to make it easier for a modern audience, mostly changing "whence" to "where did ... come from."

poetry and reality."[99] Gunkel describes the early questions about the world and the answers given by ancient people like this:

> The child looks into the world with wide eyes and asks, Why? The answer which the child gives itself and with which it is for the time satisfied, is perhaps very childish and hence incorrect, and yet, if it is a bright child the answer is interesting and touching. . . . In the same way a primitive people asks similar questions and answers them as best it can. These questions are usually the same that we ourselves are asking and trying to answer in our scientific researches.[100]

The last sentence captures exactly the sentiment of many theistic evolutionists today on the relation between the account of origins in Genesis and the theory of evolution. Genesis contains appropriate answers to the questions primitive people were asking. Modern evolutionary theories contain answers to those same questions, only in factual, scientific terms.

Form criticism was also applied to the New Testament. The principle is the same as with the Old Testament. The New Testament is read with attention to its individual forms—parables, sermons, history, sayings, miracle stories, confrontations, etc. George Ladd explains: Form criticism "studies the Gospel tradition in its oral form before it was written down in our Gospels or their sources."[101] For example, after Jesus died and rose, the early church started remembering what Jesus said and did. These remembrances became "legends" and "myths" about the man on whom the early church based its faith. In time, this oral history was written down and became the four gospels. And so, the bulk of the gospels is not based on eyewitness accounts but consists of "reliable hints as to what the early Christian communities believed about Jesus, whom they acknowledged as Lord and Christ."[102]

This is a particularly effective tool for theistic evolutionists. When Jesus and the other New Testament writers spoke about creation and the flood as events that really happened, those reports can be relegated to the shadowy world of the early church's oral history of Jesus and the apostles. Therefore, you cannot blame Jesus or the New Testament writers for this or that statement that treats creation and the flood as fact. This is only what the early church thought Jesus said or wanted him to have said.

---

[99] Herman Gunkel, *The Legends of Genesis*, loc. 524.

[100] Herman Gunkel, *The Legends of Genesis*, loc. 347.

[101] George Eldon Ladd, *The New Testament and Criticism*, p. 199.

[102] Henry P. Haman, *A Popular Guide to New Testament Criticism* (St. Louis: Concordia, 1977), p. 55.

More types of historical criticism

Redaction criticism

Redaction criticism is yet another form of historical criticism. Scholars try to study the work of the editors (redactors) who, it is claimed, organized and edited the written and oral source material and created the Scriptures. Redactors have always been part of the mix of historical criticism, but in the early years not much attention was paid to them. They were merely the behind-the-scenes people who assembled the sources. But in redaction criticism, their work is given a much more important role.

Redaction criticism asks questions like: Why did the editor include this or that material and why did he include it at this point in the narrative? Was the editor trying to make some point by what he included in Scripture and by the order in which he organized the material? Might he have had an agenda? If the Bible scholar can begin to answer those questions, he will better be able to understand when the text was written and perhaps glean insights into its meaning.

For example, in the creation/evolution debate, theistic evolutionists often throw out the idea (certainly, a cliché) that *everyone* realizes that Genesis 1 contains one creation account and that Genesis 2 contains a second, distinct, and somewhat different creation account written by a different author. These two accounts, they claim, were pasted together by the redactor. Supposedly, all modern Bible scholars are in agreement on this.

John Barton (Oxford professor emeritus of biblical interpretation and advocate of higher criticism, including redaction criticism) notes this common opinion, and interestingly, Barton uses redaction criticism to support a straightforward reading of Genesis 1:

> Biblical critics have often countered a fundamentalist insistence on the exact details of the events of creation in Genesis 1 by maintaining that none of these details matters, since the chapter is "really about" the *fact* that God is creator, not the *process* of creation. But this kind of casual indifference to the verbal form of the text finds no echo in the painstaking work of redaction critics who are as concerned with every minute verbal nuance as is the most committed proponent of verbal inspiration.[103]

Barton points out that a number of modern redaction critics take pains to show that the phrase in Genesis 2:4: "These are the generations of the heavens and the earth when they were created," was inserted by a redactor to tip off the

---

[103] John Barton, *Reading the Old Testament*, p. 52 (emphasis author's).

reader that the following material is more information (not a second account) about the creation of man and woman on day six. Barton explains that this was inserted to ensure that the narrative "will be read (as in fact it was read by most readers before the rise of source criticism, and as it is still read by many today) as simply a detailed exposition of the part of Genesis 1 that most nearly concerns mankind, the account of its own origins." Barton continues: "The redactor who achieved this aim was clearly no mere collector, pasting various creation stories into an album." [104]

Literary criticism[105]

Up to the middle of the 20th century, most scholars tried to learn the meaning of Scripture by reconstructing its history—who wrote it, when it was written, and what were the sources on which it was based.

Scholars in the latter half of the 20th century have been working with another form of Bible criticism called literary criticism. Literary criticism refers to a variety of methods scholars have developed to understand literature in general. These methods have been put to use by Bible scholars. C. John Collins explains: "In the late twentieth century, many Bible scholars came to a fresh appreciation of the literary qualities of the Biblical books; thus we have come to favor literary readings oriented toward the text as we have it."[106]

Exploring the literary qualities of Scripture is a worthwhile pursuit. For centuries Bible scholars have explored the various kinds of literature God had his inspired writers use. Scripture contains narrative, poetry, conversation, prophetic proclamation, and more. This gives Scripture beauty, simplicity, and the kind of complexity that begs ongoing study. Chapters and books are sometimes structured in interesting ways that move the reader along. A book might build to a climax in the middle and then taper off to a satisfying conclusion. Sometimes words are used a specific number of times in a chapter and organized in intriguing ways, for example, psalms in which each verse begins with the next letter of the alphabet, going from "A to Z." These devices often have to be pointed out to non-Hebrew readers. In other cases, a Hebrew teacher might have had

---

[104] John Barton, *Reading the Old Testament*, p. 51.

[105] Literary criticism is also used as a synonym for biblical criticism or higher criticism, or even lower (variant reading) criticism. Here it refers to one kind of biblical criticism, namely, using the text itself as one's critical tool.

[106] C. John Collins, *Did Adam and Eve Really Exist?* (Wheaton: Crossway, 2011), p. 23. Also see "Reading Glasses: Literary Criticism" https://www.sbl-site.org/assets/pdfs/TBReadingGlasses_BB.pdf (Accessed February 2019). This is a good article on literary criticism from the Society of Biblical Literature. It explains its context and presents its basic principles. Credit goes to this article for the analogy of "reading glasses" used in the next section. For a very accessible treatment of this difficult topic, see John Barton, *Reading the Old Testament*, pp. 140-235.

to point out a literary method to his Hebrew students and then watch them sit back and marvel in amazement at the beauty and ingenuity of how God chose to communicate to us through his inspired writers.

At first glance literary criticism might seem to be a return to the traditional way of approaching Scripture, but that is not exactly the case. In the hands of a Bible critic, literary criticism gives the scholar yet another platform outside of Scripture on which to stand and evaluate it.

Collins gives us a feel for the position the literary critic takes. He claims that literary criticism gives us "the means by which the Biblical authors communicate their point of view."[107] He then describes the kind of conclusions literary critics come to about Scripture. A study of the text reveals to the literary critic that the narrator of Scripture is "reliable and omniscient" and "serves as the voice and perspective of God." The author tells us when he is writing something significant by using "heightened speech." He may use this heightened speech to indicate that his words are divine. [108]

Literary criticism as Collins describes it can lead to the same kind of speculation and discussion as other forms of Bible criticism. At the very least, one senses that literary critics look behind the words of the text to discover clues to the meaning of Scripture that can't be discovered by an average reader reading the text in a straightforward way. The subjective nature of this critical tool is evident in Collins' admission: "Not everyone who is aware of these literary features will agree on just what they mean in a particular passage, and thus, we cannot avoid the kind of discussion that evaluates proposed ways of reading."[109]

Many glasses to choose from

Picture a box in which you see many pairs of glasses, each with a different shade of colored glass. Each represents a method of interpreting Scripture. As they study the Bible, Bible critics choose which pair of glasses they prefer to wear. Moreover, they reserve the right to take off one pair and put on another if they wish.

Jesus and the writers of Scripture used the pair of glasses Scripture itself provides: God is the author of Scripture, the words of Scripture are inspired by God, Scripture is a single document and one part can be used to interpret another, Scripture leads us to Christ, and it was written for people of all ages to understand and take to heart.

---

[107] C. John Collins, *Did Adam and Eve Really Exist?*, p. 24.

[108] C. John Collins, *Did Adam and Eve Really Exist?*, p. 24.

[109] C. John Collins, *Did Adam and Eve Really Exist?*, p. 25.

If your head is spinning because there are so many glasses to choose from, you are not alone. Critical scholar John Barton shares the experience of those who teach historical criticism: "The common experience of Old Testament teachers [is] that their students cannot remember which method is which: no logical progression is perceived from each method to the next, no common themes are noticed."[110]

Barton provides a helpful framework for organizing the many different glasses critics have to choose from. Critics attempt to find meaning from three basic sources: (1) the history of the text, (2) an analysis of the text as it stands, and (3) how a reader responds to the text (a contemporary method we will not touch on in this book).[111]

In Barton's first category are methods that focus on the *history of the text*. This is the kind of criticism we have been focusing on in this chapter. These include "source criticism," "form criticism," and "redaction criticism." In all three, Barton writes, "Biblical scholars cease to ask about the divine meaning of Scripture and begin to ask, 'What did the *author of this text* mean?'"[112]

Source criticism concentrates on the meaning that the *authors of the original sources* put there. Form criticism concentrates on the meaning the *religious community* put there through the myths and legends of its past. Redaction criticism concentrates on the meaning the *editor of Scripture* had in mind when he chose which sources to include and how to assemble them into a single document. None of them takes Scripture at face value.

A second group of critical methods, broadly called literary criticism, attempts to find the meaning of Scripture *in the text of Scripture* itself. It uses methods similar to those used by scholars to analyze all forms of literature. Another method called "canon criticism" analyzes why certain books might have been included in Scripture and others not.

A third set of critical methods, not discussed in this book, tries to discover the meaning of Scripture in *the response* Scripture evokes from people who read it. Barton writes, "Rhetorical criticism, reader-response criticism, and deconstruc-

---

[110] John Barton, *Reading the Old Testament*, p. 238.

[111] The terminology in general can be confusing. Historical criticism, which deals with Scripture's history—the authorship of the books and the canon of Scripture—is sometimes called literary criticism. Historical criticism is also referred to as "higher criticism" to distinguish it from a study of the variant readings, referred to as "lower criticism" or "textual criticism" as noted above. Those who read the Bible in a traditional way sometimes refer to higher criticism as "negative criticism" because of the negative impact it has on the teaching of inspiration and on Scripture in general. Some use the term "biblical criticism" as a synonym of "higher criticism," while "historical criticism" is reserved for the critical methods that seek to reconstruct the history of the Bible text. When authors use a term in a book you are reading, it is best to determine how they are using a particular term.

[112] John Barton, *Reading the Old Testament*, p. 240 (emphases added).

tion all concentrate on the interplay between text and reader as determinative for meaning."[113] These methods are rather avant-garde, and the theistic evolutionists I read did not use them. Some of these methods are more at home in a postmodern world than in the "modern" world created by the Enlightenment.

This summary shows the broad range of tools critical scholars use to determine the meaning of Scripture. No scholar uses the tools in exactly the same way, and all the tools lead to speculation and a variety of conclusions. If nothing else, this summary helps us realize that when theistic evolutionists back up a point with the claim, "scholars say," the claim itself may not be very scholarly.

The critical methods developed over the last three centuries have created a Bible well suited to take its place in a world where the Enlightenment approach to truth is still alive and well. The meaning of Scripture, it is claimed, must never be set in stone. The process of discovery is more important than the conclusions of any one scholar. As long as the process continues, all is well. Meaning must remain in flux as scholars seek new, ever more fruitful viewpoints from which to objectively evaluate the text. The discovery of more interpretive glasses will hopefully get Bible scholars closer to Scripture's meaning. But a straightforward reading of Scripture is always out of the question.

John and Joan, continued

> *John:* Over the years, John has continued to grow in faith and has found himself able to understand more of his Bible every time he reads it. He respects his pastor's learning and the background material he brings to his Bible studies. He appreciates even more how his pastor shows him other sections of Scripture that shed light on the section they are studying. Above all, he is thankful for his pastor's spirit of repentance and faith in Christ, the Savior, which he shares with the class no matter what part of the Bible he is teaching.
>
> John just read a short book on the claims the Bible makes for itself—that it was inspired by God and that its words are true. He appreciated examples of New Testament believers, like the believers in the newfound congregation at Berea, who searched the Old Testament to see if what Paul said about Christ being the Messiah was true. This has given him confidence that, with the Lord's help, he is competent to read and understand the Bible.
>
> Jesus said to the Pharisees that the Scriptures testify about him (John 5:39). With those words of Jesus in mind, John is always on the lookout for verses in the Bible that point him to Jesus. John realizes he will always struggle to understand some passages, but he is confident that in time at least

---

[113] John Barton, *Reading the Old Testament*, p. 242.

some of those passages will become clear. At church he just finished a Bible study on Hebrews and was amazed at how much of the Old Testament has Christ at its center. During that class, many formerly dark passages from the Old Testament became clear for him. He can even read those difficult books of Moses—with all their talk of uncleanness and cleansing, of sacrifices and purifications—with understanding. They are still hard to wade through, but he sees in those sections of Scripture his own uncleanness, his own need for purification, and pointers to the sacrifice Christ made for him.

Joan: Joan, however, is having a harder time of it. Her teacher, Jack, has been explaining the Psalms. That has always been one of Joan's favorite books. The spiritual struggles of the psalmist and the psalmist's confidence in God are similar to her own hope in the midst of her struggles. She loves those places in the New Testament where the writer quotes from a psalm and explains how it predicted Jesus' suffering and glory.

One day she expresses that idea in class. Her teacher gives her a knowing sort of smile and explains, "I'm glad you find them encouraging. Remember, however, the psalms are a genre of literature found in all ancient societies. They were written for public use in worship by anonymous writers. Over the years the church has poured much meaning into these texts. Indeed, they have become vehicles of intensely personal prayer and faith, as I see you have discovered."[114]

One day the class is talking about Saint Paul. Joan's teacher is trying to explain what in Paul's writings are actually from his pen. Joan has her Bible open to Galatians. She asks her teacher, "Jack, in Galatians 1:12 Paul talks about the source of his gospel: 'I did not receive it from any man, nor was I taught it, but I received it through a revelation of Jesus Christ.' Is what Paul said true?" Jack replies, "I would put it this way: he believed it was true."[115]

Jack has just finished his session on the sources used to write our Bible: "We have to realize," he says, "that the Old Testament is a very ancient book. Much of its content was in existence long before it was written down and then finally assembled by editors into our present Bible. The New Testament came about in much the same way. After Jesus left this earth, believers began to reflect on what Jesus had said and done. Years later, some believers thought they should write down the history of Jesus lest it be lost. They wrote what we call the four gospels. Jesus may not have actually said everything

---

[114]John Barton, *Reading the Old Testament*, p. 39. This is a paraphrase of a passage in which Barton is describing the implications of form criticism.

[115]I asked that question in a community lecture on the Bible by a local ELCA professor, and that's the answer I received.

The Development of Historical Criticism

or performed all the miracles the writers included in the gospels. But in a wonderful way these books express what the early church had come to believe about Jesus and the hope they had in his life and death."

Joan becomes nervous. "So how can I hope to understand the Bible? I don't have your training." Jack responds, "I sense your struggle, Joan. Non-specialists depend on the consensus of experts who have studied the Bible with the many tools available to them. And even the experts must continually adjust their interpretations based on new historical evidence."[116]

Joan picks up on this: "Sir, then how can I know the meaning of what the Bible says? How can I open my Bible and be confident that I understand it correctly?"[117]

Jack replies, "Joan, I can't give you a definite answer to those questions. The Bible is a very old document. We cannot be completely sure of when it was written or who wrote it. Over the years it has been interpreted in many different, sometimes contradictory ways. There are many copyist errors in the text of the Bible. There are questions about whether certain books should even be in the Bible. The findings of modern science are beyond question and prove that the early chapters of Genesis are mythology. Sometimes we just have to use our common sense."

Jack continues, "Let me share another thought. You grew up in a very conservative home where you were taught that the Bible is different from all other books. But it isn't. Modern scholars are of the consensus that 'the doctrine of biblical inspiration led people to separate the Bible from all other books.' That idea 'made it impossible for them to read it impartially and with open eyes.'[118] As a responsible scholar, I can only say that if you want to read the Bible objectively, you must use as best you can the tools scholars have provided."

Cliché: It is very difficult to become a truly competent Bible reader.

This cliche is stated or implied in every book that promotes historical criticism.

---

[116] Quoted from George T. Montague, *Understanding the Bible: A Basic Introduction to Biblical Interpretation* (New York: Paulist Press, 2007), Kindle Version, loc. 1723.

[117] John Barton, *Reading the Old Testament*, p. 39. What makes Barton's book valuable, in my opinion, is his thorough understanding of historical criticism along with all the other critical methods. He is a strong proponent of critical methods to study the Bible, but he understands and asks the hard questions that beg to be answered. This paragraph is based on the questions Barton asks about the historical-critical methods described in this present chapter.

[118] Quoted from Stephen Neill, *The Interpretation of the New Testament, 1861–1961*, p. 137.

But how true is it? God gave his Word to lead people to Jesus. We understand the life of Abraham because, as Jesus said, "Your father Abraham rejoiced that he would see my day. He saw it and was glad" (John 8:56). We understand Moses because he was a prophet, like Jesus. He said, "I will raise up for them a prophet like you from among their brothers. And I will put my words in his mouth, and he shall speak to them all that I command him" (Deuteronomy 18:18). We understand Isaiah because he rejoiced in the sacrifice God would provide for the world's sins: "But he was pierced for our transgressions; he was crushed for our iniquities; upon him was the chastisement that brought us peace, and with his wounds we are healed" (Isaiah 53:5).

Jesus told the religious leaders of his day: "You search the Scriptures because you think that in them you have eternal life; and it is they that bear witness about me" (John 5:39). The apostle Peter wrote, "Concerning this salvation, the prophets who prophesied about the grace that was to be yours searched and inquired carefully, inquiring what person or time the Spirit of Christ in them was indicating when he predicted the sufferings of Christ and the subsequent glories" (1 Peter 1:10,11).

We understand the New Testament because it reveals Christ to us: "Now Jesus did many other signs in the presence of the disciples, which are not written in this book; but these are written so that you may believe that Jesus is the Christ, the Son of God, and that by believing you may have life in his name" (John 20:30,31).

I realize there is more to reading Scripture with understanding. But competency in reading Scripture does not begin with historical criticism. It begins with the knowledge that God gave us the Scriptures to make us competent to know his Son and his plan of salvation.

Chapter 4

Historical Criticism:
Theistic Evolution's Tool of Interpretation

Historical Criticism and Theistic Evolution Today

How is historical criticism used today?

In the last chapter, we traced the history of historical criticism in the 18th and 19th centuries. We also noted that 20th-century Bible scholars have been dissatisfied with the earlier research and have developed a number of new critical methods.

All these methods have found their way into a large number of seminaries throughout the world. The pastors being trained in these seminaries will prepare sermons and teach Bible studies with historical critical methods in mind. Many, perhaps most of these pastors, won't openly force historical critical methods onto the members of their congregations. In 19th-century Germany, it was said that "clergymen who on Mondays stood out as determined representatives of the higher-critical method at their [pastoral] study groups, at the same time were proud of the fact that on Sunday they had preached 'normal' sermons that were faithful to the Scriptures."[119] That is probably true in many congregations today.

But Christians cannot expect to be shielded from historical criticism. There is one place where it enters full force into the lives of many young men and women whether they are Christians or not: in the required college courses called by names like "Introduction to the Bible" or "The Bible as Literature."

Professors who teach these courses are likely aware of their role in the university curriculum. University students can excel in their liberal arts classes, it is thought, only through open-minded and critical thinking, which a preexisting belief in the inspiration of Scripture will make impossible. I attended a lecture by a religious professor at a liberal ELCA college. He said that one of the hardest things he had to do at the beginning of each semester was to get his students to approach the Bible on his terms (that is, with the help of critical tools) and not as they did in their churches back home.

---

[119] Gerhardt Maier, *The End of the Historical-Critical Method*, p. 22.

What critical methods are being taught in these classes? The starting point is usually source criticism in the form of the JEPD theory. John Barton says that the belief in four sources, each of which was originally a more or less finished work in its own right, "has so far weathered most attacks."[120] Teachers generally accept the basic outline of Julius Wellhausen's reordered history of Scripture—the Documentary Hypothesis—and use that as their starting point in reinterpreting the early chapters of Genesis.

The Documentary Hypothesis is relatively easy to teach. As we saw above, Wellhausen deduced that the "P" material, namely, the regulations for temple worship and the priesthood found in the Pentateuch, were written *after* the exile. They were attributed to Moses in order to give them credibility. Wellhausen's chronology, supported by Herman Gunkel's form criticism, provides teachers a framework that gives them both structure and freedom. The structure comes from Wellhausen's specific re-creation of the Bible's past, and the freedom comes from applying Gunkel's teaching that the Bible is comprised of legends and myths. How much in Scripture actually happened and how much is fiction is impossible to say. Each teacher will likely draw the line at a different point depending on his or her personal beliefs about the Bible. When teachers get their students to think about Scripture in terms of an ancient document whose origin is buried in the past, they give their students a structured way of thinking about Scripture along with the freedom to come to their own conclusions about it.

A visit to two modern "Bible as literature" classes

A visit to two contemporary Bible introduction courses taught by influential scholars will demonstrate how biblical criticism is being taught in universities today.[121] In both classes the teachers are introducing their students to the Bible and are using critical glasses developed over the past three hundred years. Significantly, we will see that 19th-century German historical criticism is very much

---

[120] John Barton, *Reading the Old Testament*, p. 21.

[121] Both courses are offered by The Teaching Company (www.thegreatcourses.com) in their series entitled "The Great Courses." The courses offered by The Teaching Company are comprised of lectures by contemporary college professors at some of the best-known colleges and universities in America. All the teachers have impeccable qualifications and are chosen for their ability to teach college students. Purchase of a course includes audio lectures and a text version written by the author. Quotations come from the text version.

The Old Testament course is taught by Professor Amy-Jill Levine, Vanderbilt University, Graduate Department of Religion. *The Old Testament* (Chantilly, VA: The Teaching Company, 2001). The New Testament course is taught by Professor Bart Ehrman, Department of Religious Studies at the University of North Carolina at Chapel Hill. *The New Testament* (Chantilly, VA: The Teaching Company, 2000).

Historical Criticism and Theistic Evolution Today

alive and well in our modern world. (As you read the excerpts from these two lecturers, please note that I am only focusing on their use of historical criticism.)

A course on the Old Testament

The teacher, Professor Amy-Jill Levine of Vanderbilt University, shares her excitement with the class. Scripture is "the foundation document of Western thought" (p. 1). She describes the Bible as a book "replete with genres ranging from myth and saga to law and proverb, containing dry political history and erotic love poetry, informed by a worldview much different than our own; these texts are a compendium of a people's sacred story" (p. 1). She will give attention "not only to the content of the biblical books but also to the debates over their meaning and the critical methods through which they have been interpreted" (p. 1).

This is all from page 1 of the lecture notes. In a few words the professor has introduced the class to nearly the whole historical-critical program. They've already learned that the Bible contains myths and legends. Students can expect to be bored by the dry political accounts but perhaps excited by the erotic love poetry. Due to the much different worldview of its authors, her students will have to be careful not to interpret Scripture without background material. In order to be competent Bible readers, the students will have to familiarize themselves with specialized "critical" methods of interpretation.

The lectures will "not avoid raising issues of religious concern." But she assures the class that "the goal of an academic course in biblical studies should not be to undermine religious faith. Rather, it should provide members of faith communities with richer insights into the literature that forms their bedrock" (p. 2). The professor does not admit the likelihood that at least a few of her students accept the Bible as a factual account of what God actually did for their salvation.

In lecture 1 the teacher describes her approach to Scripture. In a story that spans from creation to Judaism's life in the Greek world, we can expect to encounter various kinds of literature: "cosmological myths and stories of origin (Gen. 1-11), sagas of culture heroes (Gen. 12-50, Joshua, Judges), law codes (Leviticus, Deuteronomy)." Its authors include "storytellers, bureaucrats, prophets, priests, scribes, and visionaries." It addresses a variety of questions: "Who are we? What is our history? What are our standards of morality? How do we relate to those outside our community? How, and whom, shall we worship?" (p. 3).

The wide variety of "genres, authors, audiences, and issues requires a complex approach" (p. 4). "The wider the number of critical tools we use and the consequent range of questions we pose, the more complete our appreciation will be. . . . Historical-critical approaches seek to situate biblical material in its original context and test the accuracy of its presentation.... Archaeology has been used to prove, disprove, and understand biblical content.... The recognition of literary conventions ('type scenes')... increases appreciation of the narrative" (p. 4). "We will also look at cross-cultural comparisons. 'In the beginning'... is perhaps a response to the foundation myth of the Babylonian Empire" (p. 5). And these are only a few of the overwhelming number of tools the teacher uses, which will make her students more competent to read and understand the Bible.

Chapter 2 treats Adam and Eve. "The Garden of Eden, like the rest of the primeval history (Genesis 1-11) is 'myth,' a foundational story that undergirds cultural norms and explains communal identity. Many scholars suggest that Genesis 2-3... was composed during Solomon's reign (ca. 900 B.C.E.).... Three to four hundred years later, the P (Priestly) writer placed Genesis 1 before the J account [in Genesis 2], creating a new lens by which Eden may be understood" (p. 7).

The Mosaic authorship of the Pentateuch is discussed in lecture 6. The instructor admits: "The arguments for Mosaic authority of the Pentateuch... are scripturally based" (p. 23). But she gives all the reasons presented over the centuries, particularly during the Enlightenment, that make this doubtful. Having said that she points out the value of source criticism.

In lecture 7 we are introduced to form criticism. "The form critic, influenced by folktale analysis, focuses on the units... that comprise the larger narrative and attempts to locate the social setting of that unity in its oral stage (p. 27). "The form critic seeks the 'setting in life' of the tale before its incorporation into the biblical narrative" (p. 27). The premise is that "the stories originally circulated independently, perhaps even unconnected to the patriarchs. Although the form remains consistent, studies of oral cultures reveal that storytellers typically adapt their accounts to times, places, and audiences" (p. 27).

In chapter 7 the teacher further discusses methods of form criticism, "folklore analysis and type scenes" and applies that critical tool to the account of Jacob. "Folktales and type scenes are told less (if at all) for the sake of historicity. They are typically presented as events attested by unconfirmed witnesses. They assume different facets as they move from teller to teller, culture to culture. They reveal more about cultural and character-based issues than about "what really happened" (p. 34). She admits that folktales and type scenes are not easy to recognize or classify.

Lecture 8 continues with a discussion of the exodus: "Whether historical or not, we simply can't prove it" (p. 36). "Moses' early life, also unattested in Egyptian sources, evokes cross-cultural folktales and Israelite cosmogonic motifs" (p. 37). Source criticism helps us understand the origin of the names for God: EL and JHWH" (pp. 42,43). Some of Joshua and Judges are written in the form of "etiology." Presented as historical narrative, etiology is a saga that explains to later generations why certain things got to be the way they are. For example, how did the Dead Sea get there or why are Israel and Moab always at odds? (p. 19).

The teacher accepts a form of the JEDP theory, with the sources arranged according to Julius Wellhausen's Documentary Hypothesis. The author of one source primarily used Jehovah (J, written about 900 B.C.). A second author primarily used Elohim as God's name (E, written about 800 B.C.). A third source is the material found in the book of Deuteronomy (D, written around 600 B.C.). The P material is "marked by attention to law, Aaron, and genealogies" and was composed during the Babylonian exile or soon afterward by someone who combined (redacted) his and the other three sources into the document we call the Scriptures (Glossary, pp. 120ff).

A course on the New Testament

The teacher is Bart Ehrman of the University of North Carolina at Chapel Hill. He confesses that the Bible is an important book "whether seen as a religious book of faith or as a cultural artifact." Among books it is "probably also the most widely disputed and misunderstood." Throughout the course, the teacher will not concern himself with "questions of belief and theological truth," but will approach the text from a "historical perspective" by which the class will "acquire a historically rich grounding for our understanding of these foundational documents" (p. 1, para. 1).

Already in the first paragraph, Ehrman has introduced the class to the basic mind-set of all Bible critics: The Bible is a product of "the past" and can be evaluated like any piece of literature. We can be interested in the Bible without being interested in any of the truths it may teach. The Bible is not clear, as the history of interpretation proves, and it will take an expert in ancient history and culture to help us understand it.

In lectures 1-4 the teacher will help us understand the historical context in which the Bible was written. In lectures 5-8 he will treat the four gospels, "each with its own perspective on who Jesus was and why his life and death matter" (p. 1). In lectures 9-12 he will help the class "in a sense, move behind [the four gospels] to see what we can learn about the historical Jesus himself and what he actually said and did" (p. 1). The teacher has planted the idea that the gospels don't agree on Jesus' history, so we must reconstruct what Jesus might have said and done. The rest of the course is an exercise in analyzing the text using the tools of Bible criticism. We will confine ourselves to the lectures on the four gospels.

As the teacher moves through the chapters on New Testament background, he points out difficulties in the New Testament text. This has the effect of softening up the class and preparing them to use critical tools. His presentation of these difficulties seems fresh and insightful, but these difficulties have been used by Bible critics for hundreds of years and have been evaluated by conservative Bible scholars for just as long. Yet Ehrman does not nuance his arguments with reference to these counterarguments, something you would think college-level students deserve.

He discusses the canon of Scripture. He mentions other books that were in existence along with those that were included in Scripture. Certain books were "chosen" to be in Scripture, and he names some of the criteria the church used to make its choices. For the sake of an unbiased evaluation, he takes God's guiding hand out of the mix: "The question about whether the Christians who formulated the canon were right about their decisions is a historical one, not a theological one" (p. 6). In other words, only by taking matters of faith (theology) out of the discussion will objectivity be maintained.

The teacher emphasizes the importance of context to understand Scripture. "If we don't know the context of a work, we take it out of context. And if we take it out of context, we change its meaning.... Because context determines the meaning of words and actions, he says that we must first ask what the context was in which Jesus lived and the books of the New Testament were written" (p. 8).

So how does one determine the context if it is not from the gospel writers' words? In lecture 4 the teacher starts exploring "traditions" about Jesus. His approach is determined by the fact that Jesus died in about A.D. 30 and that the gospels were written some 35 to 65 years later. The gospels are not factual accounts of Jesus' words and deeds but "traditions" about him. Ehrman writes, "For our purposes here, I want us to consider the time gap between the death of Jesus and the first accounts of his life. The gap is 35 to 65 years, which is significant for understanding the character of these earliest accounts. This would be akin to writing the first accounts of the presidency of Lyndon B. Johnson at the turn of the 21st century—with no written sources from the time" (p. 20).

The teacher points out that oral traditions change as they are told and retold. He notes the "discrepancies" in the New Testament to illustrate how this happened in the gospels. The authors of the gospels were later writers, whose books the early church credited to those who actually were eyewitnesses or, in the case of Luke, who had direct access to the eyewitnesses. The writer who wrote the gospel we call Mark "was a relatively highly educated Greek-speaking Christian who was writing some 35-40 years after the events that he narrates." He is a Christian who "appears to have heard stories about Jesus that had been in circulation for some time, then wrote a number of them down—no doubt putting his own 'spin' on who Jesus really was" (p. 26). Mark "molded his traditions" to make his point that Jesus was an unexpected Messiah (p. 30). Mark "begins his

Historical Criticism and Theistic Evolution Today

account by calling his book a 'Gospel' (1:1). The term *Gospel* means 'good news.' Thus, by using this title, Mark doesn't claim to be writing a historically accurate biography in the modern sense, but an account of Jesus that reveals how his life and death brings 'good news' to those willing to receive it" (p. 26).

Once the oral history argument has been established, the New Testament is no longer a record of Jesus' life and teachings but a record of what the early church believed about Jesus' life and teachings. Once the gospels have been reduced to a collection of traditional sayings and deeds, rewritten and organized to suit the authors' agendas, the students realize how much they need critical methods and the help of critical scholars to understand them. The teacher asks: Since "all the Gospels embody traditions that have been more or less altered in the course of their transmission, how can we get behind the portrayals of Jesus in these accounts to see what the man himself was really like?" (p. 57). Ehrman promises that in this and the next two lectures he will analyze the gospels as "historical sources useful for the task of historical reconstruction" (p. 57).

Secular history does not yield information about Jesus, so we must depend on the gospels alone. But how reliable are they? Arguing on the basis of discrepancies he has already pointed out, he says, "These traditions were evidently changed—sometimes a little, sometimes a lot—in the course of their transmission (as we saw in the case of John and Mark on the day of Jesus' death). Sometimes even *these* authors changed the traditions they inherited. The evidence for these changes is the fact that the gospels contain accounts that appear to be irreconcilable in places" (p. 60).

The teacher defines his role as an interpreter of Scripture: "In some ways it helps to think of the historian as a prosecuting attorney who bears the burden of proof in examining his witnesses (sources) to prove his case" (p. 60). As a "prosecuting attorney," he subjects a section of Scripture to three tests. Can an account be found in more than one independent source? Does an account work against the vested interest of the author? Does an account correspond with what scholars know about the Jewish context when Jesus lived? (Chapters 10,11).

His conclusion is that Jesus was an apocalyptic prophet who was crucified as a "troublemaker." But in his case, "three days after his death, the crucified man was believed to have been restored to life. And that is the beginning of Christianity" (p. 69).

Summary

In both lectures the history behind the formation of Scripture was based on methods presented in chapter 3 of this book. Scripture itself is not allowed to tell us who wrote it or to describe the context in which it was written. The lecturers evaluate Scripture as a historical document, an approach they claim is necessary if the document is to be interpreted objectively.

I am sure that these two scholars are well versed in the more recently developed critical methods, but in addressing college students, their methods are mostly those developed 150 years ago by the German critical scholars. The teachers of these two courses will likely not agree on the details of Wellhausen's or Gunkel's research, but they both rely on them. Scripture is said to have been pieced together by redactors from remnants of oral history or written documents they had at hand. It was written by people to address timeless questions or to help believers at a certain time and place get through the problems they faced.

The students who accept the view of Scripture taught in these two courses will find it impossible to use Scripture to find the truth. Scripture has been relegated to an historic document that must be analyzed without the burden of theology. The message of Christ as the world's redeemer from sin is minimized or absent. Discussion about meaning is reduced to the merits of the theories of this or that critical scholar. The members of the class are now free to formulate their own opinions about Scripture's origin, purpose, and meaning.

How theistic evolutionists use Scripture

Secular evolutionist Michael Ruse describes the problem faced by those who read Genesis in a straightforward way: "The Darwinian reading of Genesis is going to give you major problems—insoluble problems, I suspect." But he encourages us: "There are plenty of resources open to the Christian who would move toward science and away from a literal reading of the early books of Genesis."[122] In terms used in this book, there are plenty of platforms outside of Scripture on which to stand and evaluate it—plenty of tinted glasses to put on to read it accurately.

This section will show in their own words how theistic evolutionists follow Ruse's advice. The tools of interpretation they use are not the result of recent discoveries and new evidence. They are the same resources used by Levine and Ehrman in their college lectures—resources that have been under development for the last three hundred years.

As mentioned earlier in this book, there have always been some who attempt to reconcile Scripture and evolution by reading Scripture in a straightforward way, but redefining and reinterpreting words and passages to allow for evolution. But this results in too many strained interpretations as to be workable. The easiest

---

[122] Michael Ruse, *Can a Darwinian Be a Christian?* (Cambridge: Cambridge University Press, 2001), p. 217.

Historical Criticism and Theistic Evolution Today

way to reconcile Scripture and evolution is simply to change one's approach to Scripture as a whole. And this is what today's theistic evolutionists do.

Below is a sample of how contemporary theistic evolutionists use historical criticism. I've attempted to use authors who have an Evangelical rather than a liberal background. But the dividing line between Evangelicals and liberals is quite blurred. I have also attempted to focus on authors who are in the center of the discussion and omit those who might be considered on the fringe.

Denis Lamoureux

Denis Lamoureux was raised in an Evangelical church with a belief in a six 24-hour-day creation. He became a dentist, and in the course of his medical training, he became aware of the scientific basis for evolution. He then got a PhD in theology. His book *Evolutionary Creation* was published in 2008.

His book "rests upon the time honored belief that divine revelation flows from two major sources—the Book of God's Words and the Book of God's Works."[123] Lamoureux writes, "A central issue in the origins debate involves the interpretation of the opening chapters of the Bible."[124] His position is that "the Holy Spirit descended to the knowledge level of the inspired authors by using their conceptualization of the physical world in order to communicate as effectively as possible inerrant and infallible Messages of Faith."[125] Ancient science and ancient history in Genesis 1-11 "are incidental vessels that deliver eternal spiritual insights," and "our challenge as modern readers of the Bible is to identify these ancient vessels and to separate them from the life-changing Messages of Faith."[126]

Lamoureux is quite clear on how Jesus and the writers of Scripture read the early chapters of Genesis:

> The strongest argument for a six-day creation is that a literal interpretation is the natural and traditional way to read the opening chapters of Scripture. Undoubtedly, this view of origins is closest to that held by the inspired writer of Genesis 1. Other biblical writers understood this creation account literally.... Christians throughout history have also upheld the strict literal interpretation of Gen 1. Protestant reformer Martin Luther argued, "Moses spoke in the literal sense...." Powerful evidence for the strict literal interpretation of the first chapters of the Bible comes from Jesus Himself.... Clearly, Jesus employed a literal reading of the

---

[123] Denis Lamoureux, *Evolutionary Creation*, (Eugene, Oregon: Wipf & Stock, 2008), p. xiv.

[124] Denis Lamoureux, *Evolutionary Creation*, p. xv.

[125] Denis Lamoureux, *Evolutionary Creation*, p. xv.

[126] Denis Lamoureux, *Evolutionary Creation*, p. 19.

first chapter of Genesis. Like young earth creationists, He appealed to the creation of the first humans (Gen 1:27), the marriage of Adam and Eve (Gen 2:24), the murder of Abel (Gen 4:8) and Noah's flood (Gen 6- 9). And Scripture features many similar passages.[127]

After that clear statement about what Jesus and the Bible writers believed, Lamoureux stops in his tracks in the face of evolutionary theory. The paragraph that immediately follows his fine summary of how Jesus and the Bible writers read Genesis 1-3 begins like this: "The greatest problem with a literal interpretation is that it completely contradicts every modern scientific discipline that investigates the origin of the universe and life."[128]

The evidence of science compels him to follow the path of historical criticism. He writes, "Scripture is authored by the Holy Spirit and by the ancient writers. Consequently, biblical interpretation involves identifying both the divine and human purpose of a passage."[129] Jesus and New Testament writers used the "science-of-the-day" and the "history-of-the-day," including Adam as the first man, to make theological points.[130]

Rejection of a literal reading of the early chapters of Genesis leads Lamoureux to deny a foundational truth of Scripture, namely, that Adam and Eve fell into sin, which resulted in death. "The cosmic fall," he writes, "is rooted in ancient scientific categories that do not correspond with nature. Consequently, Christians must open the Book of God's Works in order to discover the physical origins of human life, suffering, and death."[131] And of course, he means how that Book of God's Works is read by evolutionary scientists.

Genesis had its beginning in oral tradition.[132] People who live in oral cultures "do not enjoy the wide spectrum of complex intellectual categories found in societies today."[133] The description of the origin of the world in Genesis 1-3 rests on "ancient motifs" found throughout ancient Mesopotamia.[134] He accepts the JEPD and redaction theories of the German theologians we have studied.[135] He states, "Twenty-first century Christians must recognize that all events described in Gen. 3 never actually happened as stated. No woman was ever tempted in

---

[127] Denis Lamoureux, *Evolutionary Creation*, pp. 23,24.

[128] Denis Lamoureux, *Evolutionary Creation*, p. 24.

[129] Denis Lamoureux, *Evolutionary Creation*, p. 165.

[130] Denis Lamoureux, *Evolutionary Creation*, p. 274.

[131] Denis Lamoureux, *Evolutionary Creation*, p. 165.

[132] Denis Lamoureux, *Evolutionary Creation*, pp. 180,181.

[133] Denis Lamoureux, *Evolutionary Creation*, p. 182.

[134] Denis Lamoureux, *Evolutionary Creation*, p. 183.

[135] Denis Lamoureux, *Evolutionary Creation*, pp. 185-188.

an idyllic garden by a sinister talking snake; two rebellious people did not eat mystical fruit that imparted knowledge of good and evil; and God never launched suffering and death into the world in judgment for their sinfulness. Therefore, the fall of humanity into sin did not occur as stated in the Bible, and the cosmic fall never happened."[136] Yet amazingly, according to Lamoureux, none of this "in any way changes the Message of Faith."[137]

Peter Enns

Peter Enns' personal history and approach to Genesis illustrates how biblical criticism, particularly in the context of theistic evolution, is affecting conservative Christian institutions of higher learning. Because of his views, Enns was forced to leave Westminster Theological Seminary.

Enns has written a number of books. We will use his 2012 book *The Evolution of Adam: What the Bible Does and Doesn't Say About Human Origins*. Enns identifies himself and almost the entire world of biblical scholars as followers of Julius Wellhausen. After giving a good description of the advance of historical criticism since the mid-17th century, and after noting the wide divergence of opinions before and after Wellhausen, Enns has this to say:

> Wellhausen's theory brought together many generations, even centuries, of observations about the content of the Pentateuch. He posed his theory in a compelling manner, and the heart of the matter continues to be a stable element in current scholarship: *The Pentateuch was not authored out of whole cloth by a second-millennium Moses but is the end product of a complex literary process—written, oral, or both—that did not come to a close until the postexilic period.* This summary statement, with only the rarest exception, is a virtual scholarly consensus after one and a half centuries of debate.[138]

Why is it important, Enns asks, to see the Pentateuch as a work written after the Jews returned from their exile in Babylon? We customarily think of the Old Testament Bible world extending from the creation, through Abraham, to Moses and the exodus, and up to the Babylonian captivity, with a few books written after the return from captivity.

But really, Enns explains, the Old Testament world is the world of the Jews *after* they returned from captivity. He explains that during the exile, "Israel's

---

[136] Denis Lamoureux, *Evolutionary Creation*, p. 205.

[137] Denis Lamoureux, *Evolutionary Creation*, p. 188.

[138] Peter Enns, *The Evolution of Adam: What the Bible Does and Doesn't Say About Human Origins* (Grand Rapids: Brazos [Baker] Press, 2012), p. 23 (emphasis author's).

connection with God was severed: no land, no temple, and no sacrifices.... Since these long-standing ties to Yahweh were no longer available to them, the Israelites turned to the next best thing: bringing their glorious past into their miserable present by means of an official collection of writings."[139] The writings they had at hand were early records of ancient deeds, court politics, and temple liturgies. Enns says that "it is unlikely, however, that these were thought of as sacred Scripture at the time."[140]

Our Bible, therefore, "is an exercise in national self-definition in response to the Babylonian exile."[141] It was "a new national history that would be meaningful to them . . . a document of self-definition and spiritual encouragement: 'Do not forget where we have been. Do not forget who we are—the people of God.'"[142]

This, he assures us, will help us look at Scripture in the right light and find the answers to questions that the Scripture is designed to answer. That's the purpose of the Old Testament—to help us define ourselves as the people of God. To do that, the Old Testament must be "recast in the light of the appearance of God's Son."[143]

Enns concludes that when we understand that Scripture's account of creation was written to help the Jews define themselves and were "potent claims about who they were," we can accurately approach the creation account. Knowing this "lays to rest any notion that these writings have any relevance to modern debates over human origins."[144]

There is no need to speculate about Enns' relation to historical criticism. He says, "A proper understanding of the Adam story is directly affected by how we understand Israel's primordial stories as a whole in light of the nineteenth-century developments in biblical scholarship."[145] Regarding Paul's obvious belief that Adam was a literal person, Enns writes, "As unique as Paul's gospel was, he wrote as an ancient man and naturally held widely accepted views on a good number of things."[146] Our view of Adam has evolved over the years and "must now be adjusted in light of the preponderance of (1) scientific evidence supporting

---

[139] Peter Enns, *The Evolution of Adam*, p. 27.
[140] Peter Enns, *The Evolution of Adam*, p. 26.
[141] Peter Enns, *The Evolution of Adam*, p. 28.
[142] Peter Enns, *The Evolution of Adam*, p. 30.
[143] Peter Enns, *The Evolution of Adam*, p. 33.
[144] Peter Enns, *The Evolution of Adam*, p. 34.
[145] Peter Enns, *The Evolution of Adam*, p. 6.
[146] Peter Enns, *The Evolution of Adam*, p. 93.

evolution and (2) literary evidence from the world of the Bible that helps clarify the kind of literature the Bible is."[147]

C. John Collins

C. John Collins is a professor of the Old Testament at Covenant Theological Seminary of the Presbyterian Church of America. Covenant Seminary bases its faith on the Westminster Confession. Collins is the author of *Did Adam and Eve Really Exist? Who They Were and Why You Should Care*, published by Crossway in 2011.

Collins is a major player in the theistic evolution discussion. He is serious about the Bible and its authors. He rejects Peter Enns' implication that "we in the scientific world are more sophisticated than the ancients."[148] Collins may disagree with how the ancients described their world, but he will do so "without any patronizing nonsense about their naiveté."[149] He also distances himself from source and form criticism: "Because these sources no longer exist (if they ever did), each scholar had his own opinion on what they looked like." Collins identifies himself with those 20th-century critics who "came to a fresh appreciation of the literary qualities of the Biblical books" and "the text as we have it."[150] This sounds promising for an evaluation of the early chapters of Genesis.

But Collins is still in the critical camp. He lists four positions an interpreter of Genesis can take in regard to the author of Genesis: (1) The author intended to relay *"straight" history*, with a minimum of figurative language. (2) The author was talking about *what he thought were actual events*, using rhetorical and literary techniques to shape the readers' attitude toward those events. (3) The author intended to recount *an imaginary history*, using recognizable literary conventions to convey "timeless" truths about God and man." (Position 4 is a more liberal version of 3.) He concludes: "I am going to argue that option (2) best captures what we find in Genesis and best explains how the Bible and human experience relate to Adam and Eve."[151]

Collins calls the early chapter of Genesis "myth." A myth is not a fairytale, he explains, and may be based on events that actually happened. However, Genesis 1-11 is first and foremost the beginning of a Hebrew worldview to serve as an alternative to the Mesopotamian worldview. The purpose of Genesis 1-11, he

---

[147] Peter Enns, *The Evolution of Adam*, p. xiii.

[148] C. John Collins, *Did Adam and Eve Really Exist?*, p. 29. Referring to Enns' contention in *Inspiration and Incarnation*, p. 40.

[149] C. John Collins, *Did Adam and Eve Really Exist?*, p. 29.

[150] C. John Collins, *Did Adam and Eve Really Exist?*, p. 23.

[151] C. John Collins, *Did Adam and Eve Really Exist?*, pp. 16,17.

says, is "to shape Israel's view of God, the world, and mankind, and their place in it all."[152]

Drawing on literary criticism, Collins proposes that we must distinguish "history," which is a record of events that happened, and what he calls "worldview story." A worldview story may contain figurative or imaginative elements. It is not necessarily complete in every detail. It is not free from ideological bias. It is not necessarily told in exact chronological sequence.

But it is still history, at least in a sense. Collins defines Genesis 1-11 like this:

> If, as it seems likely to me, the Mesopotamian origin and flood stories provide the context against which Genesis 1-11 are to be set, they also provide us with clues on how to read this kind of literature. These [kinds of] stories include divine action, symbolism, and imaginative elements; the purpose of the stories is to lay the foundation for a worldview, without being taken in a "literalistic" fashion. We should nevertheless see the story as having what we might call an "historical core," though we must be careful in discerning what that is. Genesis aims to tell the story of beginnings the right way.[153]

Collins ends this book affirming the historical reality of a single pair, Adam and Eve. He warns that if we give up "the conventional way of telling the Christian story, with its components of a good creation marred by the fall, redemption as God's ongoing work to restore the creatures to their proper functioning, and the consummation in which the restoration will be complete and confirmed, then we really give up all chance of understanding the world."[154]

With that conviction, he presents various scenarios suggested by theistic evolutionists who place Adam and Eve somewhere in the evolutionary development of mankind. But he admits that "these scenarios leave us with many uncertainties." [155] The bottom line for Collins is that "these uncertainties in no way undermine our right to hold fast to the Biblical story line with full confidence."[156] But his confidence lies in his definition of Genesis as a "worldview story," which is broad enough to embrace both the evolution of mankind and a literal Adam and Eve.

Collins admits that Jesus and the New Testament writers treat Genesis 1-11 as a record of actual events and consider the people referred to there as real

---

[152]C. John Collins, *Did Adam and Eve Really Exist?*, p. 32, quoting himself in Collins, *Genesis 1-4*, p. 242.

[153]C. John Collins, *Did Adam and Eve Really Exist?*, p. 35.

[154]C. John Collins, *Did Adam and Eve Really Exist?*, pp. 133,134.

[155]C. John Collins, *Did Adam and Eve Really Exist?*, p. 131.

[156]C. John Collins, *Did Adam and Eve Really Exist?*, p. 131.

individuals. He writes, "It is fair to say that the Gospel writers portray Jesus as someone who believed both that Adam and Eve were actual people, and that their disobedience changes things for us their descendants"[157] and "There is little dispute among the commentators that Paul has based his discussion on the way he read Genesis 3. Paul apparently shares with his contemporary Jews the idea that Adam's sin is what brought sin and 'death' . . . into the world of human experience."[158]

Collins also admits that some of Paul's statements require that Adam and Eve were two literal people. Although Collins himself believes they were literal people, he will not let Paul's words prove that to him. He must come to the conclusion himself, using the literary qualities of Scripture to determine its meaning.

Vern Poythress

Vern Poythress is a professor at Westminster Theological Seminary, holding degrees in both science and theology. Below are a few quotations from *Redeeming Science: A God-Centered Approach*, published in 2006. They were chosen to illustrate that theistic evolutionists often build their arguments on their view of mankind's past.

Scripture often describes the parts of God's creation in symbolical terms, for example, "the windows of heaven." Poythress refuses to read into these symbols an ancient scientific worldview. This is refreshing; most theistic evolutionists use symbols of the universe to determine ancient scientific beliefs—in this case their belief that there were literal windows somewhere in the heavens that open when it rains.

Nevertheless, Poythress believes that Genesis is an ancient document, which must influence how we read it. Genesis 1 and 2 are "not directly addressing questions that we bring to it out of a modern scientific environment. It addresses the ancient world, with its questions about what the gods are like, and what role they had in bringing the world into its present state."[159]

Poythress says that Scripture is silent about the method God used to create the world "in order to concentrate on the main point."[160] Poythress argues that we cannot turn to Scripture for details about "the means that God may or may not have used in creating the plants and animals." So we cannot rely on Scripture alone to understand how God created the universe. "That leaves open *any* of

---

[157] C. John Collins, *Did Adam and Eve Really Exist?*, p. 78.

[158] C. John Collins, *Did Adam and Eve Really Exist?*, p. 83.

[159] Verne Poythress, *Redeeming Science: A God-Centered Approach* (Wheaton, IL: Crossway, 2006), p. 92.

[160] Verne Poythress, *Redeeming Science*, p. 255.

the three main options: fiat creationism, progressive creationism, and theistic evolution (provided that we allow for exceptions). We may tentatively decide for one of these views only by examining evidence outside Scripture, that is, evidence deriving from general revelation and the world that God rules."[161]

Cliché: We must interpret Scripture as its original readers interpreted it.

Theistic evolutionists often warn that we must be careful to interpret Scripture as its original readers would have interpreted it. This is a valid point. But we must also be careful not to come up with speculative ideas about how the original readers would have interpreted Scripture and then use those ideas to promote our own interpretation.

For example, Vern Poythress in a discussion of the meaning of "kinds" (Genesis 1:11) writes, "As modern people, interested in science, we come to Genesis 1 with scientific questions about evolution already in mind. But Genesis 1 originally addressed Israelite readers, who had no such questions."[162]

According to Poythress, an ancient Israelite herdsman was concerned about the future economic security of his children and grandchildren, and he needed assurance that he could pass his herds down to them. That was the question the ancient herdsman would be asking, and God's statement about animals being created in set divisions, "kinds," provided that assurance.

Poythress interprets the word "kinds" accordingly:

> [Genesis 1] says, in effect, that you can count on the fixity of kinds when you are dealing with the next generation, and the generation after that. It does not tell us what may or may not happen over millions of years or generations.[163]

Poythress starts with the assumption that evolution is true. Since evolution teaches a uniform development and differentiation of the species from a common source, there can be no such thing as "kinds," that is, fixed types of animals. So that is settled. But the truth of Scripture still needs to be maintained. So he comes up with a question an ancient herdsman might have asked, then shows how

---

[161] Verne Poythress, *Redeeming Science*, p. 256 (emphasis author's).

[162] Verne Poythress, *Redeeming Science*, p. 255.

[163] Verne Poythress, *Redeeming Science*, p. 255.

Historical Criticism and Theistic Evolution Today

> the word "kinds" would have given that ancient herdsman an assuring answer. Therefore, the word "kinds" does not say that the animal world was divided into permanent groups.
>
> Poythress and others give the impression that they were there, observing the ancients and listening to their discussions. But they were not there. And there are no records that hint at questions the ancients might have been asking. One might just as well say that ancient herdsmen were wondering why their goats were not breeding with their dogs.
>
> Poythress' imaginary question of an ancient herdsman falls short of reconciling Scripture and evolution. Genesis 1 does not say that God will keep animals at their current state of evolution relatively stable over the lifetime of ancient herdsmen and their descendants. It simply says that in the beginning God created animals in divisions called kinds. That is what an ancient worshiper of the true God would have heard and believed when he read those passages in Genesis 1.
>
> True, the ancient people did not approach the text of Scripture with the questions posed by modern scientists. So what? That just as easily proves that they accepted Scripture for what it says.

The four examples I've chosen can be multiplied many times over. There is no author who accepts evolution, which all theistic evolutionists do, who does not feel himself or herself backed into a corner when trying to fit evolution into Scripture or who does not come out fighting with the tools of historical criticism.

Caution: scholarly language ahead!

Scholars should be permitted to use scholarly language, but readers should not let scholarly language become proof that the author's point is scholarly. Readers should always be willing to take a step back and think carefully about what they are reading. To give you a bit of practice, here are a few technical-sounding quotations from various sources. Ask yourself what you think the author means. I'll offer a translation in more understandable English of what I think the author is saying.

> *Quotation:* The perceived tension between scientific description and divine action also derives in part from expectations concerning the purpose and meaning of the scriptural texts. Conflicts are bound to result if Scripture and science are understood to be addressing the same issues

in the same sort of way. Appeals to the "plain meaning" of Scripture and an emphasis on personal interpretation divorced from its historical, cultural, and literary context encourage Scripture to be read from a modern Western scientific outlook.[164]

> *Translation:* If you read Scripture literally, you will soon discover that it conflicts with modern science. You need critical tools, which scholars can supply, in order to read the Bible as the ancients would have read it. When you do that, you will find that Scripture and modern science merely approach the origin of the universe differently and are not really in conflict at all.

Quotation: If God is the ultimate author, we would expect Scripture to point to truths beyond the grasp of any individual author, indeed truths that people might not be able to understand nearly as well without the knowledge gained from modern science. Accordingly, after attempting to determine as best that we can the intention of the author of the meaning of a passage for the hearers at that time, we will use all our knowledge, including that of science, to try to understand the theological truth to which the text is pointing. This means that we will inevitably go beyond what the text actually claims, while nonetheless trying to remain grounded in a careful exegesis of the text. In other words, we properly use every resource at our disposal to search out the theological truths hidden in the text.[165]

> *Translation:* If God wrote the Scriptures, it likely contains deep truths people cannot discover without additional information. Using the new insights afforded by modern science, we can understand Scripture better than the ancients could have understood it. When we study the words of Scripture with our newfound scientific insights, we will find ourselves going beyond what Scripture says on the surface and discover the deeper theological truths that lie hidden in it.

Quotation: When we interpret the Bible, especially Genesis, we try to match the relationship of the text to the context. We try to match the biblical text and its original ancient context with our own interpretation of the same biblical text within our modern scientific context. In sum, we try to interpret the theological commitment of the Bible in light of

---

[164]Keith Miller, "An Evolving Creation: Oxymoron or Fruitful Insight," in *Perspectives on an Evolving Creation* (Grand Rapids: Eerdmans, 2003), p. 5.

[165]Robin Collins, "Evolution and Original Sin," in *Perspectives on an Evolving Creation*, pp. 474, 475.

our scientific framework. We don't try to import the science of the ancient Middle East into our theological deliberations.[166]

Translation: Scripture was written to ancient people with scientific beliefs we now know to be inaccurate. Once we understand how they would have understood Scripture in the context of their own science, we can strip away anything the text says about scientific matters and seriously search Scripture for the theological truths God wants to teach us.

Quotation: All questions regarding the particulars of the creation's physical properties and capabilities . . . are to be addressed to the creation itself and may be investigated by means of the natural sciences. The conceptual vocabularies of the scriptural text are so far removed from this enterprise that a Christian has no basis for presuming that any substantive detail could be derived from the Bible.[167]

Translation: The Bible is too old a book to answer questions about origins. We must ask the creation itself to provide those answers. Since the creation itself cannot actually speak, we must allow modern scientists to speak for it.

Quotation: [This is about Romans 5:15-19, in which Paul refers to Adam.] Thus, in expressing the revelation given to them by God, [the original Bible writers] would naturally use many of the prescientific concepts and beliefs of the time as vehicles for this revelation. Further, even if God explicitly directed the writing of the text, in general we would not expect God to override the widely held cultural beliefs in delivering the divine revelation unless those beliefs were particularly harmful. One reason for this is that, as philosopher Peter van Inwagen has pointed out, using a culture's own belief system is often the most effective way of conveying some truth. . . . Following this line of reasoning, Paul's talk of sin coming into the world through one man, Adam, can plausibly be considered a presupposition of the text—it is the common cultural framework of belief that Paul and his hearers share, and which Paul uses to make his theological points about Christ.[168]

---

[166] Ted Peters and Martinez Hewlett, Can You Believe in God AND Evolution? (Nashville: Abingdon Press, 2008), p. 70.

[167] Howard Van Till, "The Fully Gifted Creation," in *Three Views on Creation and Evolution*, edited by J. P. Moreland and John Mark Reynolds (Grand Rapids: Zondervan, 1999), p. 214.

[168] Robin Collins, "Evolution and Original Sin," in *Perspectives on an Evolving Creation*, pp. 478, 479.

Translation: God truly wanted ancient people to understand the Bible. So he had its writers use ideas their readers accepted, even if those ideas were wrong. But don't worry; Paul was using these erroneous ideas to talk about Christ, and that's what's important.

Cliché: Scholars say.

Theistic evolutionists like to introduce an idea about how to interpret Scripture with the phrase, "many scholars say." There is no doubt that at least *some* scholars would agree with any particular approach to Scripture. But from our study of historical criticism, it is clear that critical scholars hold a wide variety of positions. Even the greatest minds, like Julius Wellhausen, saw many of their ideas and interpretations overturned or modified.

Bible scholars today who want to take a critical approach to Bible interpretation—and that includes all theistic evolutionists—are forced to sift through the various approaches to reading Scripture that have been developed over almost three hundred years of historical-critical research.

The phrase "many scholars say" makes an author seem objective. But when you see that phrase, look for a footnote identifying which scholars and which approach to Scripture the author is referring to. That is the least a theistic evolutionist author can do. Anything less is an attempt to use the weight of the phrase "many scholars say" to frighten you away from reading Scripture in a straightforward way.

John and Joan, conclusion

It has been a particularly intense session, in which the teacher, Jack, has explored a wide range of critical tools the class could use to become more skilled in studying their Bible. Afterward, Joan goes home, sits down to read her Bible, but sets it aside. "What place does this book have in my life?" she wonders.

She thinks to herself, "I love the Bible, and I want to read it. But there is so much speculation about its meaning. There are so many tools to interpret it, and I'm such an amateur in using them. I just don't know anymore. And the Bible goes against everything we are told today about where the world came from—about where I came from."

Historical Criticism and Theistic Evolution Today

She decides to talk to her next-door neighbor, her friend John. He seems to have a different perspective. He always seems to be happy after he reads the Bible. Maybe John is just naïve. But then again, maybe he can help.

What is at stake?

People who want to accept evolution and Scripture *will have to accept some form of historical criticism.* One author summarized it in no uncertain terms: "The hermeneutics behind theistic evolution are a Trojan horse that, once inside our gates, must cause the entire fortress of Christian belief to fall." [169]

Historical criticism forces people to give up the ability, even the right, to interpret God's Word on their own. Biblical criticism is a highly technical field that is under continual revision. Its many methods force the interpreter to choose which ones to use, which is an impossible task unless one understands them all. A basic acquaintance with higher critical methods may help a person understand someone else's interpretation. But the right to offer one's own interpretation is granted by the academic community only to those who have thoroughly studied the whole field of historical criticism. In this way, interpreting the Bible becomes a task for the experts.

Those who accept historical-critical methodology must give up Scripture's claim to be true. They must choose among a variety of ways to combine the work of human authors, who are subject to error, with the revelation of God, who is not. They will have to accept the idea that God accommodated himself to the errors of the day and that Jesus and the Bible writers did the same.

They are left with a book stripped of historical truth and relegated to the level of myth, legend, and baseless symbolism. In the end they are robbed of the foundation God has given us on which we base our faith and are set adrift in a sea of speculation.

Book 1 of this set identified elephants that theistic evolutionism has allowed into the room of the Christian faith. If evolutionary ideas are applied consistently—if these elephants are allowed to fill the room—they will crowd out the foundations on which the message of Scripture is built and undermine our understanding of the work of God's Son, our Savior.

The first four chapters in this book, Book 2, have introduced another huge elephant. This is the elephant of historical criticism. My prayer is that these first chapters have enabled you to recognize historical-critical methods when you run across them, understand them for what they are, and ask God for his grace

---

[169] Richard Philips, quoted in "The Search for the Historical Adam," by Richard N. Ostling, in *The Origins Debate,* edited by *Christianity Today,* (Carol Stream, IL: *Christianity Today,* 2012 Kindle Edition), loc. 295.

to help you hold on to his Word. If you are troubled about evolutionary claims, there is plenty of material available to suggest alternate ways to understand the scientific data, ways that are in line with Genesis 1 and 2. But above all, read God's Word. Read it as Jesus and the New Testament writers read it—in a straightforward way. In Scripture lies the power to see the matter clearly, for it is "spirit and life" (John 6:63) and "is indeed at work in you who believe" (1 Thessalonians 2:13).

Part Three

The Ancient Near Eastern Argument

Chapter 5

The Ancient Near Eastern (ANE) Argument

What is ANE literature?

In the opinion of this author, the ANE argument is the most powerful argument at the disposal of theistic evolutionists today. It makes a serious claim to be an objective way to read the creation account in Genesis. The final chapters in this book will look at this claim in the light of Scripture.

ANE literature and resources refer to writings, sculptures, and inscriptions discovered in the Near East by archaeologists over the last 150 years. The most important finds have been in Egypt, in Mesopotamia, and in sites along the eastern and northern Mediterranean seaboard. The finds date back to at least 2500 B.C.

This material provides information about the day-to-day life and beliefs of nations like Egypt, among whom Israel lived when they were developing into a nation, and about nations like Assyria and Babylon, with whom the Israelites came into contact later in their history.

There is a wide range of material. The material includes longer works, short inscriptions in temples and tombs, epic poems about the lives of the gods, law codes, legal texts, treaties, historical accounts, poetry, and correspondence. Included is religious material in the form of liturgies, hymns, wisdom literature, oracles, and prophecies.

Most important for our purposes is ancient Near Eastern *religious* material in the form of documents, inscriptions, and carvings. These include various accounts about how the gods created the world, along with clues about how the ancients were supposed to have viewed the universe.

The problem ANE literature promises to solve

For theistic evolutionary writers, documents from the ancient Near East are not just helpful for the theistic evolutionary argument. At this point they have become nearly indispensable. To understand why, we must review the problems historical-critical scholars faced in their struggle to prove that their methods were needed in order to understand Scripture.

The inspiration of Scripture had largely been jettisoned during the first half of the 18th century. Scripture was considered to be the product of human authors with all their limitations. Its origin had been relegated to the distant past and rendered unreliable as a source of truth. Nor could it be trusted to provide readers with background material necessary to understand its audience and to interpret it as its original readers would have.

Scholars believed they had to find new tools to interpret the Scriptures. Some of the most brilliant men in the world—the Bible scholars in German universities who were recognized the world over for their keen analytical abilities and relentless attention to detail—worked tirelessly on the text of Scripture. They looked for clues about where the text came from, how the ancient sources might have been combined, and when in history the final text might have been assembled. If they understood these things, they believed, they could better understand what the Bible meant to its original readers and how it might be used today.

As we saw in earlier chapters, Julius Wellhausen introduced a theory called the Documentary Hypothesis. Wellhausen's arguments, as widely accepted as they were at the beginning, did not completely satisfy in the long term. Many of his arguments were rejected, not just by those who believed in the inspiration of Scripture but also by fellow critical scholars, who pointed out that many of Wellhausen's conclusions were mere speculations.

Scholars continued to search for other sets of "glasses" through which to view and interpret Scripture. But even then, the religious world was not satisfied. No tool had been found that yielded an objective point of view. Each method was, and still is, plagued by too much speculation to be reliable. In fact, critical scholar John Barton points out the harm done by thinking that "there is, somewhere, a 'correct' method, which, if only we could find it, would unlock the mysteries of the text."[170]

To help in their quest, scholars had begun to study the life, customs, and language of the ancient Near East. Perhaps archaeology would provide an objective viewpoint for understanding the Scriptures. In the 18th century, David Michaelis became the greatest scholar in the world in this regard. He knew everything about the world of the Bible that had been discovered in the Near East up to his time, and he worked to incorporate that knowledge into the study of Scripture.

But how much help did background material provide? By studying how words were used in other ANE languages, some light was shed on the words used in Scripture. Discoveries of ANE pottery and crops helped Bible readers better envision how a Hebrew meal might have looked. Insights into the marvels of Egyptian pyramids shed light on the wisdom of the Egyptians, which Moses learned in his years in Pharaoh's household. But none of this material replaced to any significant extent the background material provided in Scripture itself,

---

[170]John Barton, *Reading the Old Testament*, p. 5.

The Ancient Near Eastern (ANE) Argument

nor did it change any of the teachings of Scripture. Once again, nothing they found changed the fact that if you were on a desert island with only a Bible, you would find everything you needed within the Bible itself to interpret it properly.

In the end, the intense study of source documents, forms, and archaeological artifacts did not provide a satisfactory key to unlocking the meaning of Scripture. All these approaches, which were meant to replace the practice of letting Scripture interpret Scripture, included too much speculation to accomplish that goal.

ANE literature to the rescue

Throughout the late 18th and into the 19th century, historical criticism of the Bible and evolutionary science were progressing almost lockstep with each other. Wellhausen's Documentary Hypothesis appeared at roughly the same time as Darwin's *On the Origin of Species*. Many theologians had bought into the idea of historical criticism, but they were feeling pressure to find a critical tool that was truly objective, a "magic bullet" that would enable them to interpret Scripture in line with the new evolutionary theories.

During the last half of the 19th century, the discovery of a large amount of material in the Near East seemed to be that magic bullet. This material offered a fresh view of early mankind's emergence from its prehistory and promised to provide an objective context in which to study and interpret Scripture.

After all, Scripture and the writings of Egypt and Mesopotamia (ancient Babylon) have much in common. They are products of the same period in world history. They were written by people who shared the same culture. They speak about many of the same topics and do so in similar ways. Therefore, the argument goes, they can all be read and interpreted in the same way. The way we evaluate the beliefs and practices of the Hebrews should parallel how we evaluate Egyptian culture—their gods, their concept of the afterlife, their beliefs about the universe, their law codes, politics, and social life.

Important for the creation/evolution debate were insights into how the people of the ancient Near East viewed the origin and structure of the universe. The new information would provide an objective way to evaluate the Bible's account of creation and its many references to the structure of the universe. After all, the Hebrews could not be expected to view the universe any differently than the people around them.

The argument continues: Scripture was written to reject the Egyptian and Mesopotamian *gods and religious beliefs,* but the Hebrews had no reason to reject ancient Near Eastern scientific ideas about *the structure of the universe.* Scripture is valuable as a witness to the power and glory of the true God. But its views on the makeup of the universe must be discarded—along with those of

Egypt and Babylon—as views appropriate to a prescientific age but not to ours. Scripture's ancient views on the universe can be replaced with modern scientific discoveries, including the theory of evolution.

The argument is strengthened by the fact the resources discovered in Mesopotamia and Egypt were produced long before the nation of Israel came into existence. Therefore, Israel's Scriptures were likely heavily influenced by the literature of the people around them.

John Walton says that the key to interpreting the Old Testament "is to be found in the literature from the rest of the ancient world."[171] The Hebrews, he writes, "thought about the cosmos in much the same way that anyone in the ancient world thought, and not at all like anyone thinks today."[172]

In the beginning of his chapter on ancient science, Denis Lamoureux gives the theistic evolutionist's logic: "This chapter presents evidence that an ancient science of the structure and operation of the physical world appears throughout the Bible."[173] He concludes the chapter with the claim that he has succeeded in producing that evidence: "This view of the cosmos was the best science-of-the-day thousands of years ago in the ancient Near East, and it was embraced by the inspired writers of God's Word and their readers."[174] Finally, he points out the implications of this for the creation/evolution debate: "If there is an ancient science regarding the structure and operation of the world, then consistency argues that this is also the case for its origin. The use of Scripture to determine how God created the universe and life would then need to be reconsidered."[175]

Evaluating the ANE argument

The ANE argument is simple, and it sounds logical. Accepting it seems to be a matter of common sense. Nevertheless, hidden below the surface is a set of assumptions and matters of interpretation that must be explored and answered. We will begin with the assumptions.

Recall the foundation on which Enlightenment theologians studied Scripture. (1) The Enlightenment was built on a new understanding of the past, which denied the ability of ancient people to accurately analyze the universe around them. (2) It was built on the idea that the people of Israel were simply one nation among the other nations of the ancient Near Eastern world, being influenced by them

---

[171] John Walton, *The Lost World of Genesis One*, p. 10.

[172] John Walton, *The Lost World of Genesis One*, p. 14.

[173] Denis Lamoureux, *Evolutionary Creation*, p. 106.

[174] Denis Lamoureux, *Evolutionary Creation*, p. 131.

[175] Denis Lamoureux, *Evolutionary Creation*, p. 106.

The Ancient Near Eastern (ANE) Argument

and influencing them in return. (3) It was built on the idea that human reason alone could discover the structure and operation of the universe. This caused them to lose sight of the intimate relationship between God and his creation.

These are the assumptions on which historical criticism of Scripture is based. They are present in all theistic evolutionary thinking. And they are lurking behind the scenes in the ANE argument. Scripture gives its own answer to each of them.

Did early mankind lack the ability to explore and understand the universe?

According to the Enlightenment

The ANE argument is fueled by the idea that ancient people were unable to think about the world as modern people do. It was not just that they *lacked* modern tools of observation, but they were *unable* to observe the universe with our intelligence and analytical ability.

Contemporary historians of science claim that the Egyptians and Babylonians (and, of course, the Hebrews) had no interest in what might be causing things to happen. They did not search for hidden principles or natural laws that governed what they observed. Accordingly, what they saw on the surface was all that exists and all that really mattered. This was their "science."

They were creative people, to be sure, but they were only concerned with discovering what had practical applications for their lives—better methods of work, better tools, and more workable and durable materials. But they had no interest in gaining knowledge about the world just for the sake of understanding it.

That ability, it is claimed, began with the early Greeks in the sixth century B.C. For the first time, people began to study the world itself, think about it, and attempt to find natural laws that governed it. The Greek method of thinking about the universe, it is said, marked a turning point in human history. It was the beginning of Western philosophy and the scientific method.

The claim that there was a basic difference between people in the ancient world and people today tends to create a negative posture toward the pre-Greek cultures and their "science." And this, of course, includes Scripture's statements about how the world is structured and how it operates. J. Edward Wright compares the Egyptians and Babylonians (and the Hebrews) with the Greeks by how they reacted to a particular phenomenon they all would have been able to see. The sun appears lower or higher in the sky on the same day of the year depending on how far north or south one is standing. The ancient Babylonians with their intense interest in observing the heavens, should have tried to figure out why this happens—as the later Greeks would try to do. Wright explains ancient Babylonian thinking: "All Babylonian astronomy presupposed a flat earth and either did not recognize or ignored the influence of latitude on celestial observation."[176] In other words, to the Babylonians the earth looked flat, and they weren't interested in exploring anything that challenged that idea. Either they didn't observe the phenomenon (after 2,000 years of tracking the stars?) or if they did observe it, they ignored it. Case closed.

Lawrence Principe, another historian of science, in his discussion of the earliest known Greek philosopher, Thales of Miletus, says: "Thales' statement [that everything was made from water] marks a key distinction between the underlying, unseen reality of things and their external appearance. This distinction would prove key to Greek natural philosophy and is crucial to modern science." Principe explains why this was important: "Thales stands at the beginning of a tradition in Greek thought that involved the [organizing and explanation] of observations and the search for hidden causes and principles in nature. These are hallmarks of Western scientific and philosophical traditions of which we (at present) find little evidence in Egypt and Babylonia."[177] But he admits: "I would say, to be safe, that there is a huge amount of Babylonian cuneiform writing out there. Maybe in one of those texts there is something like what Thales was doing. At present, we're not aware of it."[178]

That is a fair statement. Principe at least leaves the question open. Wright's use of the argument from silence, however, closes the door to any possibility that the ancient Egyptians or Babylonians thought like the Greeks. He views the past in evolutionary terms. The Greeks had reached the point in human evolution when a more subtle way of thinking became possible.

Theistic evolutionists reflect this view of mankind's past. Throughout their literature one finds scenes of humble, unlearned Hebrew farmers, emerging from a preliterate state, who had to be addressed in simple terms on a limited range of topics. Complex or new ideas, and certainly ideas outside of what is speculated to be their worldview, had to be avoided or expressed in a simple way that they could understand. What's more, principles of scientific discovery and analysis were hardly things they considered important for their agrarian existence.

---

[176] J. Edward Wright, *The Early History of Heaven* (Oxford, Oxford University Press, 2000), p. 99.

[177] Lawrence Principe, *History of Science: Antiquity to 1700, Course Guidebook*, pp. 9,10. The words in brackets replace the author's terms: "systematization and explication."

[178] Lawrence Principe, *History of Science: Antiquity to 1700, Audible Lecture Two*. Note that the three-tiered universe model is not what people in the New Testament and afterward believed about the universe. From the time of the Greek philosophers, especially Aristotle, they believed that the earth was a sphere and that the sun, moon, and stars revolved around the earth. The Jews in Jesus' day, especially people like Paul, who we know read Greek literature, would have understood this. Theistic evolutionists sometimes get this mixed up. They speak about the authors of the New Testament believing in a three-tiered "flat earth" universe.

The Ancient Near Eastern (ANE) Argument

According to Scripture

Did scientific thinking first begin with the Greeks in the sixth century B.C.? Were they the first to have the joy of exploration and the satisfaction of discovering hidden causes? Were they the first to discuss their observations with others?

Consider the implications of what Scripture says about the earliest human beings. The first two people, Adam and Eve, were created fully developed—physically, morally, and spiritually. God gave them and their descendants the command: "Be fruitful and multiply and fill the earth and subdue it, and have dominion over the fish of the sea and over the birds of the heavens and over every living thing that moves on the earth" (Genesis 1:28). God's commands implied that Adam and Eve thoroughly understood the universe in which they lived. After all, if they were to rule over it, they would have to understand it. Such understanding implies an interest in knowing how things worked and why things happened as they did.

It would also require intelligence and a high level of analytical ability. God told Adam to name the animals. To do that properly, Adam must have had insights into their nature and the desire to give them names that reflected the qualities he saw in them.

Their fall into sin and the hardships God brought into the world, including death, would only have diminished what they would have been able to accomplish. Nevertheless, they and their descendants soon put their native abilities to use. The technical skills needed to raise animals developed quickly. At the same time, musicians and metalworkers developed their arts. Cities were built. Those who believed in God's promise of a Savior began to meet for worship, which likely involved form and structure (Genesis 4:16-26).

At the tower of Babel, shortly before God created a variety of languages to keep people from finishing it, he assessed the human mind and its potential: "And the LORD said, '. . . this is only the beginning of what they will do. And nothing that they propose to do will now be impossible for them'" (Genesis 11:6).

One might argue that God was speaking only about the technical aspects of their work—the processes, methods, tools, and drawings they might have devised. But can we separate people's desire to make objects for their everyday use from a desire to understand the underlying characteristics of the material and tools they used? What's more, it is one thing to say that the Greeks were the first to *record* their thoughts about the universe but quite another to remove this kind of thinking from other ancient people who may not have recorded their thinking processes.

Practical tasks always demand theoretical knowledge. For example, if I want to make a tool for a particular task, I must first explore which material has the right characteristics to do what I want it to do. I must understand the physics involved—*why* does a tool with one design work better than a tool with another design? *How* can I adjust the ergonomics of the tool so people can use it better? To do that, I must explore the human body.

Solomon lived long before the earliest Greek scientists. Early in his life he was given the task of administering the large nation his father, King David, had entrusted to him. He asked God for wisdom. "And God said to him, 'Because you have asked this [wisdom].... Behold, I give you a wise and discerning mind, so that none like you has been before you and none like you shall arise after you'" (1 Kings 3:11,12).

Solomon's judgment in the case of the two prostitutes showed his insight into human thoughts and motives (1 Kings 3:16-29). Solomon was also interested in the causes behind objects in the physical world, and he organized his observations and conclusions as the Greeks did later. The writer of 1 Kings summarized the extent of Solomon's wisdom:

> And God gave Solomon wisdom and understanding beyond measure, and breadth of mind like the sand on the seashore, so that Solomon's wisdom surpassed the wisdom of all the people of the east and all the wisdom of Egypt.... and his fame was in all the surrounding nations. He also spoke 3,000 proverbs, and his songs were 1,005. He spoke of trees, from the cedar that is in Lebanon to the hyssop that grows out of the wall. He spoke also of beasts, and of birds, and of reptiles, and of fish. (4:29-33)

Solomon was not alone in his desire to understand the world around him: "All the kings of the earth sought the presence of Solomon to hear his wisdom, which God had put into his mind" (2 Chronicles 9:23). These are the very people who were supposed to have had no interest in *how* the world worked—no curiosity about *why* things are like they are. Yet these people came to Solomon to better understand their world. Perhaps their goal was to create a new tool or weapon, and Solomon's insights might have helped them do that. But they may simply have been seeking wisdom about the world for its own sake.

There is nothing in Scripture to suggest that mankind has evolved to possess an ever greater ability to analyze the world. Perhaps the Lord gave the Greek nation special gifts that would help create a scientific mind-set through which he would bless future generations. But based on Scripture's description of ancient human beings, it cannot be concluded that the ability to think scientifically began at a later stage in the world's history.

The Ancient Near Eastern (ANE) Argument

The lack of tools for observation cannot prove a lack of ability or interest in observing nature. Difficulties inherent in ancient travel and exploration should not be interpreted as a lack of interest in exploring and charting the world. Lack of modern writing tools and media and the training necessary to master a more cumbersome alphabet than the Greeks had should not be interpreted as a lack of interest in recording their findings. A theistic evolutionist cannot hide behind the assumption that ancient ideas about the universe can be discarded because they were created by people who could not think and reason as we can. Scripture teaches us that the ancients were no different from us. They were intelligent; they were interested in theoretical matters; they could analyze their world.

Was the nation of Israel merely another ancient Near Eastern nation?

Kyle Greenwood defines the cultural relation between the Hebrews and their neighbors like this: "We should therefore not speak of Israel being influenced by the world—they were part of that world."[179]

In a sense, we can agree with Greenwood. The Israelites did not live in a cultural bubble. One would expect their Scriptures to reflect ancient Near Eastern ways of life, commerce, warfare, and administration. The Israelites had law codes that dealt with life in general and with the special problems faced by other people living in the ancient Near East. They shared similar ways of writing treaties. Israel and the nations around them all produced wisdom literature. They all wrote down the words of their prophets.

But the Israelites were not just one ANE nation among others. Nor were their writings just one example of ANE literature. Scripture teaches that the relationship between Israelites and the nations around them was far more complex than Greenwood suggests.

Nations like Babylon and Egypt were very different from each other, and each would defend the superiority of its culture. Each would bow to its own gods and give them credit for creating the world and for blessing them. We admit that these nations were, in fact, different instances of a common ancient Near Eastern culture. Greenwood's statement quoted above could be applied to nations like Babylon and Egypt.

But not to the nation of Israel. God started the nation of Israel from scratch. Shortly before he died, Joshua reminded the Israelites, "This is what the LORD, the God of Israel, says: 'Long ago your forefathers, including Terah the father of Abraham and Nahor, lived beyond the River and worshiped other gods. But I

---

[179] Kyle Greenwood, *Scripture and Cosmology: Reading the Bible Between the Ancient Word and Modern Science* (Downer's Grove: IVP Academic, 2015), p. 38.

took your father Abraham from the land beyond the River and led him throughout Canaan'" (Joshua 24:2,3 NIV).

A central teaching of the Old Testament is that God wanted to keep his people separate from the nations around them. They lived in the ancient Near Eastern world, but they were not to consider themselves to be a part of that world. God had removed Israel's fathers—Abraham, Isaac, and Jacob—from their ancestral home in Mesopotamia. They were to live in the land of Canaan, but they were not to live with the Canaanites or be influenced by them.

Abraham refused to get a wife for his son Isaac from the people of Canaan lest his son fall under their influence. God later transplanted Jacob's family into Egypt, where he gave them a place to live that was separate from the main Egyptian population centers. The Israelites were forced into slavery, a horribly unpleasant time for them. But this also forced them to maintain their separate identity.

During their time as slaves in Egypt, they learned firsthand the skill of building cities to add to their skill of caring for flocks (see Exodus 1:11). They were led out of Egypt by a man who grew up in Pharaoh's court where he was "instructed in all the wisdom of the Egyptians" and "he was mighty in his words and deeds" (Acts 7:22). So when the Israelites left Egypt, they were hardly a humble, unlearned group of shepherds. They were a fairly sophisticated group of people ready to build cities and able to govern.

Although the Hebrew Scriptures were written long after some other pieces of ANE literature, its content was unique., revealed by God himself. After God led the Israelites out of Egypt, he began giving them his written Word, which defined their unique purpose as a nation. The laws he gave Israel naturally covered many of the same topics covered in the law codes of the nations around them. But since they were given by God, in regard to showing justice and love, Israel's laws were far more sophisticated than other law codes. Also, their laws carefully defined Israel's worship life so as to exclude any possibility that Israel would worship alongside the people living around them.

Moses summarized what the people of the ancient Near East would someday say about the Israelites and their God: "For what great nation is there that has a god so near to it as the LORD our God is to us, whenever we call upon him? And what great nation is there, that has statutes and rules so righteous as all this law that I set before you today?" (Deuteronomy 4:7,8). When the other ancient Near Eastern people compared their laws with Israel's, they could only conclude, "Surely this great nation is a wise and understanding people" (Deuteronomy 4:6).

Israel's way of life and worship—their culture at the deepest level—was a rejection of the culture of the ancient Near East. God had told Abraham that all nations on earth would be blessed through him (Genesis 12:1-3). Only if the Israelites remained separate from the nations around them could they be a source of blessing to them—a beacon to the world of the power and love of the true God. Only then could they point the nations around them to the Savior who would come from them. Later in their history when the Israelites did act like the other ancient Near Eastern nations around them, they became unable to fulfill God's purpose for them. Nevertheless, some people from the nations around Israel still left their national gods and turned to the God of Israel.

To start discussing ANE literature and its relation to Scripture with the idea that Israel was just another nation in the ancient Near Eastern world—as theistic evolutionists often do—is to miss (and likely to dismiss) these overarching themes in the Old Testament Scriptures. It leads to confusing external similarities with the deep dissimilarities between God's people and the nations around them, dissimilarities that even the nations around them recognized.

Is the universe simply matter and energy, subject to analysis by human reason, or is there more?

There is much to our universe that we can see with our eyes and evaluate with our human reason. Genesis 1 and 2 record the creation of the physical universe. Those chapters, however, are not just about water, earth, plants, and animals—the things we can observe. Those chapters are also about the Creator, whom we cannot observe but who supports and directs his creation. Not to recognize this is to cripple our understanding of the universe. And, as we will see in the last chapter, it cripples one's ability to understand and evaluate other ANE resources as well.

Genesis 1 and 2 tell us that God spoke his Word, and the various parts of the universe came into being. The apostle John tells us that Jesus was the *Word* God used to create the world (John 1:1-3). Moses spoke about the greatness of God: "Behold, to the LORD your God belong heaven and the heaven of heavens, the earth with all that is in it" (Deuteronomy 10:14). And God's continual presence is necessary if the universe is to exist. The writer to the Hebrews says that Jesus "is the radiance of the glory of God and the exact imprint of his nature, and he upholds the universe by the word of his power" (Hebrews 1:3).

Where does God "live" as he carries out his work of upholding the universe and caring for its people? God is present everywhere. David confessed: "If I ascend to heaven, you are there! If I make my bed in Sheol, you are there!" (Psalm 139:8). God said through Jeremiah: "Can a man hide himself in secret places so that I cannot see him? declares the LORD. Do I not fill heaven and earth? declares the LORD" (Jeremiah 23:24).

Nehemiah praised God for creating "heaven, the heaven of heavens, with all their host" (Nehemiah 9:6). The psalmist tells all people to praise the Lord, and that includes "you highest heavens, and you waters above the heavens" (Psalm 148:4). Yet God is outside even the highest heavens. When Solomon dedicated the new temple in Jerusalem, he confessed: "But will God indeed dwell on the earth? Behold, heaven and the highest heaven cannot contain you; how much less this house that I have built!" (1 Kings 8:27).

The Old Testament says that God chose to be found in "the heavens." The psalmist wrote, "The heavens are the LORD's heavens, but the earth he has given to the children of man" (Psalm 115:6).[180] When the people of Israel prayed, they raised their hands upward to God who is in heaven. Whenever the Israelites sinned as a nation and then repented, Moses prayed that God would "look down from your holy habitation, from heaven, and bless your people Israel and the ground that you have given us, as you swore to our fathers, a land flowing with milk and honey" (Deuteronomy 26:15).

God, whose dwelling is in heaven, chose special places on earth where he could be found. Early in the history of the nation of Israel, Jacob, the third of the Hebrew patriarchs, had to flee from his brother. As he traveled north, he came to a place called Luz, where he spent the night. He had a dream in which he saw a ladder with one end fixed on the earth and the other end fixed in heaven. Angels of God were ascending and descending on the ladder. God was above it. Jacob named the place Bethel, or "house of God." He said, "Surely the LORD is in this place, and I did not know it" (Genesis 28:16). He had not seen God there when he arrived. Nor did he see God after he awoke, but he knew God was there in a special way: "How awesome is this place! This is none other than the house of God, and this is the gate of heaven" (Genesis 28:17). Later in Jacob's life, God would meet him in other locations on earth.[181]

When Israel became a nation, God chose to live among the people of Israel in a tent. Later he would live in a temple in Jerusalem, where both his own people and people from the surrounding nations could find him. After Solomon confessed that the highest heaven could not contain God, he prayed that God would "listen to the plea of your servant and of your people Israel, when they

---

[180]Note Jesus' words: "But I say to you, Do not take an oath at all, either by heaven, for it is the throne of God, or by the earth, for it is his footstool, or by Jerusalem, for it is the city of the great King" (Matthew 5:34,35).

[181]God would again meet with Jacob 20 years later. Before Jacob met his brother, Esau, God appeared to him and wrestled with him. He called the place Peniel, or "face of God" (Genesis 32:20). For another example, see Genesis 32:1. The angels of God appeared to Jacob, and he named the place Mahanaim. Since Jacob lived before the Israelites grew into a nation and before Moses began to write, we might ask how the patriarchs came to know the true God and to understand that he revealed himself in special places. This isn't a mystery if we accept a relatively recent common origin for mankind in Noah and his family, whom God protected in the flood.

The Ancient Near Eastern (ANE) Argument

pray toward this place. And listen in heaven your dwelling place, and when you hear, forgive" (1 Kings 8:30).

Scripture speaks about God's relation to various places in the physical universe. Yet even that confines God to a time and place. Someday, God will destroy this creation, and that includes the heavens he created. Isaiah writes, "All the host of heaven shall rot away, and the skies [the heavens] roll up like a scroll" (Isaiah 34:4). Peter says that "the heavens will pass away with a roar" (2 Peter 3:10). After the present universe was destroyed, the apostle John saw a new creation: "a new heaven and a new earth, for the first heaven and the first earth had passed away" (Revelation 21:1).

The first creation will be destroyed and replaced, but the "place" where God lives will never be destroyed. In the New Testament, this is also called heaven, but it is distinct from the heavens above us. Paul spoke about a man who was caught up into the "third heaven" (2 Corinthians 12:2). Paul was referring to himself and didn't know if his body or only his spirit was involved in this experience). There he heard things that he was not permitted to repeat on earth. Paul referred to the third heaven as "paradise," which is the same word Jesus used when he told the repentant criminal hanging on the cross next to him: "Today you will be with me in *paradise*" (Luke 23:43). Jesus also used the word when he assured the faithful that they would eat from the tree of life, "which is in the paradise of God" (Revelation 2:7).

When they saw Jesus ascend into heaven, the disciples were told: "This Jesus, who was taken up from you into heaven, will come in the same way as you saw him go into heaven" (Acts 1:11).[182] Yet even after Jesus left, he can always be found among his people. He said, "Where two or three are gathered in my name, there am I among them" (Matthew 18:20).

As we will see in the last chapter, diagrams of the ancient "science" of a three-tiered universe offered in theistic evolutionary books picture God pigeonholed somewhere above a thin dome. According to Scripture, however, God is eternal and is present everywhere. He is outside this creation. But he chooses to "live" in his creation in places where he can be found by his creatures.

God is just as much present in the universe he made as the physical objects we see around us: "The voice of the LORD is over the waters; the God of glory thunders, the LORD, over many waters. The LORD sits enthroned over the flood; the LORD sits enthroned as king forever" (Psalm 29:2,3,10). The universe cannot

---

[182]When we talk about heaven as the place where the eternal God lives, it is best to express ourselves as Scripture does and leave it at that. Sometimes we hear well-meaning Christians suggest that heaven is like another dimension. Sadly, that way of speaking is an attempt to talk in scientific terms about mysteries we don't understand. Those ideas have a way of backfiring and making Christians seem to base their faith on speculation.

be reduced to material things we can observe and analyze. Scripture tells us that God is present in his creation. Israel's "science" includes God's activity.

Conclusion

If we accept Scripture, we reject the idea that mankind slowly emerged from a prehistoric past. God created mankind fully formed, with the same intelligence, insight, and interest in the world that we have today. We understand the Israelites to be a special nation created by God to play an important role in his plan to save the world. Their Scriptures were a product of God's own Spirit and cannot be analyzed in reference to the literature of the nations around them. And we know God to be the Creator and Sustainer of everything we see around us. He lives in and around what he has made.

Chapter 6

How Does Scripture Actually Describe the Universe? Part One

Narrative and the Language of Observation

The chart below contrasts the straightforward way of reading Scripture with the historical-critical and theistic evolutionary way of reading Scripture. The chart also shows the outline for our study of what Scripture actually says about the makeup and operation of the universe, which in turn answers the ANE argument.

	Straightforward Reading	Theistic Evolutionist Reading
Method of interpretation	Genesis 1 is a narrative account of God's creating activity, revealed by God to those he inspired to write the Scriptures.	The creation account is mythology, created from the oral legends passed down from prehistoric times.
The narrative of creation	God's presence in his creation, guiding and preserving it, is the overarching theme in the creation narrative. But that theme never overrides Scripture's description of what God created. The account of creation in Genesis 1 and 2 is a narrative of events that provides a basic understanding of the structure and operation of the universe. It describes the universe in general terms, which do not rule out the results of future scientific study and observation.	Since the creation account in Genesis 1 and 2 is derived from ancient mythology, it provides us with information about what the ancients believed the universe was like. God's presence in the world is a major theme of Scripture, but the scientific opinions of God's authors must be discarded. They have been proved wrong by later observations and discoveries.

Language of observation	Scripture uses the language of observation as we use it today. It helped them express what they observed about the relationships between the objects in the universe.	In Scripture statements that we would consider to be the language of observation actually reflect ancient scientific beliefs. As such, they can be gleaned for information about what the Israelites actually believed about the structure and working of the universe.
Symbols in Scripture	Symbols in Scripture are based on the creation account as recorded in Genesis 1 and 2. Our interpretation of symbols is guided by what we know about the physical world as described in the creation account. The purpose of the symbols is to praise God's unseen—but no less real—power, glory, and lordship over all creation.	Symbols are based on what the Israelites believed about the structure and working of the universe. Along with the language of observation, we can use the symbols of Scripture to teach us about the physical objects the Hebrews believed were present in the universe, as well as how those objects worked.
Resulting cosmology	Scripture teaches the same three-tiered universe that we see around us today. Scripture teaches us to acknowledge God's invisible presence and control of his creation and to rely on his power and love.	Scripture, along with other ancient Near Eastern resources, teaches that the universe has a three-tiered structure, filled with the various physical objects the ancients believed existed. The three-tiered universe and all it contains constitutes an ancient science that we are required to discard in the face of modern science.

The questions we will ask of Scripture

The ANE argument can only be answered after a thorough exploration of what Scripture itself says and does not say about the physical universe. Those who promote the ANE argument, and this includes most theistic evolutionists, claim that the writers of Scripture accepted the "scientific" ideas of their contemporaries and that their writings are brimming with references to outmoded ideas.

Narrative and the Language of Observation

If this claim is true, Scripture's statements about the universe can be dismissed in favor of evolution.

The main question is this: Does Scripture teach a form of ancient science about the makeup of the universe that is inaccurate in the light of what modern scientists actually observe? Here we are not concerned about their analysis of what they see, only the observations themselves.

The claim is that everyone in the ancient Near East believed in a "three-tiered universe." This refers to a threefold division of the universe into (1) the sky above us, (2) the earth around us, and (3) what lies below us under the earth. In addition to this basic division of the universe, the ancients were supposed to have believed in a number of objects and structures that exist in the three-tiered universe.

The first tier is *the sky above*. The ancients were to have believed that above the earth is a dome. It is thin and hard and serves to keep the water above it from coming down on the earth. Support structures on the earth keep the dome in place. There are various levels in the area above the dome where divine beings live. In the morning, the sun enters the area under the dome through some kind of portal in the east, travels across the underside of the dome, and departs through an opening in the dome in the west. At night it returns to the east, where it is ready to make another circuit. The moon and stars do something similar as they rise and set. The gods are to have stored various elements above the dome, like rainwater, hail, and lightning. There are openings in the dome through which the gods would send these elements on the people of the earth below.

The second tier is *the surface of the world* (the land and the sea). The ancients were to have believed that the earth is flat. The flat earth was generally held to be disk-shaped. The disk shaped landmass is surrounded by an ocean, which extends under the surface of the earth. The land is kept from sinking into the sea by support mechanisms on its underside—foundations or pillars.

The third tier is *the area beneath the surface* of the earth. The landmass extends downward to an indeterminate distance. The water we see in the oceans extends under the earth and resurfaces in various places in the form of springs of water. Below the earth's surface lies another world, hidden from those who live on the land above. This is the home of the dead; various gods also live there.

Needless to say, in the light of modern science, this view of the universe must be dismissed. Ancient ideas about how the universe came into existence must also be dismissed as myth.

One More Elephant

Treating Scripture as a normal piece of literature

Historical critics like to say they are analyzing Scripture in the same way they analyze any other piece of literature. In chapters 2 through 4 we have seen that this means analyzing it in the context of Enlightenment assumptions and goals.

We, too, will analyze Scripture as we analyze any other piece of literature. The writers of Scripture used *the three normal ways of speaking and writing that all people, modern scientists and theologians included, use when they discuss any topic.*

- First, Scripture uses "simple narrative." It describes a series of events in a way readers recognize as a literal description of what took place.

- Second, Scripture uses the "language of observation;" that is, it describes the various parts of the physical world in terms of the relationships between them as viewed by people on earth.

- Third, Scripture uses "symbolical language." It describes the wonders of creation and the glory of God by using language that people recognize as symbolical.

Our conclusion is this: If we accept Scripture's (1) narrative of creation, (2) its description of the universe in terms of the relationships between the objects we see around us, and (3) its right to use symbolical language, we will see that Scripture teaches nothing that forces us to believe anything about the physical universe that runs contrary to what scientists observe today.

In the rest of this chapter and the next, we will look at each point in detail.

First, Scripture describes in narrative form how God created the world

The narrative of Genesis 1-3

There is such a thing as myth. A myth is a type of literature that teaches timeless truths using a story that is not meant to be taken literally. On the other hand there is narration, an account whose details are meant to be understood in a literal way. Both are legitimate forms of speech. In the right context, each can convey truth.

Historical criticism says that the early chapters of Genesis are myth. Critics claim to have found clues in these chapters to substantiate their claim. For thousands of years, however, readers have understood Genesis 1-3 to be narrative. There is nothing in the text to suggest otherwise. Jesus and the New Testament writers treated these chapters as a literal narrative account of what happened at

Narrative and the Language of Observation

the beginning of the world. We will follow the lead of Jesus and the New Testament writers and view Genesis 1 and 2 as they did.[183]

What follows is a close look at what Genesis 1 says and does not say. What information do these chapters, read as a literal narrative, give us about the make-up and structure of the universe? Do they support the idea that Scripture reflects an ancient scientific view of the universe? We'll take the three tiers—heaven, earth, and under the earth—in order.

The meaning of "the heavens" as described in the creation account

The following excerpt from Genesis 1 includes the material we will focus on as we describe how Scripture defines "the heavens." Remember, we are concentrating on the claim that Scripture teaches that there is a dome above the earth, which it calls heavens.

> [1]In the beginning, God created the heavens and the earth.
>
> [2]The earth was without form and void, and darkness was over the face of the deep. And the Spirit of God was hovering over the face of the waters. . . .
>
> [6]And God said, "Let there be an expanse in the midst of the waters, and let it separate the waters from the waters." [7]And God made the expanse and separated the waters that were under the expanse from the waters that were above the expanse. And it was so. [8]And God called the expanse Heaven. And there was evening and there was morning, the second day.
>
> [9]And God said, "Let the waters under the heavens be gathered together into one place, and let the dry land appear." And it was so. [10]God called the dry land Earth, and the waters that were gathered together he called Seas. And God saw that it was good. . . .
>
> [14]And God said, "Let there be lights in the expanse of the heavens to separate the day from the night. And let them be for signs and for seasons, and for days and years, [15]and let them be lights in the expanse of the heavens to give light upon the earth." And it was so. [16]And God made the two great lights—the greater light to rule the day and the lesser light to rule the night—and the stars. [17]And God set them in the expanse of

---

[183] Note the discussion of accommodationism in chapter 2. If someone wants to argue that Jesus and the New Testament writers believed that the creation account was a myth but were merely accommodating themselves to the ideas of their contemporaries, they will have to live with the idea that Jesus and the New Testament writers were willing to do that sort of thing. Nevertheless, those who make that claim are admitting that the Jewish population, after reading Genesis for centuries, understood it to be a simple narrative account.

the heavens to give light on the earth, ¹⁸to rule over the day and over the night, and to separate the light from the darkness. And God saw that it was good. ¹⁹And there was evening and there was morning, the fourth day.

²⁰And God said, "Let the waters swarm with swarms of living creatures, and let birds fly above the earth across the expanse of the heavens." ²¹So God created the great sea creatures and every living creature that moves, with which the waters swarm, according to their kinds, and every winged bird according to its kind. And God saw that it was good. ²²And God blessed them, saying, "Be fruitful and multiply and fill the waters in the seas, and let birds multiply on the earth." (Genesis 1:2-22)

We learn from Genesis 1:2 that God created an original material called "the deep" (תְהוֹם). (See below for a note on the Hebrew text included in this book.[184]) Before God created light, there was only darkness "over the face of the deep" (עַל־פְּנֵי תְהוֹם). In the next phrase, we hear that the Spirit of God was moving "over the face of the waters" (עַל־פְּנֵי הַמָּיִם). "The deep" is another term for "the waters."[185]

On the second day of the creation week, God turned his attention to the deep, that is, the waters: "And God said 'Let there be an expanse (רָקִיעַ) in the midst of the waters, and let it separate the waters from the waters.' And God made the expanse and separated the waters that were under the expanse from the waters that were above the expanse. And it was so" (Genesis 1:6,7).

How we define and picture the "expanse" will largely determine how we understand what Scripture teaches about the structure of the universe in general. Genesis says, "And God called the expanse, 'heavens'" (Genesis 1:8, my translation). We might also translate a little more loosely: "And God gave a name to the expanse, namely, 'heavens.'"[186] "Heavens" is simply *the name* God gave to the expanse he created. "Expanse" and "heavens" do not refer to two different things.

---

[184]It can be frightening to see foreign languages in a book you're reading. But no knowledge of Hebrew required! The inclusion of some Hebrew text will have no affect on your reading this book. It simply gives the Hebrew words behind the English words printed out in the text. It may prove helpful for those who know Hebrew. Even if you don't know Hebrew, in a few places it will help you see minor differences in the Hebrew that affect the translation. But you will understand the point even without knowing any Hebrew.

[185]In the Old Testament, "the deep" refers not just to the oceans, or to a particularly deep part of the ocean, but to any body of water. For example, in Deuteronomy 8:7 "the deep" refers to the springs of water in the land of Canaan, and in several places (for example, Psalm 106:9), "the deep" refers to the Red Sea through which the Israelites passed when they left Egypt.

[186]Note the parallel construction in Psalm 19:1. The first phrase speaks in terms of the name God gave to the expanse. The second phrase uses the name for the expanse itself. Translations like the ESV that translate "the sky" in the second phrase hide the parallelism, which is based on the fact that the heavens and the expanse are the same thing.

Narrative and the Language of Observation

The different ways "expanse" and "heavens" are translated in the various versions have made the matter more complicated than it need be. In his Latin translation of the Bible called the Vulgate, the early church father Jerome translated "expanse" with the word "firmamentum," from which we get our English word "firmament." This is the translation used in the King James Version. "Firmament" simply means a "firm thing," which conveys well what the Hebrew says. Genesis 1:6 says that the expanse of the heavens was "in the midst of the waters," literally, "between waters to waters" (בֵּין מַיִם לָמָיִם). The expanse was firm enough to support the waters above it and keep them from coming into contact with the waters below it.

Some translations, like the English Standard Version (ESV), capitalize "Heaven" and make it singular. This leads us to think of the expanse in the sense of the place were believers will live with God in eternity. Some translations, like the New International Version (NIV), translate "sky." This leads us to think of the lower atmosphere, which is immediately over our heads. Both of these translations point the reader in wrong directions, away from the fact that the expanse was simply the area between the upper waters and the lower waters.

The translation "sky" can lead to the idea that the heavens are made up of several different regions: Nearest to the earth is the sky. Above that is the expanse itself: a thin, hard dome that keeps the upper waters in place. Above that is Heaven: where God dwells. This is reflected in some translations. If the translator pictures the expanse to be a thin, hard structure, he might translate the Hebrew word for expanse with "vault" or "dome."[187]

In Scripture, however, heavens is the just the name God gave the "expanse." To use multiple terms—Heaven, firmament, sky, vault, dome—in addition to "heavens," departs from Scripture's way of speaking. Genesis makes no such distinctions. It simply speaks of heavens as the *name* God gave to the expanse he created. Heavens is simply the area between the waters that God separated on the second day.[188]

---

[187] Those translators who understand the Hebrew word RAKIAH in Genesis 1:6 to be an *area* placed between the upper and lower waters (which reflects the language of Scripture), simply translate it "expanse," or perhaps "space." The NIV84 (New International Version, 1984), CSB (Christian Standard Bible), and the NAS (New American Standard) translate "expanse;" the NLT (New Living Translation) translates "a space."
Other translators who assume that the Hebrews believed in a flat earth covered by *a thin, hard dome-shaped structure* reflect this idea in their translation of RAKIAH in Genesis 1:6. The NIV11 (New International Version, 2011) translates "vault" (whereas the NIV84 had translated "expanse"); the CJB (Complete Jewish Bible) and NRSV (New Revised Standard Version) both translate "dome."

[188] Scripture does use the expression "the heaven of heavens." But this is not a reference to a distinct area of heaven. It is how the Hebrews referred to the farthest extent of the heavens. Psalm 148:4 speaks of the heaven of heavens (translated "highest heavens" in the NIV and ESV) and

As the narrative continues, we find more clues as to the structure of the heavens. On the fourth day God placed the sun, moon, and stars "in the expanse of the heavens" (1:17) (בִּרְקִיעַ הַשָּׁמָיִם). The Hebrew word for "in" has a range of meanings, two of which are important for our purposes. A silversmith might embed precious stones in a metal crown. On the other hand, a group of people might live in a house. For our purpose, the question becomes, did the Lord embed the sun, moon, and stars in a thin domelike structure, or did he place them within the confines of an expansive area between the waters?[189]

Moses' description of God's creation of the birds provides some help. In Genesis 1:20 Moses relates God's command to the birds, "and let birds fly above the earth across the expanse of the heavens" (ESV). The ESV gives a fair translation. But it does a little paraphrasing, and it removes some information contained in the original Hebrew.

Literally, God told the birds to fly "upon the earth upon the face of the expanse of the heavens" (1:20) (עַל־הָאָרֶץ עַל־פְּנֵי רְקִיעַ הַשָּׁמָיִם). The Hebrew does not say that the birds flew *between* "the earth" and "the heavens." If the Hebrew had expressed it that way, it would, in fact, be saying that the realm of the birds was in the area between the earth and a hard dome above them. The Hebrew, however, equates the surface of the earth with the "face of the heavens;" they are the same thing. In other words, when the birds fly upon the earth, they are flying upon the (lower) face of the expanse, which touches the earth. [190] This fits with the understanding that the expanse is an area between the upper and lower waters. This also helps us understand the meaning of "in" in verse 17. God did not embed the sun, moon and stars *in a hard dome* but placed them *in the area between the upper and lower waters.*

---

follows that with a simple reference to "the heavens," above which are the upper waters: "Praise him, you highest heavens, and you waters above the heavens!" Also note that it is impossible to describe a hard, thin dome as having a "highest" region on which the waters sit. But it fits nicely when the heavens are thought of as the area between the waters above it and the waters below it.

[189] Much of the ancient world, at least since the days of the great philosopher Aristotle (382–324 B.C.), knew that the earth was a sphere. They believed that the sun, moon, and stars were objects embedded in spheres, which rotated around the earth. Those who teach that the "expanse" is a thin dome in which the sun, moon, and stars are embedded ought to find some indication in Scripture that the expanse rotates. But its purpose is not to carry the sun, moon, and stars as they rotate but to keep the upper and lower waters separate.

[190] The older Keil and Delitzsch commentary says that the birds flew "on the front" of the expanse, that is, "the side turned toward the earth." Keil and Delitzsch, *Commentary on the Old Testament, Vol. 1: The Pentateuch* (Grand Rapids: William B. Eerdmans Publishing Company, reprint, 1976) p. 60. (The commentary on Genesis was written by C. F. Keil and originally published in 1861.) A more recent commentary on Genesis by H. C. Leupold puts it this way: "The firmament is regarded as having a face, that is a side turned toward and, as we say, 'facing' the earth. Across this the birds are to disport themselves." H. C. Leupold, *Exposition of Genesis, Vol. 1* (Grand Rapids: Baker, 1942), p. 79.

Narrative and the Language of Observation

In summary, the expanse in Genesis 1 is an *area*. Its lower extent ("face," verse 20) is on the sea and the land. God populated the expanse with birds that fly on its lower face and with the sun, moon, and stars, which can be seen to vary in altitude above the earth. Accordingly, the upper extent of the heavens would be at the outer boundaries of our universe. We might object that this would put the waters above the heavens extremely far away from the surface of the earth. If that is a problem, then we must wrestle with that idea but not with how Scripture speaks about the expanse.

All of this corresponds to how the word "heavens" is used throughout Scripture. Scripture speaks of the "birds of the heavens" (Psalm 8:8).[191] Heaven is where the dew on the ground comes from (Genesis 27:28) as well as the frost (Job 38:29); where Moses threw soot to begin the plague of boils (Exodus 9:8); where the rain comes from (Deuteronomy 11:11); where the clouds form (1 Kings 18:45); where the wind blows (Psalm 78:26); and where things like the sun, moon, and stars are located, which many worship as gods (Exodus 20:4). A bit of an exception to this might be the description of Absalom entangled in a tree. He was left "suspended *between* heaven and earth" (2 Samuel 18:9). We might put this in the category of Scripture's use of the language of observation as discussed below. He was suspended between the earth and *what appears to be* a structure arching above us. Other than that, in Scripture "heavens" always refers to the *area* above us, which contains things that are found closer to the surface of the earth as well as things that are farther away.

The claim that the ancient Hebrews believed that the firmament is a dome is a chief reason that their cosmology is dismissed as bad science. But in Scripture, heaven is never defined as a hard dome. And if any Hebrew scholar did believe there was a dome covering the earth, he did not get it from Scripture.

Scripture's basic description of the heavens as the space above us *is not at odds with past or present observations of the universe.* People of all ages are invited to explore what's above us without fearing that something they find out there will be at odds with what they read about in Scripture.

---

[191] Note that translations regularly translate in modern terms, which confuse "the heavens" with a more modern designation for the area above us. For example, the NIV84 translates "birds of the air," and the NIV11 changes that to "birds in the sky." But the Hebrews knew only "the heavens," the name God gave to the entire expanse between the waters. The ESV is quite consistent in translating "the birds of the heavens," but it translates the phrase in Proverbs 30:19 "the way of an eagle in the sky," where the Hebrew has "in the heavens."

The creation of dry land

As recorded in Genesis 1:9-13

Genesis 1 also describes the creation of the surface of the earth, where mankind lives. God gathered the water under the heaven "into one place" (אֶל־מָקוֹם אֶחָד). There is no explanation of what the waters under the heavens looked like before they were gathered into one place. But once the waters were where God wanted them to be, he commanded dry land to appear (וְתֵרָאֶה הַיַּבָּשָׁה). The dry land appeared out of the water.

God gave names to the dry land and the gathered waters. He called the dry land "earth" (אֶרֶץ) and he called the water "seas" (הַמַּיִם). The ESV translates the name God gave to the dry land "earth," while the NIV translates it "land." Both are acceptable translations, but it is clear that Genesis is referring to the landmass (or masses) that appeared out of the gathered waters.

At this point we have no indication of the size of the landmass or whether it was relatively thick or thin. There is no indication as to its shape, whether it was round or irregular. There is no indication of how much dry land there was in relation to the seas. There is no indication of how the land was distributed within the seas. Was it a single landmass surrounded by the sea? Or were there a number of landmasses? Since the water was created first and the landmass appeared out of it, something or someone must be supporting the earth on the water, but Genesis 1 does not speak of that. It describes the creation of the land and sea in very general terms. Nothing scientists today observe about the land and sea is at variance with what we find in the creation account.

Additional information from the book of 2 Peter

Before we move on, we should look at a New Testament passage that gives further information about a change that took place sometime after Adam and Eve fell into sin.

Peter rebuked certain people of his day who had forgotten that God long ago judged the world with a flood. He urged people to repent in view of the coming judgment that God would send on the ungodly. Peter wrote,

> For they deliberately overlook this fact, that the heavens existed long ago, and the earth was formed out of water and through water by the word of God, and that by means of these the world that then existed was deluged with water and perished. But by the same word the heavens and earth that now exist are stored up for fire, being kept until the day of judgment and destruction of the ungodly. (2 Peter 3:5-7)

Note Peter's description of the creation of the dry land: "The earth was formed [or "existed"] out of water and through water by the word of God" (2 Peter 3:5). This parallels the account in Genesis. God first gathered together the water under the expanse, which he called "Seas." Then God used the water to create the dry land, and the dry land appeared out of the water. God called the dry land "Earth." Water existed under the earth.

Today, however, we see a relatively thin crust of earth and sea resting on molten rock, which surrounds a central core. On the basis of what scientists observe today, they assume that the world began as a hot, molten mass, slowly cooling over time. Peter, however, reminds us that God created the world out of water and through water, and that God used this water to judge the world for its wickedness. Peter also tells us that at some point God changed the makeup of the world and substituted the water with fire, which he will use to destroy the world when Jesus returns in judgment. At that time not only the surface of our world but the entire universe will be destroyed (2 Peter 3:10).

When we add this information from Peter to what we learn in Genesis, there is nothing that we observe today that is at variance with Scripture. Scientists will make new discoveries about the earth and sea but will not observe anything that contradicts Scripture. Scripture's description is too general for that to happen.

The creation of what is under the earth

Clearly something exists below the surface of the earth. Scripture, however, says little about it. The sea extends downward and is lower than the surface of the earth. How today's seabed might have been reshaped to accommodate the fire below the surface of the earth (which Peter tells us about) is not explained in Scripture.

Scripture gives a few more pieces of information about what lies below the surface of the earth. We learn from Genesis 2 that "a river flowed out of Eden to water the garden, and there it divided and became four rivers" (Genesis 2:10). The source of this river may have been a spring, whose source might have been the water below the surface of the earth. Genesis also tells us that "the earth brought forth vegetation" (Genesis 1:12). We realize that parts of those plants, the roots, stretch down into the earth. Later, when people began to mine the earth for metals, a bit more of what's below the surface of the earth was exposed.

Scripture speaks about the place where the dead go called "Sheol." Sheol is defined in Scripture as the place where all people eventually go when they die. It is not heaven or hell; it is more of a synonym of the grave. The Old Testament Scripture says little about it and certainly doesn't define it as an underworld like that of the Egyptians, Greeks, and Romans.

Once again, scientists today observe nothing below the surface of the earth that is at variance with what Scripture tells us about it.

Summary

When Genesis 1 comes to a close, we have a universe made up of two bodies of water kept separate from each other by an area called the expanse, or "heavens." The sun, moon, stars, clouds, and birds are located in this area. We are given no information on how high the expanse reaches or where the waters above the expanse are located. Nor is there any indication that we can actually see the waters above the expanse. Below the expanse is a body of water and dry land. Since the water was created first and the landmass appeared out of it, the earth must have been supported on the water. Scripture does not tell us about anything, much less an underworld, that might be found under the surface of the earth.

The *narrative of creation* contains nothing more or less than this. It does not describe the universe in any way that would conflict with the observations of people living in either ancient or modern times. It does not teach a scientific three tiered universe as theistic evolutionists claim.

Second, Scripture uses the language of observation

What is the language of observation?

The people of Israel would have spoken about the world around them in terms of the narrative account in Genesis 1 and 2. But there are other ways of talking about what they saw around them. One of those ways is the "language of observation."

The language of observation is a normal part of everyday speech. The technical name is *phenomenology*, that is, a description of something based only on the *phenomena* that we see. For example, "The sun rises and the sun sets." Everyone talks that way, including modern meteorologists. Sometimes at night we see a full moon, sometimes a half moon or a quarter moon. Montana is Big Sky Country. It really is! Just visit there sometime if you haven't. True, today we understand *why* the sun appears to rise and set. We know *why* the moon appears in different ways at different times of the month. And there is likely a scientific explanation for why the sky in Montana looks big. But when we speak about these phenomena, we continue to use the language of observation.

People in China *stand* and so do people in the United States. Both are describing an action in terms of what they see happening. When a person stands,

Narrative and the Language of Observation

he or she is working against the force of gravity and moving toward the sky above, and when a person sits, he or she is experiencing the force of gravity and is moving toward the center of the earth. People in China and in the United States are actually moving in opposite directions when they stand and sit, but we speak about what they are doing in the same way—according to what we see happening.

The language of observation might better be called the language of relationships. The sun does, in fact, rise. As the day progresses, the sun rises higher in the sky in relation to the horizon, and then it sets, also in relation to the horizon. We speak of north, east, south, and west, but we use those terms in relation to where we are at the present. If I travel five miles to the east, some of what had been to the east of me is now to the west of me.

We call certain groups of stars constellations. Today we know that the stars in some constellations are much closer or farther away from us, scattered throughout the universe. But when I say these stars are close to each other in a constellation, I am accurately describing their relation to each other as I see them in the sky.

Evaluating the theistic evolutionists' approach to the language of observation

Theistic evolutionists are well aware that we use this kind of language today. But to sustain their argument for an ancient and inaccurate science, they must make a distinction between how we use it and how the ancients used it. Denis Lamoureux explains it this way:

> What the biblical writers and other ancient peoples saw with their eyes, they believed to be real, like the literal rising and setting of the sun. In contrast, we view the world from a modern phenomenological perspective. When we see the sun "rising" and "setting," we know that it is only an appearance or visual effect caused by the rotation of the earth.[192]

In other words, when the ancients used the language of observation, they were in error because to them that was their science, but when we use it, we can be excused because we understand the reality behind it. Lamoureux applies this logic to Saint Paul: "Did Paul use phenomenological language in the manner that we do today? Would he agree with us if we asked him, 'The "rising" and "setting" of the sun are only visual effects caused by the rotation of our spherical planet, right?' History reveals that Paul would disagree."[193]

---

[192] Denis Lamoureux, *Evolutionary Creation*, p. 109.
[193] Denis Lamoureux, *Evolutionary Creation*, pp. 108,109.

This is the kind of argument that is hard to refute. The author is creating a situation in which Paul is answering a question we have no evidence he was ever asked. The author then claims the right to determine how Paul would have answered the question based on what he thinks Paul believed. Then the author puts words into Paul's mouth—which makes Paul an example of an ancient person who believed in something that today we know is wrong. Lamoureux's argument is maddening because it is based on pure speculation and guesswork. Sadly, this is the kind of logic one finds in many theistic evolutionary books.

What history does prove is the opposite of what Lamoureux claims. Paul lived some six hundred years after the Greeks began to discuss the structure of the universe. Chances are that he was familiar with the Greek philosopher Aristarchus of Samos (ca. 310–230 B.C.) who taught that the earth and the rest of the planets revolve around the sun. In Greek philosophy, the choice between a sun-centered and an earth-centered universe was just that, a choice each philosopher had to make for himself. An earth-centered universe held sway with the weight of Aristotle behind it.

Paul was considered one of the most learned men of his day. He lived in the midst of Greek culture, and he was able to cite Greek sources (see, for example, Acts 17:28). Perhaps Paul and his companions did discuss the Greek science of their day while sitting around a campfire at night, including the opinions of the philosophers about what lay at the center of the universe. Nevertheless, even if we didn't know the history of science in Paul's day, his use of the language of observation was a normal way of speaking without implying that this was a formal scientific opinion. The language of observation served his communication needs nicely.[194]

The language of observation or relationships fills a normal role in human discourse. It is not meant to express a scientific truth. It is a kind of shorthand to describe what we see. Ask yourself, if I didn't have this language tool, how would I tell someone about a sunrise or sunset? How would I talk about what I see on the horizon in the morning and in the evening? How would I speak about a distinctive group of stars in the sky? And if I visited Montana, how would I tell someone about the sky as I saw it there?

When Joshua asked the Lord to give him more time to defeat his Amorite enemies, the Lord granted his request. He described what happened: "And the sun stood still, and the moon stopped, until the nation took vengeance on their enemies. Is this not written in the Book of Jashar? The sun stopped in the midst of heaven and did not hurry to set for about a whole day" (Joshua 10:13). Instead of centering that event on Joshua's supposed ancient scientific views, why not

---

[194]Note that the only time Paul refers to the sun going down is in Ephesians 4:26: "Be angry and do not sin; do not let the sun go down on your anger."

begin with the question: "How would Joshua have described that event without the language of observation?" Or relating that to our day: "How long would the evening weather report drag on if the meteorologist was forbidden to use the words 'sunrise' or 'sunset'?"

When Solomon wanted to illustrate that there is nothing new under the sun, and that events repeat themselves over and over again, he used the example of the sun: "The sun rises, and the sun goes down, and hastens to the place where it rises" (Ecclesiastes 1:5). He was describing what we all see—that every day the sun departs from view, but the next day, there it is, back to where it was the day before. If Solomon was alive today, would he say it any differently?

Today's scientists who observe the universe and seek to understand it are in the same shoes as the ancients. When scientists today speak about a "black hole," we all know that this is not their final word on what is actually out there. They remain open to further discoveries that may prove that what they observe is neither black nor a hole. They are simply describing something as their instruments record it. They know that intelligent people in the future will not look down on them for being unable to separate their temporary use of the language of observation from a final scientific description of what they see.

The language of observation is not an inferior way of speaking about the universe. It would be cumbersome to express ourselves without it. Scientific explanations for what we see will change from century to century. But talking about objects in terms of what we observe and the relationships we see between them will always be accurate and understandable. To claim that the ancients' use of the language of observation was an expression of their scientific beliefs disregards the normal way all people describe the relationships of the things they see around them.

Chapter 7

How Does Scripture Actually Describe the Universe? Part Two

Third, the Scripture uses symbolic language

Introduction

Symbolism is a third type of language found in Scripture. There are various types of symbols, and explaining the structure of symbols is as difficult as explaining the structure of language in general.

But we know symbols when we see them. Scripture often uses metaphors. A metaphor is a figure of speech in which the quality of one object is applied to another object. King David knew that God was his source of security, so he called God his "rock of refuge" (Psalm 94:22). In his mind, David saw a large rock outcropping where soldiers could take a secure position and easily defend themselves against an attacker. David also knew that God would always stand in front of him to ward off enemy attacks, so he called God his "shield" (Psalm 119:144).

In another place, David described God as traveling "on the wings of the wind" (2 Samuel 22:11). Wings call to mind a powerful bird flying high into the sky. The wind is a powerful and unstoppable force. Nor can anyone program in what direction it must blow. Just as an eagle is carried aloft on its wings by the wind, so God enters the heavens with fast-moving, unstoppable power in a direction known only to him.

These examples show the power of metaphors. They can say a lot in a few words and do it in a beautiful way.

The ANE argument and Scripture's symbolism

We've already defined the ANE argument, but let's do that again in the context of Scripture's use of symbols. First, note what the argument is *not* about: It is not about whether Scripture uses symbolism. Everyone agrees that it does. Nor is it about the main purposes of symbolism in Scripture, which is to picture the glory and power of God.

The argument is this: The symbols of Scripture are said to reflect what the ancient Hebrews believed about the physical makeup of their universe. For example, when Hebrew writers spoke about the "windows of heaven," it is claimed that they believed there were literal openings in the dome of the heaven through which God pours rain down on the earth. Theistic evolutionists have created a list of Hebrew symbols that supposedly reflect their science of the universe.

If it can be established that the symbols of Scripture reflect the ancient science of the day, the truth of Scripture can be challenged. One can make the claim that the scientific beliefs of the Hebrews were obviously wrong, and we have a duty to replace them. To add punch to the argument, the Hebrews' view of the universe as culled from its symbols is compared to similar beliefs culled from the symbolism of the other nations living around Israel, especially Egypt and Babylon. This makes possible the claim: Now we know where the Hebrews got their scientific beliefs, and we have a framework for interpreting the Scripture's references to the universe. If we can discard the science of Egypt and Babylon, we are required to discard the science reflected in the symbols of the Hebrew Scriptures.

We will briefly discuss the literature of the other ANE nations in the postscript. What they believed or did not believe does play a role in addressing the ANE argument. But for a believer reading the Bible, that is only a matter of interest. If Scripture teaches faulty science, it deserves to be judged on the basis of what it says regardless of what the nations around Israel believed. In this chapter we will ask the question: Does the symbolism of Scripture reflect erroneous "scientific" ideas about the universe?

Historical criticism makes it difficult, if not impossible, to interpret symbols

When we read Genesis 1 in the traditional, straightforward way, we discover what God created in the beginning. This is our "reality." God created an expanse above the earth that separates the upper and lower waters. God created the sun, moon, and stars and placed them in this expanse. Scripture speaks of dry land sitting in the midst of the sea out of which it arose. It tells us that birds fly in the expanse, that fish live in the sea, and that a variety of creatures live on the land.

This non-symbolical description of God's creation gives us the reality behind the symbols found in Scripture.

But the entire Enlightenment mind-set that plays an important role in historical criticism changes this. When Genesis 1 is considered to be mythology, we no longer have a literal description of the structure of the universe. A void is created. And voids always seek to be filled. Once the literal description of God's creation is dismissed, the "reality"—that is, what the Hebrews believed about the structure of the universe—must be found in other places. We have already located one of those places, the language of observation. Instead of being viewed

The Symbols of Scripture

as the normal way people speak about the relationships between what they see in the universe, the language of observation is mined for information on what the Hebrews believed about the universe. The second source of reality is the symbols found in Scripture. Instead of being allowed to play their normal role of symbolizing what people know to be true, they too are pressed into service of providing information about what Hebrews believed actually existed in the universe.

The basic way we interpret symbols

A symbol cannot be interpreted unless we understand the symbol and what it is symbolizing

Our ability to understand a symbol depends on two things. We must first understand what we are symbolizing. And we must understand the characteristics of the symbol we use. For example, to use the symbol of God riding on the wings of the wind, we must first know that God is fast, powerful, and in control of his creation. That's the reality. Then we must understand that wings can carry things aloft and that the wind is fast, unstoppable, and uncontrollable. Knowing that, we can accurately interpret "wings of the wind" to symbolize God's power and speed in a beautiful and stunning way.

Now suppose that we have no literal statement about the reality but only statements that symbolize the reality, which is the problem we have in regard to the universe if Genesis 1 is considered to be a myth. Now we are forced to find our information about what is real in the symbol. Consider the metaphor of God riding on the wings of the wind. Without Scripture's nonsymbolical description of God, we are on shaky ground if we try to define him by looking for clues in the symbol. When we hear that God rides on the wings of the wind, we wonder: "Why does God need the wind to get from one place to another? Can't he move about by his own power? How does God control in which direction the wind goes? Might God literally have wings?" Those questions may sound silly, but that's only because we understand things about God as revealed in the non-symbolical sections of Scripture. With Scripture's literal description about God in mind, we can easily interpret the symbolism contained in the phrase "wings of the wind."

Interpreting complex symbols

The example of God riding on the wings of the wind is a fairly easy symbol to understand. The reality, which is God's power on display in Scripture's record of what God has done, is symbolized nicely by the wings of the wind. We understand both the reality and the words used to symbolize the reality.

But symbols can be more complex. Some symbols can *symbolize* something that is real, and at the same time *reflect* something else that is also real. For example, consider two present-day statements that contain symbolical language: "Yesterday I was running around like a chicken with its head cut off," and "It is so hot today that you can fry an egg on the pavement."

In the first sentence, the point of comparison is aimlessness. The person is saying: "A chicken that has had its head cut off might run around for a few seconds, but it has no sense of where it is going. I was like that yesterday." The point of comparison in the second narrative is excessive heat. The person is saying: "It takes a lot of heat to fry an egg. It is so hot out today that the pavement has become hot enough to do that."

In one sense, those metaphors are similar. They both symbolize a particular truth, in the first case aimlessness and in the second case the high temperature outside. But in another sense, they are quite different. The first *does* reflect something that really happens. People have seen chickens with their heads cut off running around aimlessly for a few moments. The second metaphor *does not* reflect something that really happens. People don't fry eggs on hot pavement.

Those who claim that the symbols of Scripture reflect Hebrew science about the universe handle Scripture's metaphors as if they were like our first example. They symbolize something (yesterday I was aimless), but in the process they reflect something that is true (a chicken with its head cut off sometimes runs around).

But might a particular symbol in Scripture be just a symbol of something (it's hot out) without reflecting something that the Hebrews believed to be literally true (people fry eggs on pavement)? The real question is, how can we know which symbol (or parts of a symbol) reflects something that is real (or something a person believes to be real) and which don't? The answer is that *we can't* unless we have first learned about the reality in nonsymbolical language. In the symbol of frying an egg on the pavement, I want to say that it is hot, not that I have the practice of frying eggs on my driveway. But a person who hears me say that *could* conclude that I do fry eggs on my driveway on hot days. The only way a person can sort out what is real and unreal in my symbol is by knowing the literal "narrative" of the day-to-day life in my culture. Without that, even if a person gets the point of the symbol—that it's hot outside—that person cannot construct a picture of what I'm in the habit of doing.

The narrative of creation in Genesis 1 and 2 is the only place where we can learn what the Hebrews believed about the physical world around them. If we reject the literal, straightforward nature of those chapters, we will consign ourselves to trying to discover Hebrew beliefs from the symbols themselves. In trying to do that, we will doom ourselves to guesswork and speculation.

If we believe that Genesis 1 and 2 contains a literal narrative of God's creation of the world, we know and understand what really exists. Scripture's symbolical language, which draws on our common knowledge of the world around us (like our understanding of "wind" and "wings"), is easily understood. We are on a solid footing, and the symbols of Scripture can do their job of symbolizing God and his creation in beautiful ways.

God is at the heart of Scripture's symbols

The heart of the ANE argument is about the "incorrect scientific beliefs" the Hebrews had about the physical universe around them. So we will stick with that and analyze what the symbols say or do not say about the physical reality of the universe. But we should remember that the purpose of Scripture's symbolism is to glorify God: to acknowledge his presence in the universe, to praise him for blessing his creation, and to warn about his power when he comes in judgment.

This realization will have a general effect on how we interpret Scripture's symbols. The theistic evolutionist who is searching the symbols for hints about Hebrew science will likely find hints on which he or she can speculate. But a reader who is impressed with God's power and glory and comes across a symbol that speaks of that glory, will very likely approach the details of the symbol differently.

For example, in one symbol we will look at below, the writer refers to the pillars of the earth. People are generally familiar with the pillars of a palace or temple that keep the roof from falling down. That symbol, taken by itself, *might* reflect an ancient belief that there are similar pillars under the earth that hold it up. On the other hand, that symbol may simply convey the message that God is keeping the earth from falling back into the sea by his almighty power. If I am looking for evidence of scientific beliefs, my interpretation will be pulled in the first direction. If I am focused on God's glory and power, my interpretation will be pulled in the second direction.

That, of course, is not the final answer to the interpretation of the symbols. The symbols must speak for themselves. But as we proceed, keep in mind the purpose of the symbols found in Scripture. The writers are invariably using the symbols to glorify God.

One More Elephant

The goal: to demonstrate the erroneous nature of the Hebrew science

Let's briefly return to the theistic evolutionary claim that the Hebrews, like the nations around them, erroneously believed in a three-tiered universe.[195] Theistic evolutionists want to prove that the Scriptures teach a three-tiered universe that contains unscientific elements.

The issue, however, is not whether the universe as we observe it has three tiers. We all see the sky above us, the earth around us, and we know that there are things under the earth. The issue is really about the details theistic evolutionists have added to the three tiers—details they claim to have found in Scripture's use of the language of observation and in its symbolical language.

Here is what the scriptural version of the three-tiered universe looks like *with the additional details added in:* Above us there is a dome arching over the earth, and above the dome there is water. The dome is thin and hard and serves to keep the water above it from coming down upon the earth. The dome rests on pillars or mountains at the edges of the earth. The sun, moon, and stars become visible when they enter the area beneath the dome through an opening in the east. They travel across the underside of the dome and depart through an opening in the west. At night they reposition themselves in the east, where they are ready to make another circuit. God stores various elements, rainwater for example, in storerooms above the dome, which he uses to help or punish the people living on the earth. These elements come through windows in the dome. There are various levels of heaven above the dome. The surface of the earth (land and sea) was believed to be flat and generally thought to be disk-shaped. The earth is surrounded by the sea. The earth floats on the sea and is kept from sinking into it by support mechanisms—foundations and pillars. Below the land is the water on which the land floats. There is also a hidden world there, the home of the dead called *Sheol*, distinct from the world above the surface.

We will want to keep this picture in mind as we examine Scripture's symbolism. Do the symbols of Scripture reflect ancient scientific ideas that must be discarded? Or do the symbols of Scripture merely use the qualities of what we see around us to symbolize the glory of God.

Where we are at and where we are going

In the last chapter, we examined the narrative account about the creation of the world in Genesis 1 and 2. We saw what those chapters do and do not say about the physical structure and operation of the universe. Unless details are

---

[195] We will primarily cite two proponents of the ANE argument who have written extensively on the subject. Kyle Greenwood wrote an entire book on the subject, and Denis Lamoureux included a lengthy treatment of it in his book.

read into that account, no scientific observation contradicts the description of creation found in those chapters. We also evaluated the language of observation. We saw that this kind of language is in common use today just as it was when the Old and New Testaments were being written.

Now we will look at the symbols found in Scripture. We will ask if Scripture's symbolism reflects a different view of the universe from the one described in Genesis, or at least a view in which the universe as described in Genesis 1 and 2 is supplemented with various structures not mentioned there.

Our discussion of the symbols is organized around the three parts of the world as we observe them today: the heavens, the earth, and what's under the earth. Theistic evolutionists sometimes quote a number of passages to prove their point, often with little discussion. The amount of detail included in the rest of this chapter is important in view of the lack of detail found in theistic evolutionist literature.

Analysis of the symbols found in Scripture

Symbols for "the heavens"

The structure of an expanse, which God named "the heavens," is at the heart of the matter. In illustrations of the ancient three-tiered universe, how the heavens are pictured will set the pace for the rest of the diagram.

Scripture sometimes says that God "stretched out" the heavens. Jeremiah writes, "It is he who made the earth by his power, who established the world by his wisdom, and by his understanding stretched out the heavens" (נָטָה שָׁמָיִם) (Jeremiah 10:12; also see Jeremiah 51:15). God stretching out the heavens is sometimes compared to an Israelite pitching a tent. The psalmist says that God covers himself with light as with a garment "stretching out the heavens like a tent" (Psalm 104:2).

The idea of God stretching out the heavens can be interpreted in two ways: (1) God stretched out a hard, thin dome from one end of the earth to the other. This is how theistic evolutionists interpret it. Or (2) God stretched out the heavens from the bottom up, that is, from the surface of the lower waters to the surface of the upper waters and then outward so that the expanse, called the heavens, was an area resting on the earth's surface and keeping the upper waters in place.

An ancient Hebrew reader, who accepted Genesis 1 as a literal account of the creation, would have understood the heavens to be an area above him, not a thin dome. A Hebrew person would have chosen option (2). That would have been the reality he or she had in mind when coming across a symbol for the heavens.

Let's examine a number of passages in which the heavens are symbolized by God stretching out a tent. The passages will help us evaluate the two options. These passages reveal other symbols that are used in reference to the heavens.

Two difficult passages

Some passages are difficult to translate. It is easy for theistic evolutionists to quote translations of those passages that support their claim that the Hebrews believed in an ancient and erroneous view of the universe. Translators look for words and expressions that are easy to understand. Sometimes their translations reflect the three-tiered universe with the additional structures we noted above. We will start with two verses in which translators do just that, Isaiah 40:22 and Job 37:18. Theistic evolutionists often use these two verses to support the ANE argument. I've put a summary statement at the beginning of each verse followed by details you can read if you wish.

Isaiah 40:22

"It is he who sits above the circle of the earth, and its inhabitants are like grasshoppers; who stretches out the heavens like a curtain, and spreads them like a tent to dwell in."

Summary: We sympathize with Bible translators and the difficult choices they must make to help us understand the original Hebrew. In this verse, some translators use "canopy" instead of "circle" as in the ESV, which makes the verse easy to understand. But the word canopy leads us to envision a completely unscientific structure in the universe, a thin dome over our heads.

Yet the words and expressions Isaiah uses in 40:22 symbolize quite well the reality described in Genesis 1 and 2. They also reflect what Scripture says about God dwelling in the heavens. We might paraphrase this verse: "The Lord sits high above the earth's horizon, looking down on mankind, who look so small from there. God stretched out this area for himself like we set up a tent; it's the home in which he lives."[196]

Details: Isaiah says that God sits above "the circle of the earth." This passage is used to prove that the ancients believed that the earth was a flat, circular landmass. But it does not have to be interpreted that way. Interpreters have two choices. "Land" is the proper name God gave to the dry land he created on the third day (Genesis 1:10). The word Moses used in that verse was the same word

---

[196]Note Young's Literal Translation, a very literal translation that includes little or no interpretation. Young translates: "He who is sitting on the circle of the earth, And its inhabitants are as grasshoppers, He who is stretching out as a thin thing the heavens, And spreadeth them as a tent to dwell in" (Isaiah 40:22 YLT).

The Symbols of Scripture

he used in verse 1: "God created the heavens and *the earth*" (Genesis 1:1; 2:1). The word *circle* can refer to different things depending on what we understand by earth. If earth refers to the landmass created on the third day, it might possibly reflect an ancient Hebrew belief that the landmass was a flat, circular disk. But if earth refers to the entire world (as Moses used it in Genesis 1:1 and 2:1), it could just as easily prove that the Hebrews knew the earth was a sphere. But perhaps it is best to interpret "circle" as an example of the language of observation: it is the circular horizon we all see around us, which God sees from his dwelling place in the heavens.

The second half of the verse reads, *"who stretches out the heavens like a curtain, and spreads them like a tent to dwell in"* (Isaiah 40:22). Theistic evolutionists use this clause to show that the Hebrews believed in a bowl-shaped dome that God stretched out over the earth. The well-supported ceiling of a tent could symbolize a thin, hard dome. In reference to this verse, Greenwood writes, "God has spread the tent canopy of the heavens over the earth, such that it is taut and will not sag or be blown off its support poles by a gust of wind. In other words, the canopy is firmly fixed in place."[197] But does the verse actually say this?

The NIV translates the first phrase like this: "He stretches out the heavens like a *canopy*." This translation focuses our attention on the ceiling of the tent. It definitely supports the idea that the heavens are a dome-shaped structure over our heads. The ESV, however, translates, he "stretched out the heavens like a curtain." The translation "curtain" makes it easier for readers to link this phrase with the next, where Isaiah compares the heavens to a tent. In other words, the curtains are not just the ceiling curtains of the tent, but all of the tent curtains.

The Hebrew word translated "curtain" or "canopy" literally means "a thin thing" (דֹּק).[198] Does this refer to a thin canopy over us or to the thinness of the

---

[197] Kyle Greenwood, *Scripture and Cosmology*, p. 83.

[198] Note that even this word has its difficulties. Sometimes there are complications in the Hebrew text, and this is a good illustration of that. Translators must do some guessing. Theistic evolutionists use passages that are quite clear in the English translation, but that's only because the translators have used a word or phrase that makes sense in English.

Isaiah 40:22 is a good example of the difficulties translators sometimes face. The passages I used to describe the meaning of the word "thin thing" use a slightly different word than the one found in Isaiah 40:22. They use the more common Hebrew word דַּק. This is *almost* the word Isaiah used in 40:22, which is דֹּק, which is used only here in the Hebrew Bible. If you look very closely, you can see the difference, not in the big letters but in the little markings above and below them. Translators must decide if the rare word Isaiah used here in 40:22 is the same word as the more common word used elsewhere. Or is it a different word with a possibly different meaning?

The authors of the current standard Hebrew dictionary (HALOT) treat it as a different word, but even they must guess at its meaning. They end their short discussion like this: veil ? gauze ?, || אֹהֶל Is 40₂₂. †. They are telling you that the word only appears here in the Hebrew Bible. Based on a similar word in other languages, the Hebrew word could mean "veil" or "gauze," but they are not certain. It is used in a passage, Isaiah 40:22, that speaks of a "tent," so its meaning is likely

space above us in the heavens? This Hebrew word is used in a variety of ways. The bad cows and bad ears of corn that Joseph saw in his dream were "ugly and thin" (Genesis 41:3). The manna the Israelites ate in the desert was thin in the sense of "a fine [thin], flake-like thing, fine as frost on the ground" (Exodus 16:14). The incense Aaron was to offer was "sweet incense beaten small [thin]" (Leviticus 16:12). The Lord's voice, which Elijah heard in the wilderness, is described as "the sound of a low [thin] whisper" (1 Kings 19:12). God would destroy Israel's enemies and make them "like small [thin] dust" (Isaiah 29:5).

So what meaning shall we choose as our translation in Isaiah 40:22? Before we answer, we should look at a passage a few verses earlier in this chapter, Isaiah 40:15, in which Isaiah had just used this word. In that verse Isaiah wrote, "Behold, the nations are like a drop from a bucket, and are accounted as the dust on the scales; behold, he takes up the coastlands like *fine* [thin] *dust*." To God, the people of the world are like a drop in a bucket and like dust on a scale, which doesn't weigh much. And that is the comparison—the people of the world are like "fine dust."

We return to Isaiah 40:22. The Hebrew only says that God stretches out the heavens like a "thin thing." The ESV's translation "curtain" may suggest something thin; curtains are thin. The NIV's translation "canopy," however, has veered away from the basic meaning of the Hebrew word. This creates a problem when Isaiah describes God's action as setting up a tent "to live in." In that case, it would refer to all the curtains of the tent, not just its ceiling. Also, the word "thin" hardly conveys the idea of something hard, as in a hard dome.

The "thin thing" can just as easily symbolize the heavens themselves, the *space* between the upper and lower waters. Isaiah is telling us that God "stretched out" not just the ceiling of a tent, but the whole tent. When a Hebrew person set up a tent, he was setting up a three-dimensional object; he pitched the entire tent, including its walls, floor, and ceiling. When he pitched a tent, he created a space to live in. This is how Isaiah concludes the verse: God spreads out the heavens "like a tent to dwell in" (Isaiah 40:22).

Now the symbol is doing its job of picturing in a striking way the firm but "thin" expanse God created on the second day. It is as if God pitched a tent in between the upper and lower waters in which to live. And who lives in this tent?

---

something associated with a tent.

In the discussion above (in the main text), I assume that the word we find in Isaiah 40:22 is at least related in meaning to the other similar and more common word. In addition to this, we need to keep in mind that the Hebrew "pointing," which is the only thing that makes these words different, was added later by Hebrew scribes. Isaiah only wrote the large letters. Also, Isaiah had used the common word a few verses earlier (40:15). But all of this only complicates the matter, potentially making the verse less able to support the ANE argument.

The Symbols of Scripture

Other Old Testament verses tells us that God's dwelling place is in the heavens—and that he has given the earth to mankind as their dwelling place (Psalm 115:6).

Job 37:18

"Can you, like him, spread out the skies, hard as a cast metal mirror?"

Summary: Some passages in Scripture are just plain difficult to translate. Job 37:18 is one of them. In this verse Elihu is challenging Job: "Job, are you as powerful as God? Could you have created the expanse?" That is the main point, and it is easy to get that out of the passage. It is only the details that are unclear. But it's the unclear details that theistic evolutionists use to prove that the ancient Israelites believed that the heavens were a thin dome.

Of course, not all passages used by theistic evolutionists are difficult to translate. But when difficult passages like Job 37:18 are used as proof of what the ancients believed about the universe, readers have a right to expect at least a footnote—one that admits the presence of difficulties, especially when the author is using that word or phrase to make an important point.

The explanation of the difficulties in Job 37:18 is found in the details section below. Read it if you wish. It is included only to demonstrate why it is important for theistic evolutionists to alert their readers to the difficulties in passages like Job 37:18 if they want to use them. As we discuss these difficulties, it becomes clear that this passage does not force a view of the heavens that is different from what is described in Genesis 1.

Details: In Job 37:18 Elihu challenges Job's right to question the way God is dealing with him. He points to God's wisdom and power: "Can you, like him, spread out the skies, hard as a cast metal mirror?" If I were a theistic evolutionist, I would certainly want to use this passage. It clearly seems to say that the skies are hard like a mirror, which in those days was made of metal, beaten thin and polished. But I would also want my use of this passage to rest on a solid linguistic foundation.

Elihu begins with a word the ESV translates "spread out." But it is not the word normally used for stretching out a tent. Rather, it is the verb we encounter in Isaiah 42:5 (רָקַע), the verb associated with the noun "expanse." There, however, Isaiah used the word to describe God's creation of the earth, not of the heavens. He said that God "spread out the earth" but obviously not in the sense of making it hard and thin. Isaiah was using the basic meaning of the verb, namely, to put pressure on something. He was telling us that God gave the earth the firmness it needed to fulfill its purpose.

Getting back to Job 37:18. After Elihu says that God spread or beat something out, he does not give us the object of the verb. In other words, God beat *something* out, but Elihu does not tell us what he beat out. Elihu simply says that God "beat out *for clouds*."

So we must guess at what "for clouds" means. The Hebrew verb associated with the word "clouds" means "to rub away, beat fine, or pulverize." This would accurately describe clouds, especially when they touch the ground in the form of fog and lay down frost on the ground. But the meaning of that word seems to have been expanded to include *the place* where the clouds are found, which we call sky. Most translations choose "sky."

But which is it? Did God beat out clouds or sky? This word is not common in Scripture but is found four times in Elihu's speech to Job. In 35:5 Job is told to look up and see "something" higher than he is. The translators use "cloud." In 36:28 Elihu is referencing "the place" where rain comes from. The translators normally use "cloud" here also. In 37:21 Elihu speaks of the wind clearing "them" away. Either the wind has cleared the clouds away or the wind has cleared up the sky. Here the translators are divided, since both options make sense. The fourth instance is the verse we are looking at, 37:18. Should we translate "clouds" or "sky"? Based on evidence from Elihu's speech, there is good reason to translate "clouds." Twice it is fairly clear that Elihu means "clouds," and another time the translation could go either way. That would tip the scales in favor of the translation "clouds" in our verse, and "clouds" makes good sense here also.

But there is more to consider. The word *clouds* has a prefix (a word attached to the beginning of another word), in this case a single letter, which can be translated "to" or "for." So the Hebrew could be translated, "He beat out *for clouds*." But sometimes that little letter tells us that the word is the object of the verb. So our verse could be translated "beat out *clouds*."

But there is yet another option. Recall that Elihu doesn't use the normal verb for "stretch out," the one normally used for setting up a tent. Rather, he uses the verb RAKAH, the verb associated with the noun meaning "expanse" (RAKIAH), which carries the idea of pressing something and making it firm. So it might be legitimate to supply "heavens" in the present verse, even though it is not there in the original. In that case we would translate: "beat out [the heavens] for clouds."

We also have options for interpreting the next phrase: "hard as a cast metal mirror." This phrase could either refer back to "clouds" or to "heavens" (if we choose to supply that word). So again we have a choice. The idea of clouds being hard like a cast metal mirror doesn't make good sense. So we might want to supply "the heavens" in the previous phrase, which after all, is the firm thing God created to separate the upper and lower waters. In that case God beat out the heavens, the expanse he created on the second day (Genesis 1:6,7), hard as a cast metal mirror.

But there is yet another wrinkle. As mentioned above, the word for "clouds" seems to have taken on the meaning of "sky." So we might translate the verse like the ESV does: "Can you, like him, spread out the *skies*, hard as a cast metal mirror?" But what would Elihu have meant by "sky"? In the ANE argument, this passage is used to prove the thin, domelike shape of the expanse, not characteristics of what we call sky. We might think that the words *expanse* and *sky* are synonyms. But would the Hebrews have thought that? For them there was but one expanse stretching from the lower to the upper waters.

A final point to consider: What does "hard as a cast metal mirror" symbolize? Do we focus on the thinness of the mirror and let it picture for us a thin dome over the earth? Or do we focus on its hardness and let it symbolize the firmness of the heavens, that is, the expanse? The difficulties involved in interpreting this verse should caution against thinking about the thinness of a mirror, no matter how convenient that thought might be. We might limit the symbolism to picture something hard. In that case it would direct our attention to the firm area God "beat out" to separate the upper and lower waters.

If your head is spinning, you're not alone. All translators are aware of these difficulties and must wrestle with them. Denis Lamoureux and Robert Price use this passage to support their arguments. Kyle Greenwood does not, possibly because of the difficulties.[199]

Other often used passages

Isaiah 42:5

"Thus says God, the LORD, who created the heavens and stretched them out, who spread out the earth and what comes from it, who gives breath to the people on it and spirit to those who walk in it."

This passage is often used to support the ANE argument. God is to have stretched out the heavens like a thin dome covering the circle of the earth.

The meaning of the word "expanse" in Genesis 1 is the key to understanding how the Hebrews viewed their universe. Our English word "expanse" or "heavens" is a translation of the Hebrew word RAKIAH (רָקִיעַ). In Scripture, this noun is *only* used to refer to the expanse God created on the second day. Therefore, to find help in understanding the nature of the expanse, we must look in other places.

---

[199] Robert Price and Edwin Suominen, *Evolving out of Eden: Christian Responses to Evolution* (Valley, WA: Tellectual Press, 2013 Kindle Version), p. 54. Denis Lamoureux, *Evolutionary Creation*, p. 123.

This noun, RAKIAH, also has a verb form (similar to how many English nouns also have verb forms: for example, the noun *bath* has a verb form *to bathe*). Since the noun RAKIAH is used only for "the expanse," it makes sense to study how the verb form, RAKAH, is used. RAKAH means "to make an expanse."

The verb, unlike the noun, is used in a variety of ways with a variety of meanings. Kyle Greenwood uses some of those to support the idea that the expanse was viewed as a hard, thin dome overhead. After listing some instances where the verb is used in Scripture, he concludes, "So we see from these examples that the firmament [the expanse] was compared to hammered metal, like the tin roof on a home."[200] Here are the verses Greenwood uses: Exodus 39:3, where gold leaf is hammered out; Numbers 16:38, where bronze censers were being hammered out; and Jeremiah 10:9, where a craftsman hammers out silver for making an idol. From these three examples, Greenwood makes a pretty convincing case that the expanse was a hard, thin bowl-shaped dome.

But Greenwood forgets to tell us that the Hebrew verb has a wider range of meanings than that found in the verses he quotes. The basic meaning of the word is to apply pressure or force. For example, Ezekiel was told, "Clap your hands and *stamp* your foot [as a sign of God's anger] and say, Alas, because of all the evil abominations of the house of Israel" (Ezekiel 6:11; also see 25:6). David used the verb when he described a victory against his enemies: "I beat them fine as the dust of the earth; I crushed them and *stamped them down* like the mire of the street" (2 Samuel 22:43).

Therefore, when an author uses the verb RAKAH, "to beat out," he is focusing on the action of beating something out, not the result of the action, which is what Greenwood is thinking about. How thick or thin something becomes is not the point. That is determined by what is being beaten out. If it is gold, it may come out as a thin sheet. If it is the ground under one's foot, it will result in an indentation and some dust being moved. If it is one's enemies, they lie fallen on the battlefield.

God created an "expanse" to separate the waters below from the waters above. For that reason it had to be firm, with enough strength to keep the waters in place. Just because the expanse is not thin does not mean it didn't need the pressure—we might say the pressure of God's Word—to give it the firmness it needed.

What is interesting is that in this verse the verb RAKAH is not used for what God did in the heavens but on the earth. Since the discussion is about the heavens, we may miss this and assume that God is beating out the heavens. Yet we

---

[200] Kyle Greenwood, *Scripture and Cosmology*, p. 84

are told that God stretched out the heavens but "beat out" the earth so it had the firmness it needs to rest on the water and to support the beings that live there.[201]

Psalm 19:4,5

"Their voice goes out through all the earth, and their words to the end of the world. In them he has set a tent for the sun, which comes out like a bridegroom leaving his chamber, and, like a strong man, runs its course with joy."

In Psalm 19:4,5 David uses the symbol of a tent in a completely different way than Isaiah used it in the previous verse. Here the tent does not symbolize the expanse but something else. David wrote that in the heavens God has "set a tent for the sun, which comes out like a bridegroom leaving his chamber, and, like a strong man, runs its course with joy." Here David wants us to envision a bridegroom who has just enjoyed his wedding night. In the morning he emerges from his tent. He is filled with the freshness and joy of a new marriage. He enters this new day with a spirit of strength and confidence. Here the tent symbolizes the place on the horizon where the sun starts its day. Every day the sun emerges from its tent. Every day it runs its course like a strong runner who does not stop until he has reached the finish line.

If symbols reflected scientific beliefs about the makeup of the universe, for the sake of clarity we would expect the writers of Scripture to be fairly consistent in how they use a particular symbol. But they aren't. Isaiah uses the picture of pitching a tent to symbolize the creation of the expanse. David uses the picture of a tent to symbolize a place in the heavens where the sun emerges every morning with freshness and strength. But in both cases "tent" symbolizes realities we have already learned from Scripture: that the heavens are like a tent in which God dwells and that the sun continues without fail to mark the days and provide light for those who live on earth.

Psalm 104:1-5

"¹Bless the LORD, O my soul! O LORD my God, you are very great! You are clothed with splendor and majesty, ²covering yourself with light as with a garment, stretching out the heavens like a tent. ³He lays the beams of his chambers on the waters; he makes the clouds his chariot; he rides on the wings of the wind; ⁴he

---

[201] Only once in the Old Testament is the verb "to beat out" or "to create an expanse" (RAKAH) used in reference to the expanse itself. This takes place in the difficult verse, Job 37:18, which we examined previously. Otherwise, when the verb is used to describe God's creation of a part of the universe, it is used to describe God's creation of the earth, as it is in the verse we are looking at, Isaiah 42:5.

makes his messengers winds, his ministers a flaming fire. ⁵He set the earth on its foundations, so that it should never be moved."

Those who use the ANE argument have no objective criteria for determining when a symbol seemingly reflects ancient science and when it is simply a symbol of God's presence and power at work in this creation. It usually boils down to mentioning those passages that easily lend themselves to proving their point and ignoring the rest.

Sometimes a verse contains a symbol that obviously *does not* reflect a literal Hebrew scientific belief placed next to one that supposedly *does*. Consider the use of symbolic language in Psalm 104.

Psalm 104 praises the glory of God, the Creator. It uses the days of creation as its outline. In verse 1 the psalmist says, "You are clothed with splendor and majesty, covering yourself with light as with a garment, stretching out the heavens like a tent." The first part of the verse symbolizes God's splendor and majesty as clothing that he wears. The second part of the verse adds to God's wardrobe the light he created on the first day. This is pure symbolism.

On the second day, God created the heavens as we might pitch a tent. The fact that the first symbol does not reflect some scientific idea about God might caution us against reading ancient science into this verse. It can be understood as simply another symbol of God's power and majesty: God created the vast expanse of the heavens as his dwelling place.

The next verse is more complicated: "He lays the beams of his chambers on the waters; he makes the clouds his chariot; he rides on the wings of the wind" (verse 3). The "beams of his chambers" is used in the ANE argument to prove an ancient belief that God provided for himself a physical structure to live in. In illustrations of the three-tiered universe, this structure is located above the hard, thin dome of the heavens. But note that the following two phrases are symbolic. The clouds are his chariot. He rides the wind. So we have three symbols linked together in a single verse. It is arbitrary to say that one of them, "the beams," refers to a literal structure God made for himself but that the other two are symbols of God's power that do not reflect an ancient Hebrew belief.

Verses 4 and 5 also combine pure symbolism with what theistic evolutionists think reflects a Hebrew belief about the structure of the world. In verse 4 David writes, "He makes his messengers winds, his ministers a flaming fire." God's angels are symbolized in two ways. They are as fast as the wind, and they do their work with the brilliance and force of flaming fire. No one will say that this reflects an ancient idea that angels are made up of wind and fire. But in the next verse, David says that God "set the earth on its foundations, so that it should never be moved." This verse is regularly used by theistic evolutionists to prove

The Symbols of Scripture

that the Hebrews believed that somewhere under the earth there are physical structures designed to keep the earth in place. But might not "foundations" under the earth serve the same purpose as wind and fire do as descriptions of God's angels? Might not these foundations symbolize God's power to keep the earth where he wants it, just as wind and fire are used to symbolize the power of angels?

So we go back and forth from pure symbolism to symbols that supposedly reflect what the Hebrews believed were physical parts of the universe. Theistic evolutionists characteristically gather all the passages that *might* take on a literal meaning, and then piece by piece assemble them into the ancient Hebrew science of the universe. But they neglect nearby verses that can only be interpreted symbolically. If they did include those passages in their list, their list would result in an inconsistent mix.

Symbols that supposedly reflect ancient scientific beliefs about the structures in the heavens

In this section we will look at symbols that supposedly refer to various objects or structures in the universe, which theistic evolutionists use to create an ancient Hebrew scientific view of the universe. Do these symbols force us to conclude that the Hebrews believed that certain physical objects or structures really existed? Or did the Hebrews understand these to be symbols of what they knew about God?

"Windows of heaven"

According to theistic evolutionists, the ancients believed that God created various structures in the heavens. One of these structures is "windows." When God wants it to rain on the earth, he opens a window in the thin dome and allows some of the water above the dome to fall to the earth. Greenwood writes, "The ancient Israelites believed that above the firmament were heavenly reservoirs where precipitation was stored for the proper time."[202] Referring to passages that speak about the windows of heaven, Greenwood says, "Moreover, if we read these passages in light of their Near Eastern context, it is clear that these are the slits in the firmament by which precipitation exited the upper heaven."[203]

Here is the question: Did the ancient Hebrews believe that God created literal windows in the heavens so the waters above could exit and fall to the earth? The short answer is no; they didn't. The narrative of God separating the waters on the second day of creation would be their reality and what they meant by "windows

---

[202] Kyle Greenwood, *Scripture and Cosmology*, p. 96.
[203] Kyle Greenwood, *Scripture and Cosmology*, p. 96.

of heaven" would be conditioned by that reality, not by ideas gleaned from the literature of their neighbors

The Israelites understood the basics of the water cycle. If God created windows through which some of the upper water could permanently rejoin the waters on earth, the sea would, in fact, eventually be "full." But it wasn't. Solomon said what everyone knew: "All streams run to the sea, but the sea is not full; to the place where the streams flow, there they flow again" (Ecclesiastes 1:7).

How is the phrase "windows of heaven" used in the Bible? The phrase is first used when God flooded the world: "On that day all the fountains of the great deep burst forth, and the windows of the heavens were opened. And rain fell upon the earth forty days and forty nights" (Genesis 7:11,12). The idea that the expanse is a thin dome makes it easy to picture God opening slits in the dome and using the water above the firmament to flood the earth. But if "the heavens" was viewed as the expanse in which the clouds are located, it is just as easy to interpret the "windows of heaven" as a symbol for God sending down rain from the clouds, which, of course, hold some of the water located below the expanse.

The Hebrews knew rain came from clouds. Psalm 18:11 says, "He made darkness his covering, his canopy around him, thick clouds dark with water." At the time of the flood, God could certainly have prepared the clouds to hold enough water to accomplish his purpose. But most important is the fact that the expanse was created to keep the upper and lower waters separated. We learn this from Genesis 1. This should direct our interpretation of Genesis 7:11,12.

The phrase is used a second time in the Old Testament account of a siege of Samaria. There was no food at all in the city. Elisha, however, promised that by the end of the next day food would be dirt cheap. The king of Israel's servant objected: "If the LORD himself should make windows in heaven, could this thing be?" (2 Kings 7:2). If we consider the context, the servant was not asking for rain because rain would not have helped the people. What the Israelites needed was mature grain. In this context, opening the windows of heaven could only be a symbol of God in heaven blessing the people with what they needed at that moment and what they would, in fact, receive *by the end of the next day.*

The NIV paraphrases the sentence like this: "Look, even if the LORD should open the floodgates of the heavens, could this happen?" This conjures up the idea of God using openings that are already in place, that is, the windows already in the dome of the expanse. And the translation "floodgates" instead of "windows" leads the reader to think of water and not grain as the blessing God would give the people. The ESV's more literal translation better reflects the Hebrew: "If the Lord himself should *make windows* in heaven." The servant did not say what would come through those windows, and he was saying that such windows did not exist. They would have to be created.

We find "windows of heaven" in Isaiah 24:18-20:

> He who flees at the sound of the terror shall fall into the pit, and he who climbs out of the pit shall be caught in the snare. For the windows of heaven are opened, and the foundations of the earth tremble. The earth is utterly broken, the earth is split apart, the earth is violently shaken. The earth staggers like a drunken man; it sways like a hut; its transgression lies heavy upon it, and it falls, and will not rise again."

A reading of the whole chapter will confirm that Isaiah is describing God's final judgment on the world. The phrase "the windows of heaven" is set in a group of symbols based on the flood. Note the above comments on Genesis 7:11,12. Considering the purpose of the expanse, to keep the upper and lower waters separate, it makes sense to think of God's judgment as a deluge of rain from the clouds of heaven, picturing the horror and complete destruction of the last days.

"Windows of heaven" is used in Malachi 3:10. The Jewish people had been withholding their tithes from the Lord, and the Lord had withheld blessings from them. God urged them to give their offerings to him: "And thereby put me to the test, says the LORD of hosts, if I will not open the windows of heaven for you and pour down for you a blessing until there is no more need" (Malachi 3:10). Here the reference is not just to rainfall, although that may have been one of the blessings God had in mind, but to the whole range of blessings that God would give his people. The NIV again translates "floodgates of heaven," which leads the reader to think only of water. But the ESV's more literal "windows of heaven" leads us to think of the wide range of blessings God would pour out to replace what he had withheld from them.

A similar symbol is used to describe the source of manna, the food Israel ate in the desert. "Yet he commanded the skies [or 'clouds'] above and opened the *doors of heaven*, and he rained down on them manna to eat and gave them the grain of heaven" (Psalm 78:23,24). Note the change in symbolism from "windows" to "doors." Do "doors" reflect another Hebrew belief that there were doors in heaven through which God pours down food? Or is it better to interpret "doors of heaven," "grain of heaven," and "the skies above" as symbols of how God (who dwells in the heavens) miraculously provided food for his people in the desert?

We can get some insight from another symbol God used to describe his power to send rain on the earth. He rebuked Job: "Who can number the clouds by wisdom? Or who can tilt the water skins of the heavens?" (Job 38:37). When God caused rain to fall from the clouds—and every Jewish person knew that rain came from the clouds—he was figuratively tilting the water skins of the heavens. If the ancients believed in literal "windows" in heaven through which the water came, one could argue that they also believed in literal water skins in the heavens where God stored rainwater. If the tilting of "the water skins of the heaven" symbolizes God opening the clouds and letting rain come down, then why not consider his opening "the windows of heaven" to symbolize the same thing?

Considering the wide range of things that come out of the "windows of heaven" and considering the parallel expression "water skins of the heavens" to which no one would assign an ancient scientific view, it is clear that God's people would understand these expressions as symbols of God, who lives in the heavens, graciously providing for their needs.[204]

"The storehouses of heaven"

Scripture refers to storehouses in which God keeps various things before he chooses to use them. The Hebrew word translated "storehouses" is the place where a king would store his nation's riches or where food was stored. The word can also refer to the treasures themselves.

God has storehouses of his own. Moses promised that if the Israelites lived as his obedient children, "The LORD will open to you his good treasury, the heavens, to give the rain to your land in its season and to bless all the work of your hands" (Deuteronomy 28:12). Notice that Moses did not say that God has storehouses or treasuries "in" heaven but that "the heavens" itself is his "good treasury." And not just rain would come down, but the power of God's will to bless them.

A number of things can be found in God's storehouses. Jeremiah praised God's power: "He makes lightning for the rain, and he brings forth the wind from his storehouses" (Jeremiah 10:13). Yet the Israelites knew that thunder and lightning accompanied rain and originated in the same place: "The clouds poured out water; the skies gave forth thunder; your arrows flashed on every side" (Psalm 77:17). In his challenge to Job, God said: "Have you entered the storehouses of the snow, or have you seen the storehouses of the hail?" (Job 38:22). Storehouses for snow and hail might possibly be viewed in literal terms, but storehouses for wind in Jeremiah 10:13 can only be interpreted as a pure symbol of God's ability to stir up the atmosphere whenever he wishes. That being the case, it is more reasonable to interpret the storehouses of lightening, snow, and hail also as symbols of God's power to send these powerful forces on the earth whenever he wishes.

But the storehouses of God are not only found in the heavens. The psalmist said, "He gathers the waters of the sea as a heap; he puts the deeps in storehouses"

---

[204]See Verne Poythress, *Redeeming Science,* p. 95. When Poythress discusses "the windows of heaven," he refuses to read into them any ancient scientific belief about the structure of the universe. It was refreshing to read his comments.

The Symbols of Scripture

(Psalm 33:7). The "sea" (a synonym of "the deep") is the name God gave to the waters under the expanse, which God separated from the dry land on the third day of creation. So the water in the sea is said to be guarded in storehouses, kept by God's power in the place where he put them on the second day of creation.

There are also storehouses for God's knowledge. Moses warned the Israelites about what would happen if they rejected him. He noted the root of Israel's wickedness, the evil fruits that result, and the bitterness they would experience:

> For their vine comes from the vine of Sodom and from the fields of Gomorrah; their grapes are grapes of poison; their clusters are bitter; their wine is the poison of serpents and the cruel venom of asps.... Is not this... *laid up in store with me, sealed up in my treasuries*? Vengeance is mine, and recompense, for the time when their foot shall slip; for the day of their calamity is at hand, and their doom comes swiftly." (Deuteronomy 32:32-35)

God's record of the evil his people have committed and the knowledge of how he could punish them are stored up in his "treasuries," clearly a symbol for the knowledge that God keeps in store for the right time to act on it.

It is clear from Scripture that the Hebrews did not think that God's treasures were stored in physical rooms located somewhere in the universe. Rather, the word "storehouses" is a symbol for wherever God sets aside things for his own use, whether in the heavens, in the seas, or in his own mind.[205]

"God sits enthroned"

In order to link Scripture with what ANE literature is supposed to teach, theistic evolutionists try to locate God's throne in the scheme of the various levels of heaven, which are separated by pavements of various kinds of stones. In Exodus the elders of Israel accompanied Moses up Mount Sinai to see the Lord. There "they saw the God of Israel. There was under his feet as it were a pavement of sapphire stone, like the very heaven for clearness" (Exodus 24:10). Ezekiel was given a similar vision of the glory of the Lord: "And above the expanse over their heads there was the likeness of a throne, in appearance like sapphire; and

---

[205] Also note the alternative symbolism in Job 38:29 about the source of ice and frost: "From whose womb did the ice come forth, and who has given birth to the frost of heaven?" Also note Amos 9:5,6, where the symbol of God's upper chambers is located in a verse that contains a variety of symbols: "The Lord GOD of hosts, he who touches the earth and it melts, and all who dwell in it mourn, and all of it rises like the Nile, and sinks again, like the Nile of Egypt; who builds his upper chambers in the heavens and founds his vault upon the earth; who calls for the waters of the sea and pours them out upon the surface of the earth—the LORD is his name." The translations differ greatly on verse 6, another example of a difficult passage that ought not—indeed, cannot—be used as proof of some Hebrew cosmological belief.

seated above the likeness of a throne was a likeness with a human appearance" (Ezekiel 1:26).

Scripture makes it clear that in both these passages Ezekiel was seeing symbols. Under the Lord's feet was "as it were" a pavement of sapphire stones. Ezekiel saw the "likeness" of a throne, "in appearance like" sapphire, and above the throne was a "likeness" of a human being. Even though Ezekiel told his readers that he was seeing a vision (Ezekiel 8:4), those who press the ANE argument still want this to reflect the ancient Hebrew belief that God sat on a physical throne in a specific place in the universe. In the process, the rich meaning of God's sitting as king over all things is lost.

The NIV's and ESV's usual translation "sit enthroned" is legitimate, but it entails a bit of interpretation. But in Psalm 2:4, the ESV alters its pattern. It translates "He who *sits* in the heavens laughs," while the NIV translates "The One *enthroned* in heaven laughs." The ESV is more literal. When Scripture wants to say that someone sits enthroned, it simply uses the word "sit." It's the context that tells us what position of leadership that person holds—judge, king, or the Lord of all.

So where does God "sit"? In Scripture God is not pictured as sitting in a particular location. Rather, he sits wherever he wants to display his glory. The psalmist wrote, "The LORD *sits enthroned over the flood*; the LORD sits enthroned as king forever" (Psalm 29:10). The word "flood" is found only here and in Genesis 6-11 in reference to the flood in Noah's time. The psalmist is saying that God sat as king over the floodwaters when he judged the world.

The Lord sits enthroned in the heavens—in the expanse he created on the second day—where he can see all the powerful people who mock and reject him: "He who *sits [enthroned] in the heavens* laughs; the Lord holds them in derision" (Psalm 2:4). In Psalm 11:4 we are told that God rules from heaven, where he sees and examines all people: "The LORD is in his holy temple; *the LORD's throne is in heaven*; his eyes see, his eyelids test the children of man" (Psalm 11:4). Note that the heavens is pictured as the temple of the Lord.

God, who sits enthroned as king over all, will answer the prayers of the righteous. The psalmist writes, "Evening, morning and noon I cry out in distress, and he hears my voice. He rescues me unharmed from the battle waged against me, even though many oppose me. God, who *is enthroned from of old*, who does not change—he will hear them and humble them, because they have no fear of God" (Psalm 55:17-19 NIV84). The symbol "enthroned from of old" symbolizes God's eternal power and his knowledge of everything that happens. On that basis the psalmist continues with the encouragement: "Cast your cares on the LORD and he will sustain you; he will never let the righteous fall" (Psalm 55:17-22 NIV84).

Once when the Israelites were in trouble, they tried to use the ark of the covenant as a good luck charm. Why? Because that's where God was sitting enthroned among them: "So the people sent to Shiloh and brought from there the ark of the covenant of the LORD of hosts, who is *enthroned on the cherubim*" (1 Samuel 4:4).[206] God was pictured as sitting in a position of power in the special place where he chose to reveal himself to his people Israel. From that place God would put his power on display and call people from all over the world to honor him and to live in his love. Later, when the Philistines, Israel's enemies, captured the ark, they discovered firsthand the power of Israel's God, who was sitting between the cherubim of the ark.

In some passages God's throne *cannot* be considered a physical structure. The psalmist wrote, "Yet you are holy, *enthroned on the praises of Israel*" (Psalm 22:3).[207] When the people of the world see God's people praising him, they will be inspired to bow down before him, if not now then on the Last Day.

In Psalm 89 the psalmist wrote, "Righteousness and justice are the foundation of your throne" (Psalm 89:14; 97:2). For God's people, the most important throne is the throne of David. God promised David that he would "establish the throne of his kingdom forever" (2 Samuel 7:13). That, of course, is the throne on which David's greater son, Jesus, would sit: "Of the increase of his government and of peace there will be no end, on the throne of David and over his kingdom, to establish it and to uphold it with justice and with righteousness from this time forth and forevermore" (Isaiah 9:7; also see Ezekiel 43:7).

Summary of how Scripture describes the heavens

God created the heavens on the second day of creation to separate the upper and lower waters. The creation of the heavens is symbolized by God stretching out a tent in which he lives and from where he blesses his creatures on the earth below. Although God lives in the heavens, he is outside the whole universe and is larger than it. He also dwells in a variety of places within his creation, where he

---

[206] In the Hebrew the phrase literally reads, "sits the cherubim." It does not contain the word *between* or *on*. So it is up to the translator to decide. In the tabernacle God chose to sit in the Most Holy Place in a position above the ark and between the cherubim, whose wings were spread over the ark. So the translation "between" the cherubim rather than "on" the cherubim is to be preferred. That keeps our focus on the tabernacle, where God lived among his people Israel.

[207] Here again, we must be careful of the translation. The Hebrew simply says, "sitting the praises of Israel" similar to "sitting the cherubim." Translators must pick a word that shows the relationship between God's sitting and the praises of his people. The ESV uses the word "on," which works but still leads us to ask how God can sit on something intangible like people's praises. But we understand the point. The NIV translation departs from the point that God is enthroned on the praises of Israel, "Yet you are enthroned as the Holy One; you are the praise of Israel" (Psalm 22:3 NIV84).

blesses his creation and his people. The windows of heaven symbolize the source of his many blessings and the judgments that God pours out on the world. The storehouses of heaven symbolize the places where God stores up what he uses to bless us. God sits enthroned as king, but his throne is not a physical throne like that on which the kings of the world sit. For example, righteousness is the foundation of his throne; he sits enthroned on the praises of people who have experienced his righteousness.

We have examined several difficult passages whose details might fit nicely into a modern diagram of the ancient's view of the universe but whose interpretation is uncertain. We have examined symbols that in some passages might refer to a physical part of the universe but in other passages cannot. We have seen the lack of strict uniformity in the use of symbols.

Symbols of the heavens describe the universe in terms that neither contradict nor add additional structures to the simple expanse God created on the second day. They are symbols of God's glory and power in action.

Symbols that picture the earth

On the third day, God caused dry land to appear from out of the waters below the expanse. Moses wrote, "Let the waters under the heavens be gathered together into one place, and let the dry land appear." And it was so. God called the dry land Earth, and the waters that were gathered together he called Seas" (Genesis 1:9,10). This is the extent of what the creation account reveals about the earth.

On the basis of the symbols used in Scripture, it is claimed that the Hebrews believed that God created literal foundations for the earth (and for the heavens) and that the surface of the land was flat and circular in shape.

The earth (and the heavens) have "foundations"

When we read about the creation of the expanse and the dry land in Genesis 1, we might ask (1) What is keeping the expanse in place above the earth? (2) What is keeping the earth from sinking back below the water, and (3) What is keeping the water from encroaching on the earth?

Scripture says that heaven is supported over the earth below it and that the earth is supported upon the waters below it. As means for support, Scripture speaks of "foundations" and "pillars." The question is, how do the Scriptures intend those terms to be understood? Are they purely symbolical or do they reflect an ancient belief that there were literal support structures under the heavens and under the earth?

In describing God's creation of the earth, Scripture says that God "founded" (יסד) and "established" (כון) it. In Psalm 24:2 David uses both of those terms: "The earth is the LORD's and the fullness thereof, the world and those who dwell therein, for he has *founded* it upon the seas and *established* it upon the rivers" (Psalm 24:1,2). In Psalm 89 the psalmist Ethan uses "founded" in reference to the creation of both the heavens and the earth: "The heavens are yours, and yours also the earth; you *founded* the world and all that is in it" (Psalm 89:11 NIV84).

Scripture uses the word "founded" (יסד) in a number of other contexts. It can refer to the founding of a country (Exodus 9:18); of choosing men for an office, and then "establishing" them in that office (1 Chronicles 9:22); and of "establishing" a proclamation as a king might do (Esther 1:8). When the topic is building a city or putting up a building, the simple term "founding" is sometimes translated "lay foundations." The idea conveyed by that translation is that people first laid foundation stones and then build the city on them. But it does not have to mean that. It can simply refer to choosing a location for a city and then building one there.

English translations are not consistent in how they translate the word "foundation." Some give a simple translation while others add some information to make it easier for the reader to picture the thought. A verse often used by theistic evolutionists to prove that the ancients believed in literal foundations under the earth is God's challenge to Job in Job 38:4: "Where were you when I laid the foundation of the earth? Tell me, if you have understanding." However, the Hebrew simply says, "Where were you in my founding of earth?" All the verse says is that God created the world; he set it in place. The idea of the earth having foundations as we think of them is not found in the text.

Consider how Psalm 24:2 is translated. The psalmist uses the word "founded" (יסד). The ESV and most translations of Psalm 24:2 simply read: "He founded it upon the seas." This is a neutral picture of God creating the earth and situating it on the seas. Compare that with the New Living Translation: "For he *laid the earth's foundation* on the seas and built it on the ocean depths." That translation presents a different picture. The NLT leads us to envision some kind of foundational structure under the earth.

However, a few verses do contain a separate word for "foundations." Psalm 104 describes the glory of God with reference to the six-day creation of the world. In verse 5 the psalmist writes, "He set the earth [or, "founded the earth" (יסד)] *on its foundations*, so that it should never be moved." That might be a legitimate translation, in which case we are led to think of a physical foundation on which the earth rests. However, the word used in Psalm 104:5 (מָכוֹן) does not necessarily refer to physical foundation stones. Its basic meaning is "a place" where something is located. It is most often used in reference to God's "dwelling *place*." It

181

can also refer to the basis on which something rests: "Righteousness and justice are the *foundation* of your throne" (Psalm 89:14).

In Psalm 104:5, it makes good sense to keep the basic meaning of the word and translate like this: "He set the earth upon its *place*, so that it should never be moved." The emphasis, then, is not on God setting down foundation stones on which the earth rests. The verse is simply saying that God established the earth in the place where he wanted it to be. He gave the world a permanent place to exist and made it immovable.

Nevertheless, in certain places it is correct to say that God "laid the foundations." The normal Hebrew word for "foundations" (מוֹסָד) is often joined with parts of the physical universe in two-word phrases. It is joined with "earth" five times: "the foundations of the earth" (מוֹסְדֵי אֶרֶץ); twice with "mountains": "the foundations of the mountains" (הָרִים מוֹסְדֵי); and once with "heavens": "the foundations of the heavens" (מוֹסְדוֹת הַשָּׁמַיִם). Might these passages reflect a "scientific" belief that there are literal foundations under the earth, mountains, and heavens?

First, note that all these verses are found in symbolical settings. That doesn't prove that they do not reflect something that literally exists. It only shows that they do not appear in contexts where they must refer to something that literally exists. Through Jeremiah the Lord assured Israel that although he would punish them, he would never forsake them: "Thus says the LORD: 'If the heavens above can be measured, and the foundations of the earth below can be explored, then I will cast off all the offspring of Israel for all that they have done,' declares the LORD" (Jeremiah 31:27). Micah called on the mountains and foundations of the earth to be witnesses to his accusations against Israel: "Hear, you mountains, the indictment of the LORD, and you enduring foundations of the earth, for the LORD has an indictment against his people, and he will contend with Israel" (Micah 6:2; see also Deuteronomy 32:22).

Some of the passages in question are found in even more highly symbolical sections of Scripture. The turmoil of God's anger over unbelief and the oppression of his people are sometimes symbolized by turmoil in creation. In Psalm 82:5 the Lord expresses his anger over the turmoil wicked rulers have caused among his people. The problems they caused God's people are symbolized in physical terms: "All the foundations of the earth are shaken" (Psalm 82:5). The opposite is also true. When God's people are blessed, the earth is stable. In her song of praise to the Lord for God's gift of a son, Samuel's mother, Hannah, said, "He raises up the poor from the dust; he lifts the needy from the ash heap to make them sit with princes and inherit a seat of honor. For the pillars of the earth are the LORD's, and on them he has set the world" (1 Samuel 2:8).[208] These verses

---

[208] In this verse "pillars" is not the normal word Scripture uses. It can also be translated "foundations." In either case, the point is the same. (Passages that use the normal Hebrew word for

do not prove that the Hebrews did not believe in these physical structures. But neither do they prove that the Hebrews did believe in them.

Also note the symbolism of Job 38:4-8 where God pictures himself as a builder: "Where were you when I laid the foundation of the earth? Tell me, if you have understanding. Who determined its measurements—surely you know! Or who stretched the line upon it? On what were its bases sunk, or who laid its cornerstone?" (Job 38:4-6). If the reference to the foundations of the earth reveals an ancient scientific view of the world, did the Hebrews also believe that there is a literal cornerstone somewhere in those foundations or that God used a plumb line to square them up? These are legitimate questions. In describing a supposed Hebrew science of the universe, it is easy to include something like a foundation in that description, but it is not so easy to include a cornerstone in those foundations. This is another example of Scripture placing a pure symbol (a cornerstone) side by side with a symbol that *might* reflect an ancient scientific belief. If one symbol *might* be understood to reflect an ancient scientific belief, but the symbol next to it obviously *does not*, it seems logical to understand both of them in the same way.

In Proverbs 8:29 Solomon uses another picture to describe God's action in creating the sea: "He assigned to the sea its *limit*, so that the waters might not transgress his command, when he marked out the foundations of the earth." The important word is "limit." The Hebrew word for "limit" is often used to describe the Law of Moses, translated "statute" in the ESV and "decree" in the NIV. God set a *limit* for the sea; that is, he *made a decree or statute* that the sea should go only so far and no farther. This is pure symbolism for God's power to control the sea. God's marking out the foundations of the earth should be viewed in the same way, namely, as a symbol for God's decree that the earth must stay where he wants it.

"The earth cannot be moved"

It is said that the ancient Hebrews believed that the earth was immovable, firmly fixed in space. During the 16th and 17th centuries, the ancient earth-centered systems of Aristotle and Ptolemy were being challenged by the new philosophy of Copernicus and Galileo. Aristotle had taught that the earth was in a fixed position at the center of the universe. But it was becoming clear that the sun, not the earth, was at the center of the solar system.

Unfortunately, the Catholic Church had adopted the philosophy of Aristotle, and some in the Church were reluctant to abandon his earth-centered view. The

---

"pillar," for example, the two pillars in front of the temple, are Job 9:6, Job 26:11, and Psalm 75:3.)

Church had assembled a short list of Scripture passages, which, according to their interpretation, supported Aristotle's view.

Various passages in the Old Testament contain the Hebrew word for "move" (מוֹט) and use it in reference to the earth. "He set the earth on its foundations, so that it should never be moved" (Psalm 104:5). "The LORD reigns; he is robed in majesty; the LORD is robed; he has put on strength as his belt. Yes, the world is established; it shall never be moved" (Psalm 93:1). When David brought the ark of the covenant into Jerusalem, he wrote, "Tremble before him, all the earth; yes, the world is established; it shall never be moved" (1 Chronicles 16:30).

The problem in the 16th and 17th centuries stemmed from the mistaken idea that "move" (מוֹט) was referring to physical movement through space. The word does not have to mean that. It can refer to not being put to ruin or destroyed. A couple of the many passages that use the word in that sense will illustrate this: David wrote, "For the king trusts in the Lord, and through the steadfast love of the Most High he shall not be moved" (Psalm 21:7), and "Cast your burden on the LORD, and he will sustain you; he will never permit the righteous to be moved" (Psalm 55:22).

As mentioned earlier, in Scripture the moral and spiritual state of the world is symbolized by the physical world being in a state of upheaval or in a state of rest. When the wicked are sinning or when God is punishing sin, the world is said to be in a state of disorder. And when things are right with mankind and when God is pouring out his blessings, the world is said to be firmly established. In Psalm 82 Asaph prays: "Rescue the weak and the needy; deliver them from the hand of the wicked. They [the wicked] have neither knowledge nor understanding, they walk about in darkness; all the foundations of the earth are shaken" (verses 4,5).

In Psalm 93 and 96, we see the opposite. The permanence of God's reign and the perfection of his justice give the earth stability: "The LORD reigns; he is robed in majesty; the LORD is robed; he has put on strength as his belt. Yes, the world is established; it shall never be moved" (Psalm 93:1). "Worship the LORD in the splendor of holiness; tremble before him, all the earth! Say among the nations, 'The LORD reigns! Yes, the world is established; it shall never be moved; he will judge the peoples with equity'" (Psalm 96:9,10).

When Scripture speaks about the earth as immovable, it is not talking about physical movement through space. It is saying that the world is in upheaval whenever the wicked have their way and in a state of rest under God's care. And since God has the final word, the earth cannot be moved.

The Symbols of Scripture

"The landmass God created is circular"

There is nothing in Genesis 1 or in any other narrative in Scripture that says the landmass God created is circular (or even whether there is one landmass or several). However, there are three passages in the poetical books that might be interpreted to say that.

None of these passages is easy; all of them are open to various interpretations. We looked at Isaiah 40:22 in detail: "It is he who sits above the circle of the earth." There we noted two possible interpretations of "circle" depending on whether "earth" refers to the landmass God created on the third day or to the earth as a whole. If the latter, it is either a reference to the earth's circumference or to the earth as we see it, as bounded by the horizon.

The same is true for the other two passages. Each of them uses the Hebrew noun (חוג) that can be translated "circle." But it is not easy to be sure of what the word means.

In one of his speeches, Job describes God's power: "He stretches out the north over the void and hangs the earth on nothing. He binds up the waters in his thick clouds, and the cloud is not split open under them. He covers the face of the full moon and spreads over it his cloud. *He has inscribed a circle on the face of the waters at the boundary between light and darkness.* The pillars of heaven tremble and are astounded at his rebuke" (Job 26:7-11). What does Job mean by "a circle on the face of the waters"? Is he saying that the landmass God created is circular in shape? It is hard to imagine how a circular landmass surrounded by the sea can be at the boundary between light and darkness (literally "at the limits of light with darkness").

This results in a rather confusing set of ancient scientific ideas. If the ancients viewed the earth as a flat disk over which God placed the "dome" of the heavens, they would have believed that the sun, moon, and stars enter and leave the dome in the morning and evening. This would have been the boundary between light and darkness. If so, the landmass would have to extend all the way out to the edge of the dome in order for it to be at the boundary between light and darkness. This, of course, makes no sense if the Hebrews believed the land was surrounded by water, which we will look at below. In that case, the sea—and not the land—would be at the boundary between light and darkness. It makes more sense for Job to be thinking of the horizon, where he saw the sun rise and set. If so, it is the horizon that is circular, not the land.[209]

---

[209] This section from Job contains another difficult passage that deserves a brief comment: "He stretches out the north over the void and hangs the earth on nothing" (Job 26:7). What Job meant by "the north" and God's hanging "the earth on nothing" is difficult to say. The verse has been interpreted and translated in several ways. One thing is clear, however. Job is giving God the credit for doing this. The earth is not simply floating free in a void that contains nothing. God is

In the book of Proverbs, Wisdom is speaking about the creation of the sea and the dry land. Wisdom says,

> Before the mountains had been shaped, before the hills, I was brought forth, before he had made the earth with its fields, or the first of the dust of the world. When he established the heavens, I was there; *when he drew a circle on the face of the deep,* when he made firm the skies above, when he established the fountains of the deep, when he assigned to the sea its limit, so that the waters might not transgress his command, when he marked out the foundations of the earth. (Proverbs 8:25-29)

These verses refer to God's creation of the expanse on day two and to his creation of the sea and dry land on day three. This verse might refer to the original shape of the landmass God created on the third day. However, the immediate context of the phrase "drew a circle on the face of the deep" is the creation of the expanse and the separation of upper and lower waters on day two. In Genesis 1:3, we are told that the earth was "without form and void" and that "darkness was over the face of the *deep*." The Hebrew word for "deep" (תְהוֹם) refers to the earth itself, which in the beginning was void and without form. In Proverbs 8 Solomon says that God "drew a circle on the face of the deep" (תְהוֹם). In the context of the creation of the expanse on day two, the word "deep" must refer to the original "deep" that was in existence at the beginning and not to the lower waters out of which God created the dry land on day four. Therefore, God's drawing a circle refers to something he did when he began giving order to the original deep, not to something he did on the fourth day when he marked out the foundations of the earth that had emerged out of the waters below the expanse.

None of these verses say that God created a circular landmass.

"The earth has four corners"

Scripture also speaks about the four corners of the earth: "He will raise a signal for the nations and will assemble the banished of Israel, and gather the dispersed of Judah from the four corners of the earth" (Isaiah 11:12; also Ezekiel 7:12; Revelation 7:1; 20:8). For the sake of consistency, it should be argued that the expression "four corners of the earth" reflects an ancient belief that the earth is square. My impression is that even those who use the ANE argument take this phrase in a symbolical sense: the earth's farthest locations. We will return to this point when we look at the phrase "the ends of the earth."

---

present in that void. He is holding the cord, so to speak, that keeps the earth hanging on nothing that might be viewed as a physical support.

"The earth is surrounded by a cosmic sea"

Scripture clearly says that the dry land appeared out of the sea. Therefore, according to Scripture, water did surround the dry land. But calling this sea a "cosmic sea" creates a nice effect. Reference to a "cosmic sea" instead of merely a "sea" creates a sense of mystery. We imagine an ancient people, living in a world filled with many mysteries, reading sacred myths that told about the men who dared to travel to the ends of the earth, where they saw a "cosmic" sea that seemed to go out in all directions. The phrase "cosmic sea," when applied to Genesis 1, gives it the aura of myth and strips it of its claim to be a literal account of how God created the world.

"The earth has ends, proving it is flat"

In ANE resources, the ends of the earth are located on the shore of the cosmic sea. But how does Scripture use "the ends of the earth"?

In times of trouble, King David considered himself far removed from God's presence among his people in Jerusalem. But no matter how far from home he was, David knew he could pray to the Lord: "Hear my cry, O God, listen to my prayer; *from the end of the earth* I call to you when my heart is faint" (Psalm 61:1,2).

God called Abraham out of a place well known in the ancient world, Ur of the Chaldees. Isaiah describes God's call of Abraham and his descendants like this: "But you, Israel, my servant, Jacob, whom I have chosen, the offspring of Abraham, my friend; you whom I took *from the ends of the earth*, and called from its farthest corners, saying to you, 'You are my servant, I have chosen you and not cast you off'" (Isaiah 41:8,9). The earth extended far beyond Ur, but it was a long way off—symbolized by the phrase "ends of the earth."

Jesus himself used the term: "The queen of the South will rise up at the judgment with this generation and condemn it, for she came *from the ends of the earth* to hear the wisdom of Solomon, and behold, something greater than Solomon is here" (Matthew 12:42).

Isaiah describes God gathering the Medes to overthrow the Babylonians: "The sound of a tumult is on the mountains as of a great multitude! The sound of an uproar of kingdoms, of nations gathering together! The LORD of hosts is mustering a host for battle. They come *from a distant land, from the end of the heavens*, the LORD and the weapons of his indignation, to destroy the whole land" (Isaiah 13:4,5; see verse 17). The nations God summons come from "the end of the heavens." If the earth is literally surrounded by a cosmic sea with the dome of the heavens extending to its very limits, as the Hebrews supposedly believed, it makes little sense to speak of people coming from the "end of the heavens."

The same can be said about Moses' use of the phrase "end of heaven." He told the Israelites to find out whether the gods of the other nations had blessed their people as God had blessed Israel: "For ask now of the days that are past, which were before you, since the day that God created man on the earth, and ask from one end of heaven to the other, whether such a great thing as this has ever happened or was ever heard of" (Deuteronomy 4:32). Here we see the pure symbolical nature of this statement, coupled with the language of observation. If the earth was a flat disk surrounded by a cosmic sea, covered with a dome called heaven, then the people living at the "end of heaven" would refer to people living in the cosmic sea.

The phrases "ends of the earth" and "end of the heavens" symbolize either places far away from Israel or the full extent of the populated world. To claim that these phrases reflect some ancient cosmological belief is to overlook how they are actually used in Scripture and even to create contradictory ideas.

"The earth is flat"

There is no place in Scripture that says the earth is flat.

Theistic evolutionists, however, claim to find hints in Scripture that the Hebrews believed the earth was flat. One example is found in the account of King Nebuchadnezzar's dream in Daniel 4. The king had a dream in which he saw a tree. He told the dream to Daniel: "The visions of my head as I lay in bed were these: I saw, and behold, a tree in the midst of the earth, and its height was great. The tree grew and became strong, and its top reached to heaven, and it was visible to the end of the whole earth" (Daniel 4:10,11). Kyle Greenwood writes, "One option [to interpret the vision] was that the earth was considered flat. No matter how tall a structure may be, for it to be visible across the earth, the earth must not have a convex surface. . . . A second option is that all the inhabitants of a spherical earth dwell in a relatively small landmass in the vicinity of Babylon."[210] Greenwood opts for the first option and says that since Daniel didn't correct the king when he reported his dream and then explain to the king that the world was a sphere, Daniel also believed that the earth was flat.

This is wooden analysis. Anyone who can imagine Daniel correcting the king for his faulty cosmology has a better imagination than I have. This was a dream, and dreams don't necessarily reflect reality. The king was reporting what he actually saw in his dream. Even if Nebuchadnezzar had had a modern globe in his office, he still would have reported his dream as he saw it. The dream made

---

[210] Kyle Greenwood, *Scripture and Cosmology*, p. 75.

the point God wanted Nebuchadnezzar to learn. Nebuchadnezzar had been given power over the entire world. But he had put himself on a level equal with the God of heaven, and he claimed authority over the entire world, which only God has. God would soon humble him.

That is a relatively innocent example. But this approach to Scripture can become dangerous. Consider how theistic evolutionists handle two statements involving Jesus. One is Matthew 4:8: "The devil took him to a very high mountain and showed him all the kingdoms of the world and their glory." According to Greenwood, this passage "depicts the entire populated world as an observable plane, when viewed from the heights."[211] Revelation 1:7 is supposed to reflect the same idea: "Behold, he is coming with the clouds, and every eye will see him, even those who pierced him" (Revelation 1:7). According to Greenwood, Jesus' ability to reveal himself to all people throughout the world at his second coming also depends on the earth being flat.

So either Satan had a faulty cosmology or Matthew was making up the words Satan spoke to Jesus. And either Jesus was mistaken about the shape of the earth or someone else must have authored Revelation and stated his own faulty view of the world. Some might say that Matthew and Jesus were merely accommodating themselves to how the people of their day thought about the world. But that idea makes the matter worse. If Satan could tempt Jesus as he did only if the earth were flat, then he could not have tempted the Son of God as he did. And if all people will be able to see Jesus on the Last Day only if they are standing on the same flat plane, our knowledge that the earth is round will force us to deny that all people will see Jesus when he returns.

Greenwood's interpretation denies the miraculous. Satan could certainly show Jesus things in a vision beyond what Jesus could see with his human eyes. And Jesus certainly can make himself visible on the Last Day to *all people* living on a spherical earth as he says he will.

Greenwood also seems to ignore the fact that people in Matthew's and John's day had been exposed to Greek philosophy for several decades, and both Aristotle and Ptolemy taught that the earth was a sphere. These men were well known throughout the world, which by Jesus' time had become thoroughly acquainted with Greek culture.[212]

---

[211] Kyle Greenwood, *Scripture and Cosmology,* p. 136.

[212] The Greek philosopher Pythagoras (ca. 569-475 B.C.) taught that the earth was a sphere. He was followed by Plato (427-347 B.C.) and Aristotle (384-322 B.C.). Aristotle based his teaching on the shape of the earth largely on philosophical grounds. But he also based it on observation. He noted that when the earth comes between the moon and the sun, it causes a circular shadow to fall on the moon. Aristotle observed that "there are stars seen in Egypt and ... Cyprus which are not seen in the northerly regions" and that the circumference of the earth was "of no great size, for otherwise the effect of so slight a change of place would not be quickly apparent." He also

Denis Lamoureux sees an erroneous ancient Near Eastern cosmology in Philippians 2:9,10: "Therefore God has highly exalted him and bestowed on him the name that is above every name, so that at the name of Jesus every knee should bow, in heaven and on earth and under the earth." According to Lamoureux, in this verse Paul was teaching a three-tiered universe. Indeed, Paul was. But he was simply speaking about the universe in same terms that we use today: the heavens above us, the earth around us, and what lies under the earth. Those who use the ANE argument have so bloated the simple concept of a three-tiered universe with a variety of objects and structures that for Paul to speak of things in heaven, on the earth, and under the earth as he does in Philippians 2 must mean that he believed in all these objects and structures. In fact, Paul's simple words can be accused of reflecting bad science only because Lamoureux and others have turned his words into bad science.

Lamoureux, too, completely ignores the history of science. He says that "the inspired ancient authors believed the earth was flat"[213] As noted above, a spherical earth had been proposed already in the 6th century B.C. and in Paul's day the theory had the weight of Aristotle (384–322 B.C.) behind it. Perhaps not everyone was aware of the Greek science of the day, but it would be hard to argue that Paul, a highly educated man whom we know had read the Greek poets, was ignorant of the basics of Aristotle's philosophy of the universe.[214]

Symbols that picture what is under the earth

ANE literature, and that includes the later writing of nations like Greece and Rome, describes the underworld in great detail. The various belief systems picture a realm inhabited by a selection of gods. These systems support the natural belief that the morally good are rewarded for their deeds and the morally bad are punished.

What Scripture says about this area bears little relation to the beliefs of other ancient Near Eastern nations. The Hebrews knew a little about what lay under their feet. Job describes mining activity: "Man puts his hand to the flinty rock

---

thought that the stars were much larger than the earth.

Another Greek, Erastothenes (276–194 B.C.) calculated the circumference of the earth to within 15 percent of what we know it to be. He accurately measured the tilt of the earth's axis. Aristarchus of Samos (310–230 B.C.) proposed that the sun was at the center of the solar system and that it rotated on its axis. His views were largely forgotten in view of Aristotle's greater popularity. Aristotle was Alexander the Great's personal tutor. Alexander conquered much of the known world, and Greek learning and culture spread in his wake. To say that Paul, a man of the greatest learning, still thought in terms of a flat earth flies in the face of history, not to mention the inspiration of Scripture.

[213] Denis Lamoureux, *Evolutionary Creation*, p. 107.

[214] See Acts 17:28, where Paul quotes a Greek poet.

The Symbols of Scripture

and overturns mountains by the roots. He cuts out channels in the rocks, and his eye sees every precious thing. He dams up the streams so that they do not trickle, and the thing that is hidden he brings out to light" (Job 28:9-11).

But regarding the dead, Scripture simply says that they go to "Sheol." Scripture does not describe Sheol in terms of an elaborate underworld where people can expect good or bad depending on how they lived on earth. Nor is it a place of purification or a place where the dead are turned over to the care of the gods who rule there. It is simply the place where people go when they die. We depend on the rest of Scripture for more details.[215]

Scripture uses various symbols to describe Sheol. David pictures death as a place where gates will shut behind him. He thanks God for enabling him to escape the gates of death and to praise God in the gates of Jerusalem: "Be gracious to me, O LORD! See my affliction from those who hate me, O you who lift me up from *the gates of death*, that I may recount all your praises, that in *the gates of the daughter of Zion* I may rejoice in your salvation" (Psalm 9:13,14). David foretold how Jesus would thank his Father for giving him victory over his enemies, including death: "The cords of death encompassed me; the torrents of destruction assailed me; the cords of Sheol entangled me; the snares of death confronted me" (Psalm 18:4,5).

When Jonah was in the belly of the fish, he called that place the "belly of Sheol." He saw himself in "the land whose bars closed upon me forever," and he thanked God for raising him "from the pit" (Jonah 2:2-6).

Gates and bars serve well as symbols when speaking about Sheol. Once you die and enter Sheol, you cannot get out. Cords and snares serve to symbolize the rapacious nature of death. But these are symbols. It is hard to imagine a Hebrew person thinking that when a person was placed into his or her grave, literal gates opened up through which that person passes before actually arriving "in" Sheol. If Sheol had literal gates and bars, people would see them, perhaps when the ground was opened at a burial. What is more, literal bars and gates cannot hold spirits, and it was clear that physical bodies go no farther than their graves.

---

[215] Sheol is pictured as being below the surface of the earth, which, of course, is where people are buried. Isaiah strikes the contrast between the heavens and Sheol in his command to Ahaz: "Ask a sign of the LORD your God; let it be deep as Sheol or high as heaven" (Isaiah 7:11; see Psalm 139:8). Solomon describes the end of life: "The dust returns to the earth as it was, and the spirit returns to God who gave it" (Ecclesiastes 12:7). In the account of Lazarus, Abraham and Lazarus were in heaven and the rich man was in hell. There was a gulf between the two that the dead could not cross. David foretold the physical resurrection of Jesus: God would not abandon his body to Sheol and let his body decay in the grave. He would raise him from the dead. The psalmist knew that he would share in Christ's victory over Sheol: "You make known to me the path of life; in your presence there is fullness of joy; at your right hand are pleasures forevermore" (Psalm 16:8-11). Another psalmist talks about Sheol as Hell, but his life would be ransomed from the power of Sheol: "Their form shall be consumed in Sheol, with no place to dwell. But God will ransom my soul from the power of Sheol, for he will receive me" (Psalm 49:14,15).

Evaluating the symbols as a whole

Some symbols cannot reflect belief in a literal structure

Let's separate the symbols that include physical structures and divide them into three groups.

First, there are things that we can all see, like the mountains or the sea. When these items are found in symbols, it is obvious that the symbol reflects something that actually exists.

Second, there are things we cannot see even if they might exist. In this category are symbols like the windows in the heavens or the foundations and pillars of the earth.

Third, there are things that, if they did exist, we would be able to see. And there are things we know exist, but we never see them doing the things they are said to do in the symbol. Attention to this third category provides a simple answer to the ANE argument.

Some symbols use physical objects and structures we should see but don't

Some symbols do not reflect an ancient belief that such things were a part of the structure of the universe. The reason is that if they existed, they could be seen. But they aren't seen. This shows that the Hebrews could use physical objects in symbols, knowing that those symbols do not reflect something that actually exists.

Perhaps the most obvious example is found in Job 38:8-11. God challenged Job: "Or who shut in the sea with doors when it burst out from the womb, when I made clouds its garment and thick darkness its swaddling band, and prescribed limits for it and set bars and doors, and said, 'Thus far shall you come, and no farther, and here shall your proud waves be stayed'?" This verse is rich in symbolism. The creation of the sea was like a child emerging from the womb. Clouds and darkness were the child's clothing. We understand those to be pure symbols of the creation of the sea.

But included among these symbols are "bars and doors." God is said to have used bars and doors to keep the sea within the limits he set for it. Bars and doors should easily take their place alongside such objects as foundations and pillars of the earth and windows of heaven. However, those who claim that foundations, pillars, and windows of heaven reveal ancient scientific beliefs cannot make the same claim about bars and doors that keep the waters in check. The Hebrews, like us, knew there were no such things. They are pure symbols of God's power.

The Symbols of Scripture

In Psalm 104 the psalmist describes God's act of bringing the dry land out of the waters: "You covered [the earth] with the deep as with a garment; the waters stood above the mountains. At your rebuke they fled; at the sound of your thunder they took to flight. The mountains rose, the valleys sank down to the place that you appointed for them. You set *a boundary* that they may not pass, so that they might not again cover the earth" (verses 6-9). The key word is "boundary." It is the normal Hebrew word for the border of a country or the limits of one's property, which were designated by rock walls or boundary stones. It is obvious that the Hebrews did not see these objects around the sea. They knew that the writer was using them to symbolize God's power to keep the sea in bounds.

In describing God separating the sea from the dry land Jeremiah used another physical object:

> Hear this, O foolish and senseless people, who have eyes, but see not, who have ears, but hear not. Do you not fear me? declares the LORD. Do you not tremble before me? I placed *the sand as the boundary for the sea*, a perpetual barrier that it cannot pass; though the waves toss, they cannot prevail; though they roar, they cannot pass over it. (Jeremiah 5:21,22)

The Israelites could see that the sand in some places rose only a few feet above the sea. Does Jeremiah's statement about the sand reflect an ancient belief in the power of sand? Or did they understand Jeremiah to be using the sand as nothing more than a symbol of God's power, which keeps the sea from encroaching on the dry land?

From this we see that the writers of Scripture can use an object in a symbol and at the same time know that the object does not exist. These are symbols the Bible writers used to picture God's power to keep the sea and the earth in place as he created them.

Some symbols refer to structures that do exist but that speak of things that don't literally happen to them

We can press the matter a little further. Some parts of the world that we can see, such as the mountains and the sea, are used in symbolical language. So there is, in fact, something real on which the symbolism is based. However, some of these real things are said to perform actions that we never see them doing.

For example, in Job 9:4-8, Job refers to some such actions, even indicating that they happen on a regular basis. Job writes:

> He is wise in heart and mighty in strength—who has hardened himself against him, and succeeded?—he who removes mountains, and they

know it not, when he overturns them in his anger, who shakes the earth out of its place, and its pillars tremble; who commands the sun, and it does not rise; who seals up the stars; who alone stretched out the heavens and trampled the waves of the sea.

Here Job is symbolizing God's anger and judgment on unbelief. The symbols Job uses are things that God could cause to happen if he wanted. On the Last Day, we will see these things happen. But until then we don't, nor did the Hebrews. They are pure symbols of the impossibility of a human being taking a stand against God.

Some symbols refer to structures that cannot be in place at the same time

Think again of the foundations of the world and pillars of heaven. Their use in symbolism might lead us to conclude that the ancients believed in the existence of literal pillars and foundations. But if we think about these structures a little more carefully, we realize that any Hebrew person with a little intelligence would have trouble believing that they actually existed.

The Hebrews knew the record of the creation of land in Genesis 1:9,10: "And God said, 'Let the waters under the heavens be gathered together into one place, and let the dry land appear.' And it was so. God called the dry land Earth, and the waters that were gathered together he called Seas." A Hebrew person would have understood that like Peter did: "And the earth was formed out of water and through water by the word of God" (2 Peter 3:5).

Let's imagine a conversation between two ancient Hebrews discussing the "foundations of the earth."

Ishmael: "Indeed, the Lord set the earth on its foundations."

Joseph: "But what do those foundations look like?"

Ishmael: "I've wondered that myself. It is hard to say."

Joseph: "The foundations of my house rest on the rocks below. I know my house will not fall. But if God caused the earth to rise out of the water, on what do its foundations rest? Water is certainly not stable like rock."

Ishmael: "That is indeed a good question. I never thought about it like that. My friend who lives by the sea once made a large raft out of some logs he found. One afternoon he and his family used it to float out a short way into the sea. Maybe the foundations of the earth are made of logs that God put underneath the earth to keep it afloat."

Joseph: "That seems a little far-fetched, Ishmael. But it seems more reasonable than the foundation of rock under my house. What would such foundations rest on to keep the world in place?"

Ishmael: "Well, maybe 'foundation' is just a symbol for God's power that keeps this world in place above the sea."

Or take another example. Theistic evolutionists want us to believe that the Hebrews considered the heavens to be a hard, thin dome that covered a flat earth, which was supported by pillars that rested on the earth. They also want us to believe that the Hebrews thought the earth was flat and surrounded by a cosmic sea. If these symbols reflect literal structures, it is impossible to combine them in a way that makes sense. In that case, the pillars and foundations of the heavens would be located out in the sea, where they would have nothing but water to support them.[216] Perhaps these are miraculous pillars!

Indeed, that's just the point! The foundations of the earth and the pillars of heavens are symbols of God's power and control over the entire universe that he created. It is impossible to picture how they would have functioned or where they would have been located if they were literal, physical structures.

The purpose of symbols in Scripture

Our discussion has been largely negative, showing what the symbols do not teach us. It would be good to end this chapter with some positive examples of how the writers of Scripture put symbolism to use.

Upheaval in a believer's life is symbolized by upheaval in the universe. And when things are right in a believer's life, the universe is at rest. We saw two examples of this previously in Psalm 82:5 and 1 Samuel 2:8. We add another example: David prayed in "cosmic" terms for God to deliver him from his enemies: "Bow your heavens, O LORD, and come down! Touch the mountains so that they smoke! Flash forth the lightning and scatter them; send out your arrows and rout them! Stretch out your hand from on high; rescue me and deliver me from the many waters, from the hand of foreigners" (Psalm 144:5-7).

One of the most striking examples of this pattern is found in Psalm 18. David composed this psalm after the Lord delivered him from Saul and all his enemies. The first five verses describe David's plight and how God helped him. Verse 6 begins David's prayer for help: "In my distress I called upon the LORD; to my God I cried for help. From his temple he heard my voice, and my cry to him

---

[216] An alternative is to claim that the mountains we see around us serve as the foundation of the heavens. In this scenario the heavens must rest on the periphery of the land and the sea is therefore outside the circumference of the heavens. This scenario implies that there are mountains all around on the periphery of the dry land. But the ancients knew that some of the land that bordered on the sea was a sandy shore. The other alternative is to locate mountains on a ring of land that is beyond the sea. In this case it is impossible to imagine a single landmass surrounded by a "cosmic sea." More significant, both scenarios destroy the division between the upper and lower waters, the very purpose for which the heavens were created.

reached his ears." At that point follows a rather violent picture of God coming to David's help against his enemies. That picture continues for ten verses:

> Then the earth reeled and rocked; the foundations also of the mountains trembled and quaked, because he was angry. Smoke went up from his nostrils, and devouring fire from his mouth; glowing coals flamed forth from him. He bowed the heavens and came down; thick darkness was under his feet. He rode on a cherub and flew; he came swiftly on the wings of the wind. He made darkness his covering, his canopy around him, thick clouds dark with water. Out of the brightness before him hailstones and coals of fire broke through his clouds. The LORD also thundered in the heavens, and the Most High uttered his voice, hailstones and coals of fire. And he sent out his arrows and scattered them; he flashed forth lightnings and routed them. Then the channels of the sea were seen, and the foundations of the world were laid bare at your rebuke, O LORD, at the blast of the breath of your nostrils. (Psalm 18:7-15)

This is followed by David's sigh of relief: "He sent from on high, he took me; he drew me out of many waters. He rescued me from my strong enemy and from those who hated me, for they were too mighty for me. They confronted me in the day of my calamity, but the LORD was my support" (Psalm 18:16-18). This is followed by 31 verses of praise, in which David described in concrete terms what God had done for him. David said:

> This God—his way is perfect; the word of the LORD proves true; he is a shield for all those who take refuge in him. For who is God, but the LORD? And who is a rock, except our God?—the God who equipped me with strength and made my way blameless. He made my feet like the feet of a deer and set me secure on the heights. (Psalm 18:30-33)

The entire psalm beautifully symbolizes God's anger over the enemies of his people and God's deliverance of his child.

Consider Psalm 75:2-7. The psalmist gives us a similar picture:

> At the set time that I appoint I will judge with equity. When the earth totters, and all its inhabitants, it is I who keep steady its pillars. I say to the boastful, "Do not boast," and to the wicked, "Do not lift up your horn; do not lift up your horn on high, or speak with haughty neck." For not from the east or from the west and not from the wilderness comes lifting up but it is God who executes judgment, putting down one and lifting up another.

Here we do not see God under the earth, firmly holding the pillars to keep them steady in the face of a physical event like an earthquake. Rather, we see God in heaven supporting his people who are tottering and ready to fall. He is sustaining the pillars of his mercy on which his people rely. He is executing judgment by putting down his enemies and lifting up those who hope in him.

In a similar way Deborah praised God for delivering her people from the Canaanites:

> Hear, O kings; give ear, O princes; to the LORD I will sing; I will make melody to the LORD, the God of Israel. "LORD, when you went out from Seir, when you marched from the region of Edom, the earth trembled and the heavens dropped, yes, the clouds dropped water. The mountains quaked before the LORD, even Sinai before the LORD, the God of Israel. (Judges 5:3-5)

And finally, take comfort in the words of the Sons of Korah, who praise God's everlasting deliverance in beautiful, symbolic language:

> God is our refuge and strength, a very present help in trouble. Therefore we will not fear though the earth gives way, though the mountains be moved into the heart of the sea, though its waters roar and foam, though the mountains tremble at its swelling. There is a river whose streams make glad the city of God, the holy habitation of the Most High. God is in the midst of her; she shall not be moved; God will help her when morning dawns. (Psalm 46:1-5)

The earth may give way and the mountains may tremble and fall into the sea. But believers can always be glad as they drink from the river that flows from the place where God dwells.

Conclusion

Theistic evolutionists can make Scripture reflect a so-called ancient science of the universe only by doing one or more of the following: (1) They must use a subset of passages that by themselves *might* reflect an ancient science. (2) They must ignore the large number of passages that use physical objects and structures in a strictly symbolical way, even when those passages are tightly packed together with the passages they want to use. (3) In a number of cases, they must base their argument on English translations and ignore difficulties in the Hebrew that jeopardize their point. (4) They must ignore the impossibility of combining the objects supposedly reflected in Scripture's symbolism into a single model of the universe.

There may have been some among the Hebrews or other nations in the Near East who believed that the earth was flat or that there were literal pillars under the earth, etc. But they did not get those ideas from Scripture.[217] In Genesis 1 and 2, God gives us a simple and powerful narrative. He leaves us with a basic description about the structure of the universe that invites exploration and discovery. Scripture will not allow itself to be drawn into the scientific discussions as science progresses from age to age.

Scripture records people using the language of observation, which has been used throughout history. No matter how science describes the universe, the language of observation will always be accurate and will serve as an important method of communication.

Scripture also uses the beautiful language of symbolism, which has also adorned the best literature throughout the history of the world. The complex way in which symbols are used in Scripture blocks any attempt to define what the Hebrews believed about the universe, beyond what God told them in Genesis 1 and 2. On the other hand, the symbols beautifully portray the presence, the power, and the glory of God.

The ANE argument is based on the claim that Scripture reflects an ancient science of the universe, which must be discarded in favor of modern science. And if ancient science is discarded, ancient ideas about the origin of the universe must be discarded as well. The ANE argument, however, is based on something that does not exist. Scripture does not teach any scientific idea that must be rejected. True, it runs counter to human interpretations of the data. But it says nothing that might discourage exploration, research, and the creation of technology through which God blesses his world.

Cliché: Artists' illustrations of the ancient three-tiered cosmos don't lie.

Sadly, they do.

Artists have created illustrations of how the ancients, and that would include the Hebrews, are supposed to have pictured the universe. Theistic evolutionists love to include one or more of them in their books. After all, a picture is worth a thousand words.

Sometimes these diagrams are included at the beginning of a book. In those cases, the author has conveniently proved his point even

---

[217] And as an aside, we would be wise not to try to make Scripture scientifically relevant, that is, to look into Scripture for evidence of modern scientific ideas hidden in some of its verses. For example, to speak of heaven, the place God dwells, as located in another dimension may start a Christian down a path he or she does not want to go.

The Symbols of Scripture

before he starts his discussion. Once readers have a picture in their minds, it is hard to get it out no matter what Scripture might tell them. Often the diagrams are copied from some old book, which adds to the aura of authority.

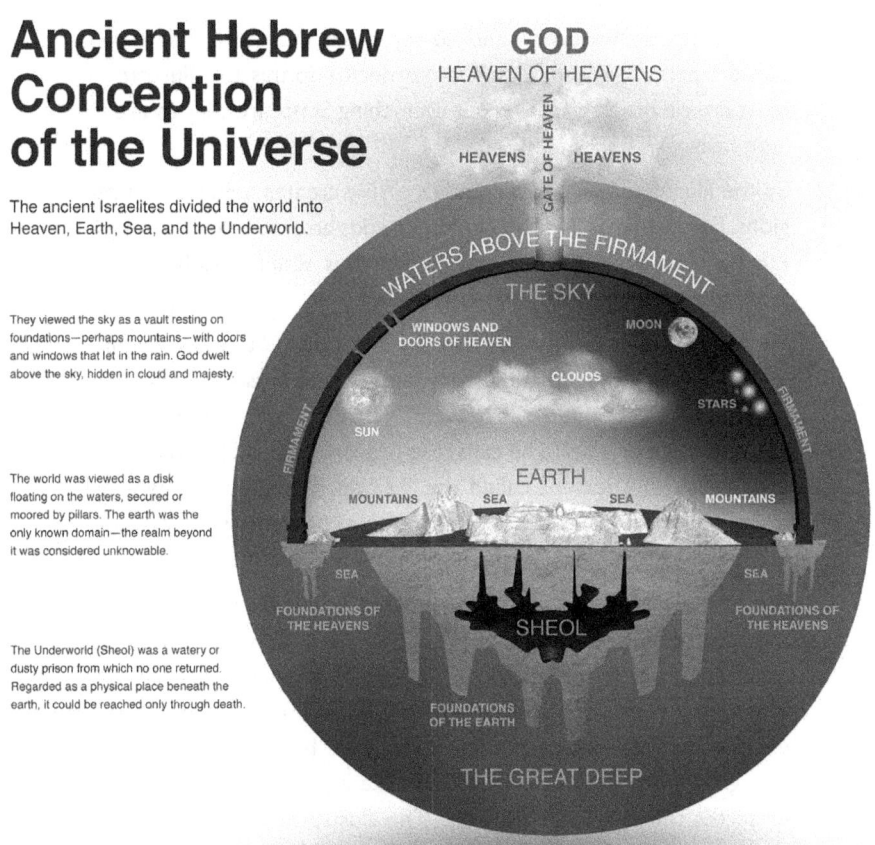

Here is one such diagram. It is entitled the "Ancient Hebrew Conception of the Universe."[218] Does it accurately reflect what we find in Scripture? Let's do a careful analysis of what we are looking at.

---

[218] Copyright Faithlife Corporation, makers of Logos Bible Software, www.logos.com. Used by permission. Please note, the author highly respects Logos Bible Software for creating Bible study tools and the Logos library system. However, the fact that a respected publisher is offering this chart gives it an aura of scholarship it does not deserve. This chart is a contemporary redrawing of an illustration copied with a couple of minor changes from a book published in 1913. See https://commons.wikimedia.org/wiki/File:The_ancient_Hebrew_conception_of_the_Universe. JPG.

The heavens as described in Scripture is the area between the upper and lower waters. Scripture tells us that the birds fly in the heavens; heaven is where the clouds are located;[219] and it is where God put the sun, moon, and stars. Scripture also tells us that God has chosen to live in the heavens.

The illustrator, however, wants to represent the heavens as a thin dome separating the waters. But in order to do this, the illustration must create other places to put everything Scripture tells us are in "the heavens."

So the illustrator must get creative.[220] He creates a number of regions. For the birds and the clouds, he adds an area called "the sky." But he overlooks the fact that "the sky" is simply another word Bible translators use for "the heavens."[221]

He places a thin dome over the sky and calls it "the firmament," which is simply the word the King James Version used for "the expanse" that God named "the heavens." Then, he creates another area above the upper waters he calls "the heavens." Finally, he creates an area above the heavens called the "heaven of heavens," where he places God. But in Scripture the "heaven of heavens" simply means the highest heaven, that is, the highest place in the heavens.

But in doing this, the illustrator creates problems. He must tuck the sun, moon, and stars under the firmament. Combined with the other structure he must add, he gives them no way to rise and set. They are just there. Also, there is no way to illustrate God's presence in the heavens, so the illustrator puts him on top of a gate that goes through the dome, almost like a passage God must use to access the creation below him. The illustrator calls this passage the "gate of heaven." But the phrase "gate of heaven" is used only once in Scripture. It's the name Jacob gave to the place he slept on his way to Haran. So an accurate, but impossible, picture of the gate of heaven would have it stretching down to that place on the earth.

---

[219] Daniel 7:13; Matthew 24:30.

[220] I'm not sure if a man or woman created this diagram. Since it was likely created by a single person, simply to make it easier to write, I use the masculine pronoun throughout.

[221] Note that the ESV translates "the heavens" with "sky" 13 times. However, the 1984 NIV translates "sky" in 72 verses. The 2011 NIV bumps that up to 84 times. The New RSV uses that translations 25 times. This shows the wide latitude translators give themselves to translate "the heavens."

The Symbols of Scripture

The pillars and foundations, which are supposed to support the earth so it doesn't sink into the waters below, are shown as protrusions under the earth that dangle down into the water. But pillars resting on water offer no support. Other pillars, which are said in Scripture to support the heavens, are shown to rest on mountains, which would provide a solid support. But the illustrator must locate these mountains on a little piece of land out in the sea, whose supports are also simply left dangling in the water below. This picture also undermines the supposed ancient belief that the land is surrounded by a "cosmic sea."

Most important, Scripture says that the expanse, the heavens, was put in place to separate the waters above it from the waters below it. In this diagram, the waters above the heavens are connected all around the dome with the waters on the earth below. Therefore, the heavens ("firmament" in the illustration) cannot perform the basic purpose Scripture gives it. And no illustration using a flat earth covered by a dome can solve that problem.

Note the little slits in the dome above the earth, which represent the "windows of heaven" where the rain comes from. This is another example of allowing the upper and lower waters to come into contact with each other. What is more, the illustrator has left out the "storehouses" in which God supposedly stores water and other things he intends to use in dealing with mankind.

The gates of Sheol are pictured as little tubes connecting the underworld with the world above. How many Hebrews thought the bodies of their dead relatives had left their graves and slipped into Sheol through a tube? And if such tubes existed, they would be visible. Remember, this diagram is titled "Ancient Hebrew Conception of the Universe."

This is nothing more than pictorial gibberish. Perhaps that statement is too harsh. But every theistic evolutionist and proponent of the ANE argument should be forced to draw a diagram that makes sense, even to the "simple and uneducated" Hebrews. They should be forced to draw a diagram of a dome-shaped heaven supported over a flat earth and draw it in a way that keeps the water above the dome separate from the water below it. Regardless of how they themselves read Genesis 1, that is what the Hebrews would have believed, and rightly so. That was the purpose of the heavens—and their diagram is supposed to be the ancient conception of the universe.

Diagrams like this do nothing more than undermine a careful study of the Hebrew text. What is more, they lead readers to assume the author's position is shared by many others, who studied Scripture seriously and took the time to illustrate it.

In a sense, illustrations like this don't lie. The diagram shows clearly what happens when Scripture's narrative of creation is dismissed and when Scripture's use of the language of observation and symbolism are indiscriminately mined to discover ancient Hebrew "science." These illustrations clearly reveal the extent to which theistic evolutionists will go to prove the ANE argument.

Postscript

The Literature of Other Ancient Near Eastern Nations

Introduction

We have made the claim that Scripture does not teach or even reflect an ancient Hebrew science that might be used to dismiss its account of the creation in Genesis 1. And regardless of what the nations around Israel might or might not have believed, we maintain that the people of Israel were a chosen nation whose Scripture was given to them by God.

But there are more players in the ANE argument. What about them? Does the ANE argument find support in the texts and inscriptions of other ancient Near Eastern nations like Egypt and Babylon?

Questions to ask about ANE literature

Before one accepts conclusions about whether or not other ANE material teaches ancient scientific beliefs, it is important to ask a few questions.

Are particular interpretations of ANE literature based on evolutionary presuppositions?

The evolutionary view of human history claims that the ancients did not possess the present-day intellectual ability to study the world. Authors who accept evolution invariably look at the ancient Near Eastern world through the eyes of the Enlightenment definition of the past. Does a particular author's approach to the past—and not the ancient material itself—determine how he or she interprets it?

And as we have seen, Scripture describes people as having great ability to study and analyze the world around them. Human reason has been corrupted by sin. But intelligence and ability were there from the beginning, on a par with the intelligence and ability of the generations that followed. Interpreters should approach the literature of the ancients no differently than they approach modern literature.

One More Elephant

Can we be sure we are interpreting ANE material correctly?

Interpreters should be careful about the conclusions they draw from ANE literature. As we have seen in our study of Scripture, it is easy to pick out a phrase from Scripture and assume the Hebrews believed this or that about the physical universe. It is just as easy to do that with the literature of other ancient Near Eastern nations. When you are told that ANE literature reveals that the ancients believed such and such about their universe, take some time to read the source material and draw your own conclusion.[222]

Ask questions about the condition of the material. How much is missing from the original? Often, major sections have been lost. Is the interpretation you are using based on the interpreter filling in the blanks? There is nothing wrong with doing that, but a more technical study will often reveal that one's interpretation of an ancient document is heavily influenced by what the interpreter assumes was in the missing sections.

Is an interpretation based on guesses about the meaning of important words that have lost their context? Do the different copies of the document (called "exemplars") all present the same story? Some of the writings were passed down from century to century, and a conquering nation might retain a myth of the nation it conquered and insert its own gods into the story. In the process it may change some of the details.

Some ancient documents are consistently cited in theistic evolutionary literature because they seem to provide clear evidence for what the ancients believed. But what does the Mesopotamian *Etana Epic* actually teach us about the ancient view of the structure of the earth? Do the missing or damaged lines of text leave unanswered questions? What does the *Gilgamesh Epic* reveal about the ancients' ideas of a sea that surrounded their world? Was it an endless ocean or did they wonder about new, undiscovered lands that might lie beyond it? What light does *The Bilingual Creation of the World by Marduk* shed on the supposed ancient idea that the earth was built on foundations extending down into the sea? Does the Babylonian "Unfinished Kudurru" (boundary stone) reflect an ancient belief that the earth *and* the heavens are supported by pillars? Ancient Babylonian mathematics proved that the stars orbited the earth in a perfect circle rather than across the surface of a somewhat oval-shaped dome. What implications does this have for their understanding of the shape of the earth?

---

[222] An excellent place to start a study of Babylonian documents is Wayne Horowitz's *Mesopotamian Cosmic Geography*. It will put you in close touch with the important primary resource material. Horowitz's writing style is very clear, but be aware that you are entering the technical world of ancient Near Eastern studies. Wayne Horowitz, *Mesopotamian Cosmic Geography* (Winona Lake, Indiana: Eisenbrauns, 2011).

The Literature of Other Ancient Near Eastern Nations

Time spent with the primary documents reveals the many judgment calls archaeologists must make to answer those and similar questions.

With Scripture's chronology there would have been shared memories

ANE literature shares common themes with Scripture. The flood is a good example, as is the creation of the world out of water.

Theistic evolutionists claim that ancient cosmology is based primarily on what ancient people observed in nature. But what in nature would have led them to the conclusion that the earth began as a single body of water and that the water was subsequently divided into two parts? What would have led to the conclusion that the dry land was created after this division? But that is how some Mesopotamian creation accounts describe it.

If we believe Scripture's description of creation and God's judging of the world by a flood, then ANE literature contains what we would expect—shared memories embodied in a variety of local accounts in which national gods play the key roles.

God chose Abraham to be the father of a new nation through whom he would bless the world. For this reason, and because of the many ANE religions in existence in Abraham's day and their varied accounts of the creation and the flood, we might expect God to reveal to Abraham the truth about how the world began. We would expect him to describe his loving relationship with Adam and Eve, the origin of sin, the first promise of a Savior, and how he used Noah to keep his promise of a Savior alive.

We would expect that God's revelation would contain accounts similar to those found in the ANE literature already in existence. In the case of ANE literature, those accounts reflected a common memory of the past, but in the case of Scripture, those accounts revealed the source of that common memory. We would expect God's Word to expose and replace the idolatry, religious legends, and spiritual darkness of the nations around Israel.

How the people in the ancient Near East viewed the universe

Did all the ancient Near Eastern nations believe in a three-tiered universe? Of course they did. We all do. We look up and see the sky arching over our heads. We see the ground beneath us stretching out in all directions. We know there are things under the earth.

But the real question is whether the ancients believed in a three-tiered universe with all the parts theistic evolutionists have added to it? Our exploration of Scripture has shown that those additions do not exist in Scripture.

But are they not pictured on the walls of Egyptian tombs and caskets? Are they not found on Babylonian carvings and in their creation accounts? There are certainly many pictures of the universe in those places. But to say that they prove ancient Near Eastern scientific beliefs about the physical makeup of the universe is no more valid than it is in regard to Scripture.

In fact, the drawings in Egyptian tombs and caskets *do not* present a uniform picture of the universe. J. Edward Wright says about the Egyptians: "There was no single dominating view of the cosmos among the Egyptians during its long history.... Reading the texts and artifacts from Ancient Egypt with an eye to discovering their views of the cosmos leaves one with the impression that Egyptian ideas on this subject were at best a confused mix of belief and images."[223]

As soon as ANE material began to be unearthed in the last half of the 19th century, artists tried to illustrate the ancient view of the universe based on the new discoveries—like the illustration we evaluated above. William Warren, author of *The Earliest Cosmologies* originally published in 1909, had this to say about attempts to diagram Babylonian cosmology that began to appear in his day: "Few studies in ancient cosmology can more entertain or instruct the investigator of today than a careful comparison of the seven diagrams published as correct pictures of the Babylonian universe in the works named below. No two of them agree."[224]

The heart of the matter

We do, in fact, see a close similarity between Scripture and other ANE literature. But it does not lie in a common ancient science about the universe. It lies, rather, in a similar pattern of how Scripture and ANE resources use symbolism. The symbols do not reflect ancient beliefs about the structure of the universe that can be reduced to an illustration. Rather, they present a simple framework made up of the heavens, the earth, and the area under the earth. And over this basic framework is laid a complex set of symbols that reflect not scientific beliefs, but religious beliefs about their gods.

For example, the Egyptians wanted to show that their gods held the universe together. They pictured that in a number of ways. One diagram pictures the heavens supported by simple columns. Another shows it supported by mountains. Another shows the sky resting on two lions. Another shows the heavens

---

[223] J. Edward Wright, *The Early History of Heaven*, p. 4.

[224] William Warren, *The Earliest Cosmologies: The Universe as Pictured in Thought by Ancient Hebrews, Babylonians, Egyptians, Greeks, Iranians, and Indo-Aryans* (New York: Eaton and Mains, 1909, reprinted in 2012 by Forgotten Books), p. 33. Warren lists seven books published between 1888 and 1902 that contain illustrations of the universe from information found in the ancient Near East.

supported by the mountains with the gods of the mountains holding it up with outstretched arms.[225] Not only did Egyptian artists picture the supports of the heavens in a variety of ways; sometimes the supports did not actually touch what they were supporting, indicating that they were symbolizing spiritual ideas.

Egyptian diagrams of the universe served to teach people about *their gods*. They symbolized the power of their gods to keep the world stable and under their control. They symbolized which gods were in control of this or that part of the universe—which gods lived in the heavens and which lived in the underworld. The pictures found on the walls of Egyptian tombs or caskets were there to help the dead person, usually a pharaoh, know where to go and what to expect in the next life, what each god did and how it should be worshiped.

In his classic work *The Symbolism of the Biblical World*, Othmar Keel gets to the heart of the matter. He includes a contemporary diagram of the universe like the one we examined in the beginning of this chapter and explains:

> Modern representations of the so-called ancient Near Eastern picture of the world overlook the fact that the ancient Near East never regarded the world as a closed, profane [purely secular] system. Rather, the world was an entity open at every side. The powers which determine the world are of more interest to the ancient Near East than the structure of the cosmic system.[226]

Keel gives his opinion about illustrations based on the ANE material:

> This openness of the everyday, earthly world to the spheres of the divine-intensive life ... is probably the chief difference between ancient Near Eastern conception of the world and our own, which views the world as a virtually closed mechanical system. The principal error of conventional representations of the ancient Near Eastern view of the world *lies in their profanity, transparency, and lifelessness*.[227]

The literature of the ancient Near East doesn't seem interested in describing "scientific" beliefs. Keel writes, "A wide variety of diverse, uncoordinated notions regarding the cosmic structure were advanced from various points of departure."[228]

The ANE argument cannot be sustained by appealing to the Egyptian and Babylonians sources. ANE literature does not yield a unified view of the structure and operation of the universe beyond the basic three tiers that we all observe. As

---

[225] See J. Edward Wright, *The Early History of Heaven*, pp. 14-17.

[226] Othmar Keel, *The Symbolism of the Biblical World: Ancient Near Eastern Iconography and the Book of Psalms* (Winona Lake, Indiana: Eisenbrauns, 1997), p. 57.

[227] Othmar Keel, *The Symbolism of the Biblical World*, p. 56 (emphasis added).

[228] Othmar Keel, *The Symbolism of the Biblical World*, p. 57.

the illustration at the end of the last chapter demonstrates, one simply cannot extract from that literature an underlying scientific belief about the structure and operation of the universe, at least one that makes sense.

In this respect, Scripture *is* like other literature from the ancient Near East. The symbols in Scripture are like the symbols in the literature and engravings of the nations living around God's people. They are symbols of the glory of whom they worship. Like the symbolism of the nations living around Israel, the symbols in Scripture tell us that the universe is not a closed mechanical system, even in the modified sense of theistic evolution. Rather, the symbols of Scripture are written to glorify God who created the universe, preserves it, redeemed it, and will someday re-create it. To use the phrase Keel applied to Egyptian literature, the Hebrews knew that their universe was not "a lifeless stage."[229]

But here is where the similarity between Scripture and ANE material ends. Unlike ANE literature, Scripture enables us to know who is the real source of life on the stage of this world. On every page it condemns the gods of the nations that lived around God's people and rejects all the power and wisdom ascribed to them. And it points all people to the Rock of Refuge worshiped by the believers in Israel.

What is lost by using ANE resources to interpret Scripture

The impact of the ANE argument can be seen in the titles of some of the popular theistic evolutionist books. John Walton's book cited earlier is titled *The Lost World of Genesis One*. ANE literature, it is claimed, has supplied insights into this "lost" world, which provides the key to the interpretation of Genesis 1.[230] But that title is based on the idea that we can no longer understand the world in which Scripture was written, yet in light of the newly discovered culture of the ancient Near East, we can now read Scripture with understanding. What is lost is the conviction that the world of Genesis 1 is, in fact, not lost. It has always been there. And under the guidance of Jesus and the New Testament writers, the world of Genesis can be readily understood by us today.

Or take another example. The full title of Kyle Greenwood's book is *Scripture and Cosmology: Reading the Bible Between the Ancient World and Modern Science*. In other words, in order to be understood, Scripture must be placed "between" the findings of ancient Near Eastern archeological discoveries and what Scripture itself tells us when read in a straightforward way. Omitted is the truth found throughout the Scripture, namely, that Scripture stands on its

---

[229] Othmar Keel, *The Symbolism of the Biblical World*, p. 56.

[230] John Walton, *The Lost World of Genesis One: Ancient Cosmology and the Origins Debate* (Downer's Grove: InterVarsity Press, 2009), p. 10.

The Literature of Other Ancient Near Eastern Nations

own. It is to be read "between" itself, as we allow one part of Scripture to help us understand another part of it.

No one denies that archaeological discoveries about the world in which God's people lived are helpful. But when people study those archaeological discoveries following the path laid down by theistic evolutionists, they are entering the world of historical criticism.

C. John Collins, who accepts a form of theistic evolution, writes the following:

> If, as seems likely to me, the Mesopotamian origin and flood stories provide the context against which Genesis 1-11 are to be set, they also provide us with clues on how to read this kind of literature. These [Mesopotamian] stories include divine actions, symbolism, and imaginative elements; the purpose of these stories is to lay the foundation for a worldview, *without being taken in a "literalistic" fashion.*[231]

According to Collins, Christians should not claim that the Babylonian and Egyptian accounts of creation are myths but that the early accounts of Genesis are not. Rather, Christians are to learn from ANE literature that all creation accounts are myths and should be interpreted accordingly. Both use "divine actions, symbolism, and imaginative elements" to teach a worldview, not an account of what actually happened.

Not all in the Evangelical world agree with how Walton interprets Genesis 1, but he summarizes in clear terms the beginning point that all must adopt if they use ANE literature to interpret Scripture:

> For the Israelites, Genesis 1 offered explanations of their view of origins and operations, in the same way that mythologies served in the rest of the ancient world *and that science serves our Western culture.* It [Genesis 1] represents what the Israelites truly believed about how the world got to be how it is and how it works, though it is not presented as their own ideas, but as revelation from God.[232]

In order for Scripture to become a player in the ANE argument, the elephant of historical criticism must be allowed into the room of the Christian faith. Scripture must be reduced to a human document that can only be understood by those who are familiar with the ancient culture in which it was written.

Those who view Scripture as one piece of ANE literature among others commit two errors. First, they misunderstand the nature of ancient Near Eastern symbols and wrongly force them to reflect an ancient science of the cosmos. The Near Eastern scholars we have quoted tell us that the symbolism in ancient

---

[231] C. John Collins, *Did Adam and Eve Really Exist?*, p. 35 (emphasis added).

[232] John Walton, *The Lost World of Genesis One*, p. 13 (emphasis added).

Near Eastern documents cannot be forced to do that. Rather, the nations around Israel used symbolism to express the belief that their national gods were in control of the world around them and were continually interacting with it. The nations around Israel saw their world alive with divine power. The Israelites did the same, but with the knowledge that their God was the one and only source of divine power. Stripped of his role in creating and sustaining the universe, God becomes a mere actor on the lifeless stage of a universe built and sustained by the mechanistic process of evolution.

Second, theistic evolutionists who promote the ANE argument read Scripture with yet another pair of historical-critical glasses. They reduce Scripture to the level of the literature of idols—idols that Scripture is working to expose and overcome. In the process Scripture is stripped of its authority to condemn sin and to reveal forgiveness through faith in the perfect life and sacrificial death of God's Son.

Works Referenced

(The complete bibliography can be found in the first of this two-book set, *Elephants in the Room: Evolution Versus the Message of Scripture.*)

Anderson, Martin. *The Adult Class Manual.* Minneapolis: Augsburg Publishing House, 1938. (Fifty-sixth Printing, 1980)

Barton, John. *Reading the Old Testament.* Louisville: Westminster John Knox Press, 1996.

Barton, John. "Verbal Inspiration," in *A Dictionary of Biblical Interpretation.* R. Coggins and J. Houldon, eds. London: SCM Press, 1990.

Becker, Siegbert W. *The Scriptures—Inspired of God.* Milwaukee: Northwestern Publishing House, 1971.

Campbell, Ted A. *The Religion of the Heart: A Study of European Religious Life in the Seventeenth and Eighteenth Centuries.* Columbia, SC: University of South Carolina, 1991.

Cassirer, Ernst. *The Philosophy of the Enlightenment.* Princeton: Princeton University Press, 1951.

Christian Worship, A Lutheran Hymnal. Milwaukee: Northwestern Publishing House, 1993.

Christianity Today. The Origins Debate: Evangelical Perspectives on Creation, Evolution, and Intelligent Design. Carol Stream, IL: *Christianity Today*, 2012. Kindle.

Collins, C. John. *Did Adam and Eve Really Exist?* Wheaton: Crossway, 2011.

Collins, Francis, S. *The Language of God.* New York: Free Press (Simon and Schuster), 2006.

Ehrman, Bart. *The New Testament, Course Guidebook.* Chantilly, VA: The Teaching Company, 2000.

Eichhorn, Johann Gottfried. *Introduction to the Study of the Old Testament.* Translated by George T. Gollop. 1803.London: Spottswoode and Co., 1988.

Enns, Peter. *The Evolution of Adam: What the Bible Does and Doesn't Say About Human Origins.* Grand Rapids: Brazos (Baker) Press, 2012.

Greenwood, Kyle. *Scripture and Cosmology: Reading the Bible Between the Ancient World and Modern Science.* Downer's Grove: IVP Academic, 2015.

Gunkel, Herman. *The Legends of Genesis: The Biblical Saga and History.* Translated by W. H. 1901. Chicago: Open Court Publishing Co. n.d. Kindle.

Hamann, Henry P. *A Popular Guide to New Testament Criticism.* St. Louis: Concordia Publishing House, 1977.

Harrisville, Roy A. *Pandora's Box Opened: An Examination and Defense of the Historical-Critical Method and Its Master Practitioners*. Grand Rapids: Eerdmans Publishing House, 2014.

Hornig, Gottfried. *Die Anfaenge der historich-kritischen Theologie*. Goettingen: Vandenhoeck & Ruprecht, 1961.

Horowitz, Wayne. *Mesopotamian Cosmic Geography*. Winona Lake, Indiana: Eisenbrauns, 2011.

"Humanism." Cambridge Dictionary of Philosophy, 2nd edition, ed. Robert Audi. Cambridge University Press, 1999.

Hurst, John F. *History of Rationalism*, New York: Carlton & Porter, 1867.

Israel, Jonathan. *Radical Enlightenment: Philosophy and the Making of Modernity 1650–1750*. Oxford: Oxford University Press, 2001.

Jacob, Margaret C. *The Scientific Revolution: A Brief History With Documents*. Boston: Bedford/St. Martin's, 2010.

Keel, Othmar. *The Symbolism of the Biblical World: Ancient Near Eastern Iconography and the Book of Psalms*. Winona Lake, Indiana: Eisenbrauns, 1997.

Keil, C.F. and Delitzsch, F. *Commentary on the Old Testament, Vol. 1: The Pentateuch*, 1861. Reprint, Grand Rapids: William B. Eerdmans Publishing Company,1976.

Kraus, Hans-Joachim. *Geschichte der Historisch-Kritischen Erforschung des Alten Testaments*. Neukirchen Verlag, 1956.

Kulikovsky, Andrew S. *Creation, Fall, Restoration: A Biblical Theology of Creation*. Ross-shire, Scotland: Mentor, 2009.

Ladd, George Eldon. *The New Testament and Criticism*. Grand Rapids: Eerdmans Publishing House, 1967.

Lamoureux, Denis. *Evolutionary Creation*. Eugene, Oregon: Wipf & Stock, 2008.

Legaspi, Michael C. *The Death of Scripture and the Rise of Biblical Studies*. New York: Oxford University Press, 2010.

Leupold, H. C. *Exposition of Genesis, Vol. 1*. Grand Rapids: Baker, 1942.

Levine, Amy-Jill. *The Old Testament, Course Guidebook*. Chantilly, VA: The Teaching Company, 2001.

Luther's Works. Edited by Jaroslav Pelikan and Helmut T. Lehmann. American Edition. Vol 1, *Lectures on Genesis Ch. 1-5*. St. Louis: Concordia Publishing House; Philadelphia: Fortune Press, 1967.

Luther's Works. Edited by Jaroslav Pelikan and Helmut T. Lehmann. American Edition. Vol. 54, *Table Talk*. St. Louis: Concordia Publishing House; Philadelphia: Fortune Press, 1967.

Maier, Gerhardt. *The End of the Historical-Critical Method*. Translated by Edwin W. Leverenz, and Rudolph F. Norden. St. Louis: Concordia Publishing House, 1974.

Works Referenced

Miller, Keith B., ed. *Perspectives on an Evolving Creation*. Grand Rapids: Eerdmans, 2003.
Montague, George T. *Understanding the Bible: A Basic Introduction to Biblical Interpretation*. New York: Paulist Press, 2007. Kindle.
Moreland, J. P., and John Mark Reynolds, eds. *Three Views on Creation and Evolution*. Grand Rapids: Zondervan, 1999.
Neill, Stephen. *The Interpretation of the New Testament, 1861-1961*. New York: Oxford, 1964.
Peters, Ted, and Martinez Hewlett. *Can You Believe in God and Evolution?* Nashville: Abingdon, 2008.
Pieper, Francis. *Christian Dogmatics*, Vol. 1. St. Louis: Concordia Publishing House, 1950.
Poythress, Vern S. *Redeeming Science: A God-Centered Approach*. Wheaton: Crossway, 2006.
Preus, Robert. *The Inspiration of Scripture: A Study of the Theology of the 17th-Century Lutheran Dogmaticians*. St. Louis: Concordia Publishing House, 1957.
Price, Robert M., and Edwin A. Suominen. *Evolving out of Eden: Christian Responses to Evolution*. Valley, Washington: Tellectual Press, 2013. Kindle.
Principe, Lawrence. *History of Science: Antiquity to 1700, Course Guidebook*. Chantilly, Virginia: The Teaching Company, 2001.
Ruse, Michael. *Can a Darwinian Be a Cristian?* Cambridge: Cambridge University Press, 2001.
Sheehan, Jonathan. *The Enlightenment Bible*. Princeton: Princeton University Press, 2005.
Sorkin, David. "Reclaiming Theology for the Enlightenment: The Case of Siegmund Jacob Baumgarten (1706-1757)" in *Central European History 36, no. 4*, 2003.
Wallmann, Johannes. *Kirchengeschichte Deutschlands*. Tuebingen: J. C. B. Mohr, 1988.
Walton, John. *The Lost World of Genesis One: Ancient Cosmology and the Origins Debate*. Downer's Grove: InterVarsity Press, 2009.
Warren, William. *The Earliest Cosmologies: The Universe as Pictured in Thought by Ancient Hebrews, Babylonians, Egyptians, Greeks, Iranians, and Indo-Aryans*. New York: Eaton and Mains, 1909, reprinted in 2012 by Forgotten Books.
Wellhausen, Julius. *Prolegomena to the History of Ancient Israel*. Translated by J. Sutherland Black and Allan Menzies, 1885. N.p.: Evinity Publishing, 2009. Kindle.
Wright, J. Edward. *The Early History of Heaven*. Oxford: Oxford University Press, 2000.

Scripture Index

Genesis
1–95
1:1–34, 165
1:2–146
1-3–144
1:3–186
1:6–147
1:6,7–146
1:8–146
1:9,10–180, 194
1:9-13–150
1:10–164
1-11–111, 116
1:11–118
1:12–151
1:17–148
1:20–148, 149
1:26–57
1:27–112
1:28–133
2–20, 95
2:1–165
2:4–95
2:10–151
2:24–112
3:15–22
3:20–21
4:8–112
4:16-26–133
6-9–112
7:11,12–174, 175
11:6–133
12:1-3–137
12:3–23
13:10–20
27:28–149
28:16–138
28:17–138
41:3ff–166

Exodus
1:11–136
4:22–11
9:8–149
9:13-16–10
9:18–181
16:14–166
20:4–149
24:10–177
39:3–170

Leviticus
16:12–166

Numbers
16:38–170

Deuteronomy
4:6–136
4:7,8–136
4:32–188
8:7–146
10:14–137
11:11–149
18:18–102
26:15–138
28:12–176
32:22–182
32:32-35–177

Joshua
10:13–154
24:2,3–136

Judges
5:3-5–197

1 Samuel
2:8–182, 195
4:4–179

2 Samuel
7:12,13–23
7:13–179
7:25–23
18:9–149
22:11–157
22:43–170

1 Kings
3:11,12–134
3:16-29–134
4:29-33–134
8:27–138
8:30–139
18:45–149
19:12–166

2 Kings
7:2–174

1 Chronicles
9:22–181
16:30–184

2 Chronicles
9:23–134

Nehemiah
9:6–138

Esther
1:8–181

Job
9:4-8–193
9:6–183
26:7–185
26:7-11–185
26:11–183
28:9-11–191
35:5–168
36:28–168
37:18–164, 167, 168, 171
37:21–168
38:4–181
38:4-6–183
38:4-8–183
38:8-11–192
38:22–176
38:29–149, 177
38:37–175

Psalms
2–13
2:4–178
8:8–149
9:13,14–191
11:4–178
16:8-11–191
18:4,5–191
18:7-15–196
18:11–174
18:16-18–196
18:30-33–196
19:1–146
19:4,5–171
21:7–184
22:3–179
24:1,2–181
24:2–181
29:2,3,10–140
29:10–178
33:7–177
40–13
45–13
46:1-5–197
49:14,15–191
55:17-19–178
55:17-22–178
55:22–184
61:1,2–187
75:2-7–196
75:3–183
77:17–176

Scripture Index

78:23,24–175
78:26–149
82:4,5–184
82:5–182, 195
82:6–14
89:11–181
89:14–179, 182
90:3–20
93:1–184
94:22–157
95–14
96:9,10–184
97:2–179
102–13
104:1-5–171, 172
104:2–163
104:3–172
104:5–181, 182, 184
104:6-9–193
104:16–13
105:4,5–172
106:9–146
110–13
115:6–138, 167
119:144–157
139:8–137, 191
144:5-7–195
148:4–138, 147

Proverbs

8:25-29–186
8:29–183
30:19–149

Ecclesiastes

1:5–155
1:7–174
12:7–191

Isaiah

3:3–12
5:39–99

7:11–191
9:7–179
11:12–186
13:4,5–187
13:17–187
24:18-20–175
29:5–166
34:4–139
40:15–166
40:22–164, 165, 166, 185
41:8,9–187
42:5–167, 169, 171
51:3–20
53–17
53:5–102
54:9,10–21

Jeremiah

1:4-8–88
5:21,22–193
10:9–170
10:12–163
10:13–176
23:24–138
31:27–182
36:4–11
51:15–163

Ezekiel

1:26–178
2–24
6:11–170
7:12–186
8:4–178
14:14–21
25:6–170
28:13–20
43:7–179

Daniel

4:10,11–188
7:13–200

Joel

2:3–20

Amos

9:5,6–177

Jonah

2:2-6–191

Micah

6:2–182

Malachi

3:10–175

Matthew

2:17–12
4:8–189
5:17–6
11:13–10
12:3-5–24
12:40–24
12:42–14, 25, 187
15:4–25
15:7–25
18:20–139
19:3-6–20
22:29–25
24:30–200
24:37-39–22

Mark

7:10–11
7:13–11
12:36–12, 14

Luke

3:38–18
4:21–23
9:31–23
11:49–12

16:31–6
20:17–8
23:43–139
24:25-27–23
24:44–6
24:44,45–24
24:45–9

John

1:1-3–137
2:22–5
5:39–23, 102
6:63–11, 16, 124
8:44–20
8:56–7
10:35,36–14
14:25,26–16
14:26–17
19:24)–6
20:30,31–102

Acts

1:8–17
1:11–139
1:16–12
4:24,25–12
7:22–136
17:1–9
17:2–6
17:9–9
17:14,15–9
17:26–19, 21
17:26,27–27
17:28–154, 190

Romans

1:1,2–6
1:1-3–24
1:19,20–21
3:2–11
4:10–14
5:14–18
5:15-17–18

215

5:15-19–121
5:18,19–14, 18
9:17–10
10:19,20–12
15:4,5–7
15:21–8

1 Corinthians

1:21-23–37
2:12,13–16
5:7–23
10:11–7
15:22–19
15:32,33–9
15:45-49–19

2 Corinthians

11:3–19
12:2–139

Galatians

1:12–100
3:16–15
3:22–10
3:26–19

Ephesians

4:26–154

1 Thessalonians

2:13–11, 124

1 Timothy

2:13,14–19
3:16,17–15

2 Timothy

3:16–9

Hebrews

1,2–12

1:3–137
1:5–13
2:11-13–13
4:7–14
5:5,6–13
9:6-8–13
10:5-7–13
10:15-17–14
11:4–19
11:5,6–18
11:7–22
11:39,40–7
12:16–7
12:24–19

James

5:11–7

1 Peter

1:10,11–16, 102
3:19-21–22

2 Peter

1:18-21–15
2:3-8–20
2:5–22
3:5–151, 194
3:5-7–150
3:10–139, 151
3:15,16–17
3:16–9

1 John

3:12–20

Jude

14–18

Revelation

1:7–189
2:7–21, 139
7:1–186
20:8–186
21:1–139
22:2–21
22:3–21
22:14,19–21

www.ingramcontent.com/pod-product-compliance
Lightning Source LLC
Chambersburg PA
CBHW071701090426
42738CB00009B/1623